# Women
# in Taiwan Politics

# Women in Taiwan Politics

Overcoming Barriers
to Women's Participation
in a Modernizing Society

Chou Bih-er
Cal Clark
Janet Clark

Lynne Rienner Publishers • Boulder & London

Published in the United States of America in 1990 by
Lynne Rienner Publishers, Inc.
1800 30th Street, Boulder, Colorado 80301

and in the United Kingdom by
Lynne Rienner Publishers, Inc.
3 Henrietta Street, Covent Garden, London WC2E 8LU

© 1990 by Lynne Rienner Publishers, Inc. All rights reserved

**Library of Congress Cataloging-in-Publication Data**
Chou, Bih-Er.
   Women in Taiwan politics : overcoming barriers to women's
participation in a modernizing society / by Chou Bih-er, Cal Clark,
and Janet Clark.
   Includes bibliographical references and index.
   ISBN 1-1555887-106-2
   1. Women in politics—Taiwan. I. Clark, Cal, 1945– .
II. Clark, Janet, 1940– . III. Title
HQ1236.5.T28C4863 1990
305.4'095124'9—dc20
                                                                                                                                                            90-8605
                                                                                                                                                              CIP

**British Cataloguing in Publication Data**
A Cataloguing in Publication record for this book
is available from the British Library.


Printed and bound in the United States of America

The paper used in this publication meets the requirements
of the American National Standard for Permanence of
Paper for Printed Library Materials Z393.48-1984.

*To Our Parents with Love and Gratitude*

*Ho-chen Chou and Joy Liu*
*Tanner and Grace Clark*
*Edward and Lois Morrissey*

# Contents

*List of Tables and Figures*     ix
*Preface*     xiii

## PART ONE    INTRODUCTION

1. The Political Underrepresentation of Women:
   A Taiwan Case Study     1
2. The Representation of Women     11

## PART TWO    THE STATUS OF WOMEN IN TAIWAN

3. Economic and Political Development in Taiwan     33
4. Development and Women's Status in Taiwan     57
5. The Reserved-Seats System and Women's Political
   Representation in the Republic of China     81

## PART THREE    ASSEMBLYWOMEN IN THE REPUBLIC OF CHINA

6. The Study and Research Methodology     103
7. The Roots of Participation: Selective Countersocialization     121
8. Political Characteristics:
   Similar Resources but Significant Gender Discrimination     139
9. Legislative Activities: Selective Emphases     159

## PART FOUR    CONCLUSION

10. The Taiwan Experience and Overcoming Barriers to
    Women's Political Participation and Representation     187

*Selected Bibliography*     197
*Index*     203
*About the Book and the Authors*     207

# Tables and Figures

## TABLES

| | | |
|---|---|---|
| 1.1 | Percentage of Women in National Legislatures, 1984 | 2 |
| 2.1 | Gender Differences in U.S. Public Opinion, Mid-1980s | 14 |
| 2.2 | Sex Differences in State Legislatures Working on Legislation Targeted at Women | 15 |
| 2.3 | Dates of Women's Suffrage | 16 |
| 2.4 | Percentage of Women in Lower House of National Legislature by Type of Electoral System, 1982 | 22 |
| 3.1 | Indicators of Development Level | 36 |
| 3.2 | Real Annual Growth | 37 |
| 3.3 | Composition of Elected Bodies | 51 |
| 4.1 | Women's Percentage of Total Employment | 60 |
| 4.2 | Percentage of All Employed Men or Women in Specific Industries | 61 |
| 4.3 | Percentage of All Employed Men or Women at Specific Levels of Occupational Hierarchy | 61 |
| 4.4 | Women as a Percentage of Total Employment at Specific Levels of Occupational Hierarchy | 62 |
| 4.5 | Percentage of All Men or Women Employed in Manufacturing with Specific Type of Employment Status | 64 |
| 4.6 | Percentage of All Men or Women Employed in Service Industries with Specific Type of Employment Status | 65 |
| 4.7 | Percentage of All Men or Women Employed in Commerce with Specific Type of Employment Status | 66 |
| 4.8 | Percentage of All Men or Women Employed in Agriculture with Specific Type of Employment Status | 66 |
| 5.1 | Women's Representation in National Legislative Bodies | 90 |
| 5.2 | Women's Representation in Provincial-Level Legislative Bodies | 91 |

| | | |
|---|---|---|
| 5.3 | Women's Representation at County/Township Level | 92 |
| 6.1 | Samples and Completed Interviews | 105 |
| 6.2 | Cross-Tabulation of Spouse-Held Political Office by Respondent Group | 110 |
| 6.3 | Social and Political Differences Among Respondent Groups | 113 |
| 6.4 | Regression Explanations of Role Conflicts, Liberalism, and Assembly Activism | 115 |
| 6.5 | Discriminant Analysis for Women Versus Men Legislators | 117 |
| 7.1 | Childhood Socialization Differences Among Respondent Groups | 122 |
| 7.2 | Regression Explanations of Family Politicization | 124 |
| 7.3 | Adult Socialization Differences Among Respondent Groups | 127 |
| 7.4 | Regression Explanations of Spouse Politicization | 128 |
| 7.5 | Regression Explanations of Political Activation | 129 |
| 7.6 | Regression Explanations of Role Conflicts | 132 |
| 7.7 | Discriminant Analysis for Women Versus Men Legislators | 135 |
| 7.8 | Discriminant Analysis for Women Winners Versus Losers | 135 |
| 7.9 | Discriminant Analysis for Old- Versus New-Generation Women | 136 |
| 8.1 | Political Resource Differences Among Respondent Groups | 140 |
| 8.2 | Regression Explanation of KMT Membership | 141 |
| 8.3 | Regression Explanations of Political Experience | 143 |
| 8.4 | Regression Explanations of Group Memberships | 146 |
| 8.5 | Regression Explanations of Groups Helping Campaign | 146 |
| 8.6 | Discriminant Analyses for Political Resource Items | 148 |
| 8.7 | Political Attitude Differences Among Respondent Groups | 150 |
| 8.8 | Regression Explanation of Political Liberalism | 151 |
| 8.9 | Regression Explanations of Perceptions of Gender Discrimination | 153 |
| 8.10 | Regression Explanations for Perceptions of Women's Political Abilities | 154 |
| 8.11 | Discrimant Analyses for Political Orientation Items | 156 |
| 9.1 | Legislative Orientation Differences Among Respondent Groups | 161 |
| 9.2 | Regression Explanation of Receiving Party Training for Legislative Office | 162 |
| 9.3 | Regression Explanations of Role Definitions | 163 |
| 9.4 | Regression Explanations of Committee Assignments | 165 |
| 9.5 | Regression Explanations of Offering Resolutions in Specific Areas | 169 |

| | | |
|---|---|---|
| 9.6 | Regression Explanation of Offering Resolutions in All Areas | 170 |
| 9.7 | Discriminant Analysis for Women Versus Men Legislators on Legislative Orientations | 171 |
| 9.8 | Legislative Activity and Success Differences Among Respondent Groups | 173 |
| 9.9 | Regression Explanation of Legislative Activity | 175 |
| 9.10 | Regression Explanations of Legislative Success | 175 |
| 9.11 | Effects of Gender in Regressions for Legislative Problems and Ambition for Office | 178 |
| 9.12 | Regression Explanations of Legislative Problems | 179 |
| 9.13 | Regression Explanation of Political Ambition | 180 |
| 9.14 | Discriminant Analysis for Women Versus Men Legislators on Legislative Activity and Success | 181 |
| 10.1 | Summary of Results About Seven Basic Factors in Assemblywomen Study | 191 |
| 10.2 | Summary of Factors Differentiating Analytic Groups | 192 |

## FIGURES

| | | |
|---|---|---|
| 3.1 | Map of Taiwan | 35 |
| 3.2 | Government Structure of the ROC | 47 |
| 6.1 | Relationships Among Central Blocks of Factors | 106 |

# Preface

Women are now grossly underrepresented among the political leaderships of every nation, reflecting their subordinate social and economic positions within widely differing types of society. Yet despite the constancy of this political underrepresentation and subordinate status throughout the world, the industrial revolution of the nineteenth and twentieth centuries has clearly transformed women's social and political roles to a dramatic extent. Interpretations of these changes remain quite controversial, however. Modernization theory argues that "the passing of traditional society" leads to an improvement in women's position and implies that full equality is just a matter of time, as the processes of social and economic development move toward full fruition. Feminist theory, in contrast, remains highly skeptical of such claims, arguing that patriarchy and capitalism are very compatible and interact to perpetuate the "marginalization" of women.

This book presents a case study of women in politics in the Republic of China on Taiwan. Taiwan provides an interesting test of these competing perspectives for several reasons. Traditional Chinese society, strongly patriarchal, would be expected to be most antithetical to women's equality. Thus, feminist and modernization theory would make opposite predictions about whether the rapid industrialization and social transformation that occurred on Taiwan during the postwar period would affect the status of women. Furthermore, the ROC has a possibly unique system that guarantees women a minimal level of representation in all its legislative bodies. Can such an institutional mechanism promote women's participation in a society where women's role in politics would be expected to be very limited because of that society's culture and development level?

We are very grateful for the financial assistance that we received for this project from the Asia Foundation and the Pacific Culture Foundation. Certainly, their generous aid made our research easier to carry out. We especially wish to thank Sheldon Severinghaus of the Asia Foundation for his encouragement and support of our study. Our home institutions, Academia Sinica in Taipei and the University of Wyoming in Laramie, provided invaluable support for the conduct of the research and the preparation of this manuscript. We are also very grateful for the research assistance that we received from Shu-huei Ho, Hwang-yen Lee, and Shu-ling Liou of Academia Sinica and Shen-shen Su of the University of Wyoming. In addition, Linda Marston did an excellent job of preparing the map used in Chapter 3. Last but by no means least, we wish to thank Martha L. Peacock of Lynne Rienner Publishers for her patience, help, and support during this project.

*Chou Bih-er*
*Cal Clark*
*Janet Clark*

# PART ONE
# INTRODUCTION

CHAPTER ONE

# The Political Underrepresentation of Women: A Taiwan Case Study

Women bear many of the marks of a "disadvantaged minority" in the social, economic, and political realms in almost all (if not all) cultures. In recognition of the special problems facing women worldwide, the United Nations proclaimed 1975–1985 as "The Women's Decade." At the end of the UN Decade for Women in the late 1980s, the status of women appeared to be changing in many nations. The majority of governments are taking steps to improve women's lot by implementing reforms mandating constitutional and legal equality for women and eliminating discrimination against them. Yet, much clearly remains to be done. According to a 1985 UN report, women, who constitute half of the world's population, still perform nearly two-thirds of all work hours but receive only one-tenth of world income. In most countries, women face substantial salary discrimination, are disadvantaged in access to educational opportunities, and remain in sex-segregated occupations to a considerable extent. They own less than 1% of world property and hold only 6% of government offices.[1]

### The Political Status of Women: The Problem

The last figure reflects the fact that a dismal underrepresentation of women in political office is a nearly universal phenomenon. This is particularly disturbing given the widespread assumption that public policy can be used to remedy discrimination and social inequities. If women were adequately represented in government, they could use their political muscle to force governments to face and ameliorate the economic and social disadvantages that are attached to their gender. The minuscule number of women who have attained public office in most nations means, however, that it is generally quite easy to leave "women's issues" off the political agenda.

Probably the most commonly used measure of women's political representation is their share of elected seats in national legislative bodies. Table 1.1 presents data on women's parliamentary office-holding for the mid-1980s. Overall, the 91 of 140 nations for which relevant data were available had an average of 10% women members in their national legislatures (compared with an average of 7% for cabinet seats). Even this low figure probably overstates women's representation because almost all the countries with missing data came from the regions with the lowest percentage of female parliamentarians.

Table 1.1  Percentage of Women in National Legislatures, 1984

| | |
|---|---|
| World | 10 |
| USSR and Eastern Europe | 22 |
|     East Germany | 32 |
|     USSR | 33 |
|     Yugoslavia | 15 |
| Developing Socialist States[a] | 22 |
|     China | 21 |
|     Cuba | 23 |
| Western Europe | 13 |
|     Denmark | 27 |
|     France | 5 |
|     West Germany | 11 |
|     Italy | 7 |
|     Norway | 26 |
|     Sweden | 29 |
|     Switzerland | 10 |
|     United Kingdom | 5 |
| United States | 5 |
| Other Developed Countries[b] | 7 |
|     Japan | 3 |
| Developing Latin America | 8 |
|     Mexico | 33 |
| Developing South Asia | 5 |
| Developing Africa | 5 |
| Developing Far East | 3 |
| Developing Middle East | 2 |

*Source:* Ruth Sivard, *Women: A World Survey* (New York: Ford, Rockefeller, and Carnegie, 1985) pp. 35–37.
[a]China, Cuba, North Korea, Mongolia, Vietnam.
[b]Australia, Canada, Israel, Japan, New Zealand.

Women's level of representation was clearly affected by development level and government system, with women much more likely to win legislative seats in more-developed countries and those with socialist systems. Only the socialist governments, in fact, gave women even a modicum of representation; they constituted just over a fifth of the legislators in communist countries, regardless of development level. Western Europe came next with an average representation rate of 13%, although within Europe there was tremendous variation between Scandinavia, where almost 30% of the parliamentarians were women, and southern Europe and the United Kingdom, where women's representation remained well under 10%.[2] Outside of Europe, women composed only about 7% of the national legislatures in developed countries. Their role in the parliaments of the developing world was even smaller, ranging from 2% in the Middle East to 8% in Latin

America (whose average was pulled upward by Mexico's 33%, one of the highest in the world). The contemporary world has witnessed some powerful women leaders: Sirimavo Bandaranaike in Sri Lanka, Indira Gandhi in India, Margaret Thatcher in the UK, Corazon Aquino in the Philippines, Benazir Bhutto in Pakistan, and perhaps most important, the "women's cabinet" of 1986–1989 led by Gro Harlem Brundtland in Norway. However, despite these individual successes—several of which occurred in unfavorable political cultures—women certainly remain grossly underrepresented in public life throughout the world.

There are two vastly differing explanations for women's subordinate status in politics and social life. Conventionally, "modernization theory" argued that the transformation from preindustrial societies to modern capitalist and (by implication) socialist ones opened up greater opportunities for women in both economics and politics. Industrialization meant that women began to work outside the home, thus eroding traditional patriarchal and kinship controls over them and increasing their self-confidence and interest in public affairs. Thus, women's "second-class status" could be viewed as a remnant of traditional societies that would gradually pass away.[3] For example, women achieve better representation in developed countries than in developing ones. This approach is quite optimistic in assuming that the increase in women's status is just a matter of time, although women's low representation in the developed capitalist world outside Scandinavia certainly challenges this optimism. Even in the Nordic nations, moreover, problems associated with the underrepresentation of women in government and the relatively low priority of "women's issues" are easy to discern.[4]

The idea that modernization almost inevitably produces more opportunities and higher status for women has been strongly challenged by "feminist theory," beginning with the pioneering work of Ester Boserup.[5] The feminist arguments were based on anthropological and historical evidence that industrial development had several important negative impacts upon women's status. Changes in agriculture, especially the introduction of advanced technology and the transformation from subsistence to cash crop production, undermined the production role of women by decreasing their participation in actual agricultural work. After industrialization commenced, women's role in the "modern sector" was "marginalized" in the sense that women were generally confined to unstable, low-paying, unskilled manufacturing jobs. Furthermore, their traditional roles and statuses and support from kinship networks were substantially eroded.[6] In short,

> Feminists see urbanization, mobility, and the conversion to the cash economy not as unalloyed benefits, but as processes that cut women off from their traditional economic and social roles and thrust them into the modern sector where they are discriminated against and exploited, often receiving cash incomes below the subsistence level. This condition, in turn, increases female dependency.[7]

In the political realm, for instance, the feminists could claim with a good deal of justification that the data in Table 1.1 support their interpretation rather than the modernization approach. Even in developed societies, with a few exceptions (e.g., the socialist countries and Scandinavia), the proportion of women's representation remains minimal; the gap in representation rates between the developed capitalist and developing worlds is relatively small in an absolute sense; and the very fact that the socialist nations are noteworthy for according women greater representation and do not differ among themselves by development level suggests that a special political will—rather than economic development per se—is the key factor promoting women's entrance into governmental positions.

Margaret Leahy provides an interesting theoretical explanation for the significantly higher representation of women in socialist societies based upon comparative case studies of Cuba, Mexico, the USSR, and the United States. She argues that both the industrial transformation of society and a basic reorientation of male-female sex roles are necessary for women to benefit from modernization. Without a redefinition of roles, women's entrance into the economy transforms their household responsibilities into a "second shift" that makes political activities even harder. Such a commitment to social equality at the expense of "economic efficiency" is probably impossible in capitalist societies.[8] Thus, while socialist countries have been criticized for not living up to their ideological commitment to women's equality,[9] they undeniably have the best record in providing political representation.

Moreover, women's increased representation in developed democracies is a relatively recent phenomenon, despite their fairly long histories of industrialization. For example, the number of women in national legislatures more than doubled between the early 1970s and early 1980s in the 23 developed democracies studied by Wilma Rule.[10] In the United States, where women's proportion in the national Congress grew only slightly, the proportion of female state legislators tripled over the 1970s and 1980s.[11] The long lag in time between industrialization and this dramatic jump in women's office-holding is usually explained by the emergence of the women's movement in Europe and North America during the late 1960s and 1970s.[12]

Feminist theory is somewhat divided, though, as to the causes and cures for the subordination and exploitation of women in industrial society.[13] Liberal feminists tend to blame the continuing patriarchal norms from traditional society and urge reformist policies prohibiting discrimination and supporting an equal position for women.[14] Socialist feminists believe that capitalism and patriarchy interact to create the economic structures that relegate women to second-class status and advocate revolutionary transformation as the only possible path that can liberate women.[15] Finally, some feminists focus upon recreating a "female sphere" where women's special skills predominate and give them a social status equal to men's.[16]

This book presents a case study about the political representation of women in the Republic of China on Taiwan. Taiwan constitutes an interesting and important context for studying the role of women for several reasons. First, the country's extremely rapid economic development during the postwar period has transformed it from a poor agricultural society to a thriving industrial one.[17] Thus, the ROC should provide a good test of the imputed consequences of industrialization for the status of women. Second, Chinese society's long history of patriarchy and the relegation of women to subordinate roles has carried over into the industrialization period.[18] If significant progress in women's political position can be observed in Taiwan, therefore, it would certainly suggest that the barriers of cultural socialization and economic structure are more mutable than feminist theory depicts them to be.

Third, the patriarchal nature of Taiwan's Chinese society has been somewhat offset by the government's ideological commitment to promoting equality for women. The leader of the Chinese Revolution of 1911–1912 and founder of the Republic of China, Sun Yat-sen, explicitly argued that women must be treated more equally in the new Chinese society that he hoped would emerge under his "Three Principles of the People"—nationalism, democracy, and people's livelihood.[19] However, Sun's Nationalist (Kuomintang) Party did not achieve power until 1928, after his death, and is not generally believed to have made great progress toward implementing these ideals on the Chinese mainland during its twenty years of rule.[20]

Nevertheless, the Nationalists did take an important and concrete step toward promoting the political participation of women in China by including in the 1947 constitution provisions guaranteeing that some seats in China's legislative bodies would be reserved for women. Subsequent legislation set these reserved seats at about 10% of total legislative membership, a level well above what now exists in the Third World and only slightly lower than in the developed capitalist countries. This possibly unique system, therefore, guaranteed women a significant but still proportionately small place in the ROC's assemblies which are less powerful vis-à-vis the executive branch than in most parliamentary systems. This raises the question of the impact of the reserved-seats system on the political status of women. On the one hand, as feminist theory would probably predict, given their minority status in relatively weak bodies, the ROC's assemblywomen might well be mere "tokens" or "placeholders" who are dominated by their male colleague leaders in the fashion of traditional Chinese patriarchy. On the other hand, unlike in other societies, some women have to be elected to office. Thus, these women could use their guaranteed political positions as a resource and become more active and effective in Taiwan's public life, as the modernization approach would expect. Taiwan's experience, therefore, should prove illuminating about both the limitations and opportunities for women to advance their political status in the contemporary world.

## Organization of the Book

This book is organized into four parts. The first provides introductory background information; the second discusses the general status of women in the Republic of China; the third analyzes the socialization backgrounds, political orientations, and legislative behavior of Taiwan's assemblywomen based on a set of interviews conducted with them in spring 1985; the fourth presents a conclusion.

Chapter 2 provides more introductory material by discussing general theories concerning the representation of women. It begins with a normative discussion about why women deserve representation in the halls of government and goes on to discuss three reasons that have been adduced to explain women's extreme underrepresentation throughout the world: (1) the effects of culture and socialization, (2) sex discrimination by political leaders and voters, and (3) structural features of a polity, such as the nature of the election system and the drag on legislative turnover produced by the great advantages that incumbents have in running for reelection in many countries. These three types of barriers, therefore, produce a baseline for evaluating women's position in the ROC in the sense that estimates of their strength are vital for interpreting women's political power and potential for increasing it.

Part 2 includes three chapters. Chapter 3 sets the stage for evaluating the status of women in the Republic of China by describing the postwar economic and political development of Taiwan. The country is certainly a development miracle—its GNP per capita multiplied manyfold from about $100 in 1950 to $7,000 in 1989. While not as dramatic, significant political change has occurred as well, with an essentially authoritarian regime in the 1950s and 1960s permitting reform in the 1970s and 1980s that set the stage for a considerable spurt toward democratization at the end of the 1980s.[21] Chapters 4 and 5 then assess the impact of these economic and political changes on women as means for seeing whether the expectations of feminist or modernization theory apply. Chapter 4 focuses on the extent of gender differences in the economy and in orientations toward political participation and values. Chapter 5 describes the reserved-seats system in some detail and presents data on the level of women's office-holding and electoral success in Taiwan. These chapters find mixed or partial support for both the modernization and feminist perspectives. Women in Taiwan have made undeniable progress along several economic, social, and political dimensions. However, their life chances remain constrained in a very real sense, and the readiest explanation for this is the patriarchal nature of Chinese society.

The third part of the book looks at assemblywomen directly and compares their characteristics and behavior with those of male colleagues in the island's legislatures and of women candidates who ran for office but lost. Chapter 6 describes the survey and research methodology, illustrated by a preliminary analysis that highlights the major themes that can be drawn from these data. Chapter 7 looks at the family and social background of the sample and concludes that women politicians in Taiwan have generally undergone "countersocialization" experiences[22] that help overcome Confucian traditions relegating women to passive and private roles. Chapter 8 examines general political characteristics and attitudes and reaches two rather divergent conclusions about women's political status. On the one hand, women were surprisingly equal to men in the possession of a variety of political resources; on the other, evidence of gender discrimination was quite clear. Finally, Chapter 9 analyzes activities within the assemblies themselves. The working hypothesis was that women would be less active and successful than their male colleagues. Some evidence of this emerged, but women turned out to score just as well (if not more so) than men on several indicators of success and to compensate for lower activity levels relative to men in some areas by being significantly more active than their male colleagues in others.

The concluding Chapter 10 seeks to integrate these results. Based on Taiwan's developmental history, neither the optimism of modernization theory nor the pessimism of feminist thought seems fully justified. Some women have clearly benefited from the industrial transformation of Taiwan, but others have proved much less able than comparable men to adjust to the new economic structures. In the political realm, those women who have entered public life have achieved a good deal of "equality" with male legislators (although the importance of this might be questioned because until quite recently legislative bodies had a limited impact on overall policy direction). There is a most important qualifier here, however, that feminists would be quick to point out. Because of the need for "countersocialization," such as high social position or having an exceptionally supportive family environment, only a small segment of Taiwan's female population would appear to be viable candidates at present. If women are to gain more equitable representation than their current 10%–15% in Taiwan's assemblies, countersocialization must occur on a much broader scale.

Still, there are at least some grounds for a little cautious optimism. Taiwan stands out, for example, in the rapid progress that women have made in gaining office relative to such longstanding democracies as the United States. The obvious explanation for this is the existence of the reserved-seats system, providing more support for the theory that the nature of the election system is a major determinant of women's electoral chances.[23] The constitutional mandate for women representatives, of necessity, brought women into politics and gave them access to political resources, in contrast to the almost total exclusion that might have been expected without the legal guarantee. Evidently, they used these resources well and became fairly equal participants in legislative politics. The growing role of assemblies and electoral competition as democratization proceeds,[24] therefore, might stimulate political involvement by broader segments of the female population and create an opportunity for electing more women to decisionmaking bodies.

## Notes

1. *China Post*, June 22, 1985, p. 3. For broader evaluations of how the UN Decade for Women affected women's status around the world, see Lynne B. Iglitzin and Ruth Ross, eds., *Women in the World: 1975–1985, The Women's Decade*, 2nd Revised Ed. (Santa Barbara, Calif.: ABC-Clio, 1986); and Ruth Sivard, *Women: A World Survey* (New York: Ford, Rockefeller, and Carnegie, 1985). Pippa Norris, *Politics and Sexual Equality: The Comparative Position of Women in Western Democracies* (Boulder, Colo.: Lynne Rienner, 1987) examines the position of women in developed nations.

2. Wilma Rule, "Electoral Systems, Contextual Factors, and Women's Opportunity for Election to Parliament in Twenty-three Democracies," *Western Political Quarterly* 40:3 (September 1987) pp. 477–498, explains these variations by such factors as the Catholic culture of southern Europe and especially by the type of election systems used in various democracies (see the discussion in Chapter 2). Norris, *Politics and Sexual Equality*, Chp. 6, reaches fairly similar conclusions, although she puts more stress on the role of leftist parties and less on the electoral arrangements. For more detailed discussions of women's underrepresentation in the developed world, see Walter Kohn, *Women in National Legislatures* (New York: Praeger, 1980); Joni Lovenduski, *Women and European Politics: Contemporary Feminism and Public Policy* (Amherst: University of Massachusetts Press, 1986) Chp. 6; and Vicky Randall, *Women and Politics: An International Perspective*, 2nd Ed. (Chicago: University of Chicago Press, 1987) Chp. 3.

3. For a good example of how this approach is applied to women in development, see Bernard Rosen and Anita La Raia, "Modernity in Women: An Index of Social Change in Brazil," *Journal of Marriage and the Family* 34:2 (May 1972) pp. 353–360.

4. Elina Haavio-Mannila et al., *Unfinished Democracy: Women in Nordic Politics* (New York: Pergamon, 1985).

5. Ester Boserup, *Women's Role in Economic Development* (London: Allen & Unwin, 1970).

6. Jane S. Jaquette, "Women and Modernization Theory: A Decade of Feminist Criticism," *World Politics* 34:2 (January 1982) pp. 267–284, provides an excellent overview. Also see Richard Anker and Catherine Hein, eds., *Sex Inequalities in Urban Employment in the Third World* (New York: St. Martin's, 1986); Boserup, *Women's Role in Economic Development;* Iglitzin and Ross, *Women in the World*, Part II; June Nash and Maria Patricia Fernandez-Kelly, eds., *Women, Men, and the International Division of Labor* (Albany: State University of New York Press, 1983); Barbara Rogers, *The Domestication of Women: Discrimination in Development* (New York: St. Martin's, 1979); Irene Tinker and Michele Bo Bramsen, eds., *Women and World Development* (Washington, D.C.: Overseas Development Council, 1976); and the Wellesley Editorial Committee, *Women and National Development: The Complexities of Change* (Chicago: University of Chicago Press, 1977).

7. Jaquette, "Feminist Criticism," p. 271.

8. Margaret E. Leahy, *Development Strategies and the Status of Women: A Comparative Study of the United States, Mexico, the Soviet Union, and Cuba* (Boulder, Colo.: Lynne Rienner, 1986).

9. Dorothy Atkinson, Alexander Dallin, and Gail Warshofsky Lapidus eds., *Women in Russia* (Stanford, Calif.: Stanford University Press, 1977); Gail Warshofsky Lapidus, *Women in Soviet Society: Equality, Development, and Social Change* (Berkeley: University of California Press, 1978); and Hilda Scott, *Does Socialism Liberate Women? Experiences from Eastern Europe* (Boston: Beacon, 1974).

10. Rule, "Women's Opportunity for Election to Parliament," p. 480.

11. Ruth B. Mandel, "The Political Woman," in Sara E. Rix, ed., *The American Woman, 1988–1989: A Status Report* (New York: Norton, 1988) pp. 90–91.

12. April Carter, *The Politics of Women's Rights* (New York: Longman, 1988); Jennifer Dale and Peggy Foster, *Feminists and State Welfare* (London: Routledge and Kegan Paul, 1986); Barbara Sinclair Deckard, *The Women's Movement: Political, Socioeconomic, and Psychological Issues*, 3rd Ed. (New York: Harper & Row, 1983); Myra Marx Ferree and Beth B. Hess, *Controversy and Coalition: The New Feminist Movement* (Boston: Twayne, 1985); Jo Freeman, *The Politics of Women's Liberation: A Case Study of an Emerging Social Movement and Its Relation to the Policy Process* (New York: David McKay, 1975); Joyce Gelb, *Feminism and Politics: A Comparative Perspective* (Berkeley: University of California Press, 1989); Mary Fainsod Katzenstein and Carol McClarg Mueller, eds., *The Women's Movements of the United States and Western Europe: Consciousness, Political Opportunity, and Public Policy* (Philadelphia: Temple University Press, 1987); Ethel Klein, *Gender Politics: From Consciousness to Mass Politics* (Cambridge: Harvard University Press, 1984); and Lovenduski, *Women and European Politics*, Chps. 2 & 3.

13. Jaquette, "Feminist Criticism," outlines these three strands of feminist theory and how they are related to each other.

14. For example, Sue Ellen M. Charlton, *Women in Third World Development* (Boulder, Colo.: Westview, 1984).

15. For example, Zillah H. Eisenstein, ed., *Capitalist Patriarchy and the Case for Socialist Feminism* (New York: Monthly Review Press, 1979).

16. For example, Elise Boulding, *Women in the Twentieth-Century World* (Beverly Hills, Calif.: Sage, 1977).

17. Cal Clark, *Taiwan's Development: Implications for Contending Political Economy Paradigms* (New York: Greenwood Press, 1989); Walter Galenson, ed., *Economic Growth and Structural Change in Taiwan: The Postwar Experience of the Republic of China* (Ithaca, N.Y.: Cornell University Press, 1979); Thomas B. Gold, *State and Society in the Taiwan Miracle* (Armonk, N.Y.: M. E. Sharpe, 1986); Shirley W.Y. Kuo, Gustav Ranis, and John C.H. Fei, *The Taiwan Success Story: Rapid Growth with Improved Distribution in the Republic of China* (Boulder, Colo.: Westview, 1981); K. T. Li, *The Evolution of Policy Behind Taiwan's Development Success* (New Haven: Yale University Press, 1988); Ramon H. Myers, "The Economic Transformation of the Republic of China on Taiwan," *China Quarterly* 99 (September 1984) pp. 500–528; and Edwin A. Winckler and Susan Greenhalgh, eds., *Contending Approaches to the Political Economy of Taiwan* (Armonk, N.Y.: M. E. Sharpe, 1988).

18. Susan Greenhalgh, "Sexual Stratification: The Other Side of 'Growth with Equity' in East Asia," *Population and Development Review* 11:2 (June 1985) pp. 265–314.

19. Chu-yuan Cheng, ed., *Sun Yat-sen's Doctrine in the Modern World* (Boulder, Colo.: Westview, 1989); Tuan-sheng Ch'ien, *The Government and Politics of China* (Cambridge: Harvard University Press, 1950) Chps. 9–11, 13, 15–18, & 21; Harold Z. Schiffren, *Sun Yat-sen and the Origins of the 1911 Revolution* (Berkeley: University of California Press, 1968); and C. Martin Wilbur, *Sun Yat-sen, Frustrated Patriot* (New York: Columbia University Press, 1976).

20. George F. Botjer, *A History of Nationalist China, 1919–1949* (New York: Putnam, 1979); Brian Crozier, *The Man Who Lost China: The First Full Biography of Chiang Kai-shek* (New York: Charles Scribner's Sons, 1976); James E. Sheridan, *China in Disintegration: The Republican Era in Chinese History, 1912–1949* (New York: Free Press, 1975); and Hung-mao Tien, *Government and Politics in Kuomin-*

*tang China, 1927–1937* (Stanford, Calif.: Stanford University Press, 1972).

21. John F. Copper, *A Quiet Revolution: Political Development in the Republic of China* (Washington, D.C.: Ethics and Public Policy Center, 1988); John F. Copper with George P. Chen, *Taiwan's Elections: Political Development and Democratization in the Republic of China* (Baltimore: School of Law, University of Maryland, 1984); James C. Hsiung, ed., *Contemporary Republic of China: The Taiwan Experience, 1950–1980* (New York: Praeger, 1981); Ramon H. Myers, "Political Theory and the Recent Political Developments in the Republic of China," *Asian Survey* 27:9 (September 1987) pp. 1003–1022; Robert G. Sutter, *Taiwan: Entering the 21st Century* (Lanham, Md.: University Press of America, 1988); Hung-mao Tien, *The Great Transition: Political and Social Change in the Republic of China* (Stanford, Calif.: Hoover Institution Press, 1989); and Edwin A. Winckler, "Institutionalization and Participation on Taiwan: From Hard to Soft Authoritarianism?" *China Quarterly* 99 (September 1984) pp. 481–499.

22. Diane L. Fowlkes, "Developing a Theory of Countersocialization: Gender, Race, and Politics in the Lives of Women Activists," *Micropolitics* 3:2 (No. 2, 1983) pp. 181–225; Diane L. Fowlkes, "Ambitious Political Women: Countersocialization and Political Party Context," *Women & Politics* 4:4 (Winter 1984) pp. 5–32; and Sue Tolleson Rinehart, "Toward Women's Political Resocialization: Patterns of Predisposition in the Learning of Feminist Attitudes," *Women & Politics* 5:4 (Winter 1985/86) pp. 11–26.

23. Susan J. Carroll, *Women As Candidates in American Politics* (Bloomington: Indiana University Press, 1985) pp. 106–120; R. Darcy, Susan Welch, and Janet Clark, *Women, Elections, and Representation* (New York: Longman, 1987) Part III; Maurice Duverger, *The Political Role of Women* (Paris: UNESCO, 1955) pp. 84–95; and Rule, "Women's Opportunity for Election to Parliament."

24. Yangsun Chou and Andrew J. Nathan, "Democratizing Transition in Taiwan," *Asian Survey* 27:3 (March 1987) pp. 277–299; Richard L. Engstrom and Chu Chi-hung, "The Impact of the 1980 Supplementary Election on Nationalist China's Legislative Yuan," *Asian Survey* 24:4 (April 1984) pp. 446–458; Arthur J. Lerman, *Taiwan's Politics: The Provincial Assemblyman's World* (Washington, D.C.: University Press of America, 1978); and Tien, *The Great Transition*, Chp. 6.

CHAPTER TWO
# The Representation of Women

One of the questions frequently asked concerning the underrepresentation of women in public office is, What difference does it make? Why should there be any concern about the fact that half of the world's population holds relatively few positions in government? There are two basic reasons for increasing the representation of women in government: First, on philosophical grounds, it is desirable that women be represented. Second, there are practical reasons why more women should serve on governing bodies.

This chapter, then, explores questions about the political representation of women. The first section provides an overview of arguments advocating equal representation for women. The basic argument here is that women form a distinct group that deserves representation according to the normal tenets of democratic theory. Furthermore, feminists have argued that women have special policy and issue interests and that they have a different political style from male politicians. The virtual exclusion of women from public office, therefore, leads to warped policy outcomes, and society loses the contribution that women leaders could make. The second section discusses the importance and immutability of the four general reasons that have been adduced for women's tremendous underrepresentation in the political elites of almost every polity: (1) biological and psychological differences between the sexes, (2) the socialization patterns created by patriarchal societies, (3) discrimination against women by political leaders and voters, and (4) structural features of the way the political processes are organized, such as the nature of election systems and the advantages that accrue to legislative incumbents. Finally, the concluding section assesses these barriers to women's political participation in general and speculates about their applicability to Taiwan in particular.

## Normative Theories About the Representation of Women

The underlying assumptions of democracy call for the participation and representation of all segments of society. Theories of what Hanna Pitkin calls "descriptive representation" argue that the exclusion of any group from positions of power may distort policy decisions and political outcomes.[1] On a theoretical level, descriptive representation justifies representative government with the assumption that a sovereign legislative assembly is a social microcosm representing all social groups proportionately and, thus, can be substituted for a democratic convocation of the whole people. This normative assumption about an entire political system is based on the presumption that office-holders represent constituents whose social characteristics they share. This occurs both because leaders empathize with such informal constituencies and identify with their interests and because members of the social group in question may feel represented just because one of "their own" holds office.

Descriptive representation certainly does not form a complete theory of democracy on either the normative or empirical level. As Pitkin argues, there are two major problems with this approach to defining representation.[2] First, there is the basic question of what social characteristics should be considered politically relevant. Second, there is no guarantee that political leaders will represent in any substantive sense social groups whose characteristics they share.

Are women a politically relevant group? If so, do women politicians generally represent that group? According to Virginia Sapiro, women can be said to form a distinct political group if they are generally viewed by themselves and others as distinct and/or if they hold distinctive political views.[3] There are many indications that gender does define politically relevant groups. Women do have a distinct position and a shared set of problems. Nevertheless, they may not be fully conscious of their difference from men, or they may agree with men on policy issues.[4]

Another normative consideration involves the importance of participation for women's self-development. According to Peter Bachrach, classical democratic theory measures public interest not only by the soundness of decisions reached but also by the "scope" of public participation.[5] The premise is that citizen participation in all aspects of public affairs is essential to the full development of individual capacities. The paucity of women in public office is a sign of a fundamental malfunction of democratic systems that are being deprived of the contributions of more than half of their citizens.[6] The very legitimacy of the democratic system, then, is at stake when women are underrepresented in government. The composition of the governing institutions is a legitimizing agency for the political regime. Predominantly male institutions cannot serve this legitimizing function in today's world.[7] Thus, there is a strong normative case for according equal representation to women.[8]

Beyond such general normative considerations, there are also practical reasons why women need greater representation on governing bodies. Women have come to have increasingly different perspectives and political attitudes from men on a wide range of social and political issues.[9] Until the

1970s, the differences between men and women in issue positions and voting patterns were generally considered fairly small, limited to such questions as public morality and the use of force in international and domestic politics. If anything, women were seen as slightly more conservative than men.[10] In recent years in the United States, differences have emerged in such areas as social compassion, protection of the environment, and basic economic issues; a significant gender gap in presidential voting and approval emerged during the Reagan administration.[11] For Europe, a recent study found that women had developed more liberal views than men on a variety of domestic issues, concluding that although this gender gap had yet to have much of an electoral impact, it could become more salient politically if European women's movements matched the success of the U.S. one in awakening women to the extent of the gender inequalities in their societies.[12] These differences suggest that women need to be represented by women if their issue positions are to receive consideration in policymaking bodies.

Table 2.1 summarizes some of the issue areas where the opinions of U.S. men and women differ significantly. There is a consistent gender gap of 7%–15% for women to be less supportive of military adventurism and harsh criminal penalties, more supportive of protecting the environment and using government to promote social and economic equality, and less confident in the "American dream." This gender gap has usually been explained in terms of the general issue interests of women. However, Susan Carroll argues persuasively that women's growing economic and psychological independence from men plays an important part as well.[13] Given these significant differences in the attitudes of the two sexes toward important political issues, therefore, women's huge underrepresentation among policymakers in the United States (and elsewhere) would seemingly bias public policy outcomes.

The women's movement, certainly, has been quite energetic in trying to get women's issues on the political agenda in both the United States and Europe.[14] Most basically, women have tried to attain equal rights through supporting such initiatives as the Equal Rights Amendment in the United States[15] or through using the judicial process.[16] In the United States, at least, abortion has been a central issue for the women's movement, although some women's groups have mobilized to oppose abortion.[17] More generally, women have been increasingly active in advocating public policies to overcome traditional disadvantages in their social and economic roles and to help the dispossessed in general.[18] Thus, women have emerged as a "special interest" with "claims" upon the public.[19] In the United States, for instance, women's lobbying has become quite important, the mark of a legitimate participant in the U.S. political processes.[20]

Female officials, moreover, appear to have become generally committed to supporting women's issues. A study of legislative candidates in the United States indicates that substantial proportions of women candidates and officeholders are committed to women's issues and to the goals of the women's movement.[21] Furthermore, a large majority of these women feel they will be better representatives of women's interests and more sensitive to the needs of women than will their male counterparts. While women in politics diverge in partisanship and ideology, large proportions in every group still support greater equity for women.[22] A recent survey of men and women in U.S. state legislatures, for example, shows that women legislators are more likely than the men to give top priority to bills focusing on women and to work on legislation to help women.[23] Table 2.2 indicates the extent to which U.S. women legislators support women's issues as compared with their male counterparts.

Table 2.1 Gender Differences in U.S. Public Opinion, Mid-1980s (by percent)

| | Women | Men |
|---|---|---|
| Agree that U. S. should take military action against nations supporting terrorism | 44 | 61 |
| Oppose U.S. aid to Contras in Nicaragua | 61 | 49 |
| Oppose the return to the military draft | 61 | 48 |
| Approve the U.S. invasion of Grenada | 48 | 68 |
| Favor stricter regulation of the sale of hand guns | 66 | 53 |
| Favor the death penalty for persons convicted of murder | 69 | 76 |
| Favor relaxing environmental protection laws to improve the economy | 48 | 58 |
| Favor building more nuclear power plants | 24 | 50 |
| Favor cutting back on operation of nuclear power plants until better safety regulations | 76 | 55 |
| Agree that government should work to reduce the income gap between rich and poor | 73 | 61 |
| Favor increased federal spending for social security program | 56 | 43 |
| Favor federal aid to relocate unemployed to areas with job opportunities | 55 | 47 |
| Favor preference to blacks in hiring and promotion where there has been past discrimination | 49 | 34 |
| Favor busing to achieve better racial balance in the public schools | 32 | 24 |
| Newsstands should not be allowed to sell pornography | 73 | 46 |
| Favor legalizing the possession of small amounts of marijuana for personal use | 25 | 35 |
| Favor the national law raising the legal drinking age in all states to 21 | 82 | 75 |
| Have a lot of confidence in the future strength and prosperity of the nation | 27 | 39 |
| Believe it possible now to start out poor and work hard to become rich | 55 | 65 |
| Satisfied with the way things are going in the United States | 42 | 52 |

*Source:* "The Gender Gap Fact Sheet," Center for the American Woman and Politics (CAWP), National Information Bank on Women in Public Office (NIP), Eagleton Institute of Politics, Rutgers University, July 1987, pp. 3–4.

Another practical advantage of increasing the representation of women in government stems from the different political psychology of women. According to Carol Gilligan, women are more likely than men to negotiate rather than engage in confrontation. They think in terms of the long-range future rather than short-term solutions to problems, and they do not see life as a zero-sum game in which one side wins at the expense of the other but consider middle solutions that can be beneficial to all. Their emphasis is on personal collaboration and issue resolution as opposed to competitive political orientations, and they stress "connectiveness"—personal and community relations—rather than abstract issues and power considerations.[24] Building upon this perspective, Janet Flammang argues that increasing the number of women in the political elites could lead to the "transformation of traditional political concepts and paradigms" both by adding new items to the political agenda and creating new role models for political activities.[25] Likewise, Elise Boulding argues that women can make a unique contribution to the current transformation of the world political economy by providing "female alternatives to [the existing] hierarchical systems."[26]

Table 2.2 Sex Differences in State Legislatures Working on Leglislation Targeted at Women (by percent)

|  | State Senate | | State House | |
| --- | --- | --- | --- | --- |
|  | Women | Men | Women | Men |
| Women's issue was top priority of session | 9.3 | 5.1 | 9.2 | 3.2 |
| Worked on legislation to help women during session | 59.3 | 39.4 | 55.3 | 33.2 |
| N = | 194 | 137 | 412 | 349 |

*Source:* Susan J. Carroll and Ella Taylor, "Gender Differences in Policy Priorities," *CAWP News & Notes* 7:2 (Winter 1989) p. 4.

Thus, although women are not homogeneous in their attitudes and women politicians are a diverse lot, they are becoming increasingly distinctive. This distinctiveness and the fact that women are a majority of the population make their dramatic underrepresentation significant for those concerned about democracy and political issues. It also raises certain practical questions: Why are so few chosen? What barriers, either internal or external to themselves, prevent women from obtaining a more equitable share of political positions?

## Theories Explaining Women's Underrepresentation

Despite the fact that women received the legal right to participate in government in many democratic countries in the early decades of the twentieth century, their progress in achieving political equity has been painfully slow. Table 2.3 lists the dates that women's suffrage was granted in various countries. Even gaining minimal entrance into the political processes was quite slow. Before World War I, women had the right to vote in only four countries. Most developed nations granted the suffrage during the interwar period, though Switzerland, an obvious laggard, held out until 1971. However, women did not gain formal access to influencing government in much of the Third World until after World War II; colonialism obviously must bear some of the blame for the slow pace of change.

Table 2.3  Dates of Women's Suffrage

| Year | Countries | Year | Countries |
|---|---|---|---|
| 1893 | New Zealand | 1952 | Belgium, Greece |
| 1902 | Australia | 1953 | China, Jamaica, Mexico |
| 1906 | Finland | 1954 | Colombia |
| 1913 | Norway | 1955 | Ethiopia, Ghana, Nicaragua, Peru |
| 1915 | Denmark, Iceland | | |
| 1917 | USSR | 1956 | Cameroon, Central African Republic, Chad, Congo, Egypt, Gabon, Guinea, Ivory Coast, Laos, Madagascar, Mali, Mauritania, Niger, Pakistan, Senegal, Sudan, Tunisia, Upper Volta |
| 1918 | Austria | | |
| 1919 | Czechoslovakia, Luxembourg, Netherlands, Poland, Sweden | | |
| 1920 | Canada, United States | | |
| 1922 | Ireland | | |
| 1924 | Mongolia | 1957 | Haiti, Honduras, Lebanon, Malaysia |
| 1928 | Germany, United Kingdom | | |
| 1929 | Ecuador | 1958 | Albania, Algeria, Iraq, Somalia |
| 1930 | South Africa | | |
| 1931 | Spain, Sri Lanka | 1959 | Cyprus, Mauritius, Morocco |
| 1932 | Brazil, Thailand | 1960 | Nigeria, Zaire |
| 1934 | Cuba, Turkey, Uruguay | 1961 | Burundi, Gambia, Paraguay, Rwanda, Sierra Leone, Tanzania |
| 1935 | Burma | | |
| 1938 | Bulgaria, Philippines | 1962 | Uganda |
| 1942 | Dominican Republic | 1963 | Iran, Kenya, Libya |
| 1945 | France, Guatemala, Hungary, Indonesia, Japan, Panama, Trinidad and Tobago | 1964 | Afghanistan, Malawi, Zambia |
| | | 1965 | Botswana, Singapore |
| | | 1966 | Guyana, Lesotho |
| 1946 | Benin, Italy, Liberia, Romania, Yugoslavia | 1967 | South Yemen |
| | | 1968 | Swaziland |
| 1947 | Argentina, Malta, Togo, Venezuela, Vietnam | 1970 | Fiji |
| | | 1971 | Switzerland |
| 1948 | Belgium, Israel, North Korea, South Korea | 1972 | Bangladesh |
| | | 1974 | Jordan |
| 1949 | Chile, Costa Rica, India, Syria | 1976 | Portugal |
| 1950 | Barbados, El Salvador | 1984 | Lichtenstein |
| 1951 | Nepal | | |

*Source:* Ruth Sivard, *Women: A World Survey* (New York: Ford, Rockefeller, and Carnegie, 1985) p. 28.
*Note:* Data not available for Angola, Bahrain, Brunei, Cambodia, Equatorial Guinea, Mozambique, Papua New Guinea, North Yemen, and Zimbabwe. There is no women's suffrage in Oman, Qatar, Saudi Arabia, and United Arab Emirates.

Gaining the right to vote, however, has certainly not been translated into equal representation for women, even after half a century in most of the developed world. Traditionally, women have been less interested in politics and less likely to vote or engage in other mass political activities in most societies.[27] However, this does not provide an explanation for their severe underrepresentation in the political leadership stratum for several reasons. First, the gender differences in participation and interest are of a far lesser magnitude than for office-holding. Second, although this gap in various types of mass participation nearly vanished in the United States during the 1970s,[28] women still remain grossly underrepresented there at all levels of government. Third, while women's participation relative to men's is higher in the United States than in most other countries,[29] the participatory gap between men and women appears to have narrowed appreciably in most other developed democracies, especially when "unconventional" types of activity are taken into account.[30] Thus, women's near-total exclusion from the seats of government power is puzzling. In response, several broad theories have been offered to explain the lower level of women's political representation.

### Innate Differences

The first theory stresses innate differences between men and women. According to this view, men and women are physically, biologically, and psychologically different. It is assumed that political leaders are those who have power-seeking, achievement-motivated personalities. These are traits believed to be found in men but not women.[31] Therefore, if these assumptions are true, women do not have the necessary personality traits to succeed in politics.[32] However, studies have not supported either assumption. People in public office do not necessarily have power-seeking, achievement-motivated traits.[33] Furthermore, studies of men and women politicians have not found significant personality differences between the sexes.[34] Thus, the explanation of the underrepresentation of women in public office does not lie in innate differences between men and women.

### Socialization Effects

A second theory does not rely on innate differences, but stresses childhood sex-role socialization. According to this theory, women and men are taught to accept different kinds of roles in life. Women are trained to be passive and home-oriented. Men are taught to be independent, assertive, and achievement-oriented. Consequently, politics and public life in general are seen as a man's world—the home is the woman's domain. As a result of this type of sex-role socialization that begins in childhood, women who challenge their designated role and actively seek public office will suffer psychological pain because they can no longer identify with nonpolitical women and are not accepted by their male colleagues.[35] Moreover, even basic Western political theory seems to assume the distinction between "public man" and "private woman."[36] For example, Rita Mae Kelly and Mary Boutilier studied the lives of women who had engaged in various levels of political activity and found that women who had taken active political roles came from nontraditional homes and had exceptional mothers.[37]

Virginia Sapiro developed a variation on socialization theory.[38] She found adult sex-role socialization to be more important in determining women's political participation than childhood socialization was. The difference in political interest between boys and girls is only slight.[39] Therefore, she hypothesized that the gap between men's and women's political participation is the result of reinforcement of childhood training by women's adult roles. She argued that childhood sex-role socialization is absorbed in the abstract and only becomes operative in the ways that males and females relate to the political system in adulthood when political behavior becomes "real." Thus, childhood socialization experiences are mediated and reinforced by the adult roles that women assume, especially family and work roles. Some of women's potential roles are much more congruent with political activities, while others are overwhelmingly privatized.

Socialization thus is assumed to discourage women's political participation in several ways. First, it creates psychological barriers to moving out of the domestic sphere. Women are conditioned to believe that their place is in the home and that public life belongs to the world of men. Thus, they are deterred from entering politics because of the internal strains that are created from breaking cultural and social norms. The result is that women in politics represent a "portrait in marginality."[40]

However, such socialization barriers are coming under increasing challenge from the women's movement and from women's increasing assumption of professional jobs. For example, a recent poll showed that while only a third of U.S. women considered themselves feminists, 62% believed that feminists had helped women and over 80% believed that the women's movement had helped women become more independent and improve their lives.[41] This certainly indicates support from a large majority of women in the United States for challenging traditional role stereotypes and socialization patterns. In addition, with the considerable growth of women's office-holding in many developed countries that occurred during the 1970s and 1980s (see Chapter 1), role strains among women politicians might well be expected to lessen.

A second perspective on role conflicts focuses simply upon the extent of women's family responsibilities. Women devote themselves to their homes and families; therefore, they do not have the time or energy for active participation in politics. Their situation as homemakers prevents their doing much outside the home beyond simply voting. However, the validity of this assumption is open to question. While homemaking may retard the political participation of some women, many women have not been constrained in this way. Most of the volunteer workers of political parties and other associations have been women. Women have historically been active as organizers, coordinators, door-to-door canvassers, project directors, lobbyists, and demonstrators in regard to local public policies.[42] Apparently, modern women continue to have time for such activities if not for holding public office.[43] This certainly suggests an invidious sexual division of labor, with women doing the thankless work and men reaping the rewards of political power.

The duties of family, however, still do represent an important constraint on holding public office. A study of elected officials found that support from spouse and family was one of the three most important factors in the decision to seek public office. Married women were even more likely than the married men to place spousal and family support uppermost in importance.[44] Furthermore, political aspiration and the ambition to hold public office still seem to be more constrained among women than men. Studies of the politically active women who make up the party elites in the United States have shown that they are less likely than the male leaders to desire elected office.[45] However, the difference in the level of political ambition has been declining in recent years.

Research has shown two of the ways that some women in public office have avoided role conflicts between being homemakers and politicians. Jeane Kirkpatrick found that women in U.S. state legislatures delayed the start of their careers until their children were in school.[46] Thus, on the average, women legislators were older than their male counterparts. A study by Carol Nechemias indicated that women's ability to hold office may depend on convenience. For example, the women in her study of sixteen U.S. state legislatures were more likely than the men to come from districts that were closer to the state capital.[47]

Another way that sex-role socialization is hypothesized to limit women's political participation is structural. By concentrating on homemaking to the exclusion of other occupations and roles, women are not found in the professions from which politicians inordinately are chosen (the law and broker-type businesses). Therefore, they do not achieve the higher socioeconomic status that forms the "eligibility pool" for elective office.[48] Susan Welch investigated the limitations asserted by career on women's representation in U.S. state legislatures. The findings were mixed: Although there were far fewer women than men in key professions that provide the career backgrounds for legislators, their levels in these eligibility pools were greater than predicted by their numbers in office.[49] Furthermore, the road to public office for women seems to diverge from that for men. Women may be able to compensate for their lower socioeconomic status by working harder in voluntary groups and political parties to prove their competence.[50]

## *Discrimination Against Women*

A third explanation attributes the low representation of women in public office to explicit discrimination against them. This "male conspiracy" theory is derived from feminist ideology. Women do not achieve equality with men because men discriminate against them. Party and interest group leaders are men, and they prevent women from achieving equality. Socialist feminists see private property and male ownership of the means of production as the cause of women's inequality. Radical feminists believe that the subjugation of women is the most basic form of discrimination. Men dominate women because they enjoy the power it gives them.[51]

Evidence of discrimination against women by political elites has not been conclusive. Although three studies have suggested that U.S. women candidates face this obstacle in running for office,[52] other writers have not concurred. One study found that while female party leaders in the United States perceived that male leaders do discriminate against women in politics, they had not personally experienced such discrimination.[53] A survey of party leaders in New Mexico uncovered little evidence of opposition to female candidates.[54] Another study in Oklahoma found that the party actually provided advantages to female candidates in terms of slating and funding.[55] Even in national legislative races, candidate gender has not been a significant factor in raising and spending campaign funds, and there is little evidence that party elites are withholding campaign funds from women candidates in recent years.[56] Apparently, discrimination by party gatekeepers has been receding in recent years as the increased legitimacy of women politicians makes overt discrimination potentially costly.

The prevailing political culture in a nation or region may also affect the degree of discrimination against women by political leaders. That is, some political cultures favor political parties that are less hospitable to women candidates, although the nature of party perspectives on women candidates seems somewhat variable. On the one hand, research in continental Europe has usually concluded that left-wing parties are more likely to slate women candidates than are more conservative ones,[57] although this trend appeared to have largely evaporated by the 1980s.[58] On the other hand, elections dominated by parties that were worker-oriented (such as the Labor Party in the UK and the U.S. Democratic Party) brought fewer women into office.[59] Yet the effects of party dominance may be changing. For example, because more women are entering the labor force, worker parties might become more amenable to the election of women; this seems to be the case in the United States.[60]

Voter discrimination, another factor seen as limiting access of women to public office, is commonly assumed to vary according to political culture. Because of socialization, voters in certain types of political culture may be more likely than those in other cultures to perceive women as less qualified than men to hold public office. In the United States, traditional political cultures are assumed to discourage the election of women. In contrast, individualistic cultures provide a more neutral setting, and moralistic cultures encourage the election of women, who are seen as having the traits that promote good government. Research in both the United States and Europe (where Catholic cultures can be assumed to be traditional ones) has supported these assumptions, but the impact of culture in the United States has undergone change over time. Nevertheless, traditional cultures still have a deleterious effect on women's political recruitment.[61]

Overall, however, voter discrimination against female candidates seems to be on the decline. While there is evidence of past voter discrimination in the United States, this problem seems to have largely vanished. At least according to public opinion polls, the general populace's acceptance of and support for women's office-holding has grown considerably since the late 1960s.[62] More importantly, the difference in voter support for male and female candidates has declined to an insignificant level since the mid 1970s. Once the candidates' party and incumbency status are taken into account, voters are now as likely to vote for women as for men in both local and national elections.[63] Similarly, candidate gender per se has been found to have almost no influence on candidates' performance at the polls in the United Kingdom,[64] and in several European countries women appear to be "equal or stronger vote-getters than men."[65]

*Political Structures*

Institutional constraints have also been adduced as a fourth barrier to the election of women. One obvious constraint is implicit in the previous findings that women candidates do as well as their male competitors once incumbency is controlled: Political incumbents have a tremendous electoral advantage in most nations because of the political resources that office-holders control, their sheer advantage in name recognition, and the fact that previous victories demonstrate an ability to appeal to the voters. To the extent that incumbents enjoy a considerable advantage in elections, women are certainly disadvantaged. Women hold only a small minority of elected posts today both because of discrimination from voters and political elites in the past and because of the internal restraints of cultural socialization. Thus, since women are much less likely than men to be incumbents who are known to and respected by constituents, it will take decades for them to achieve equality in office in most nations if the normal advantages of incumbency continue to operate.[66] However, the news about the effects of incumbency is not entirely negative—once women do succeed in winning election in a district, state, or nation, their example evidently makes it easier for other women to win elections later.[67]

The very nature of electoral systems may be limiting the election of women to public office because women clearly do better in some types of elections than in others. Table 2.4, for instance, presents Wilma Rule's findings about the proportion of women elected to the lower house of the national legislature in 23 industrial democracies at the beginning of the 1980s. Women did much better in multimember districts with proportional representation and a "party list" of candidates[68] than in single-member, winner-take-all systems. Multivariate analysis, furthermore, showed that the existence of proportional representation with party list was the major determinant of the level of women's representation in these 23 democracies, even after their other socioeconomic and political characteristics were controlled.[69] It was also significant that district size (i.e., number of seats to be elected) had a separate and independent effect, confirming earlier arguments that women do better in larger districts where voters can pick more candidates.[70]

Table 2.4  Percentage of Women in Lower House of National Legislature by Type of Electoral System, 1982

| | |
|---|---|
| *Party List/Proportional Representation System* | |
| Sweden | 27.7 |
| Finland | 26.0 |
| Norway | 23.9 |
| Denmark | 22.9 |
| Netherlands | 14.0 |
| Switzerland | 10.5 |
| Austria | 9.8 |
| Portugal | 8.8 |
| Italy | 8.2 |
| Belgium | 7.5 |
| Israel | 7.5 |
| West Germany | 7.3 |
| Spain | 5.4 |
| Iceland | 5.0 |
| Greece | 4.0 |
| *Single Transferable Vote System* | |
| Ireland | 6.8 |
| *Single Nontransferable Vote System* | |
| Japan | 1.6 |
| *Single Member District System* | |
| New Zealand | 8.8 |
| Canada | 4.3 |
| France | 4.1 |
| United States | 4.1 |
| United Kingdom | 3.1 |
| Australia | 0.0 |

Source: Wilma Rule, "Election Systems, Contextual Factors, and Women's Opportunity for Election to Parliament in Twenty-three Democracies," *Western Political Quarterly* 40:3 (September 1987) p. 483.

Several reasons have been advanced for women's advantage in multi-member districts with proportional representation. One line of argument focuses upon proportional representation itself. Parties have an incentive to place at least some women high enough on their slates to win in order to broaden their appeal, and all candidates on a list run as a team. Thus, this system overcomes the problems of gender bias by voters and leaders.[71] But another perspective views the relationship as more indirect, claiming the key factor is the political risk that a party sees in nominating a woman candidate. Research suggests that parties nominate women whom they expect to win if they are fairly sure they can secure at least three seats in a district. Thus, the key factor is the ratio of seats to competitive parties because it determines the "risk assessment" of the leaders who slate candidates.[72] This also implies, incidentally, that strong centralized parties can play a positive role in promoting women's representation, at least when they face competition and an acceptable "political risk" level.[73] In any event, whether the impact of proportional representation is direct or indirect, the correlation between election system and women's representation appears more than strong enough to justify Rule's conclusion: "The data presented in this paper make a convincing case for the superiority of party list/PR systems—in particular those with large district magnitudes—for women's opportunity for election to parliament."[74]

This analysis of the influence exerted by the election system is also relevant to another structural problem facing women candidates: The power and prestige of the political office seem to be factors in determining the level of representation of women—the more desirable the office and/or the greater the competition for it, the less likely that women will be well represented. In legislatures that are large relative to the population represented, women have more seats. Also, the degree of professionalism of the legislature determines the relative representation of women. In legislatures where the members sit full-time, receive high pay, and hold greater prestige, there will be fewer women.[75] The hypothesis that the level of competitiveness and prestige of the legislative body affects the number of women in office seems to be confirmed by the fact that there are more women in local offices than in national offices. Also, even at the same level of government, women have been more likely to be elected in places where the office is considered less desirable.[76] While the prestige or attractiveness of an office is obviously an independent factor, the election system can clearly affect the competitiveness. If there are multimember districts, whether or not proportional representation is used, competitiveness should bear an inverse relationship to the number of seats being elected. Even within the United States, for example, women gain greater representation in districts with two or more seats.[77]

## Implications

Overall, studies done in Western democratic societies have suggested many reasons why women deserve greater representation in government and why they are disadvantaged as candidates for office. Although times are changing and the numbers of women in public office are growing, much still remains to be done before women will achieve political equity. The question arises of whether studies in Western societies have validity for Eastern cultures. How much of the underrepresentation of women in Taiwan's government can be explained by theories developed for the United States and Europe?

Four theoretical perspectives explaining women's underrepresentation in political office throughout the world were reviewed in this chapter. The idea of innate biological and psychological differences between men and women appeared to have little validity. The other three theories were more promising, but none provided the entire answer. First, socialization into the roles of "public man and private woman" clearly constituted an almost insurmountable barrier for most women in the past. Changes in this situation are occurring, though: Industrialization allowed women to assume new roles, and the women's movement challenged the traditional role stereotypes in the 1970s and 1980s. Second, discrimination against women in the past was the rule (most glaringly, widespread suffrage was not granted until the 1920s and 1930s), but recent analysis from a variety of industrial democracies suggests that this is no longer a problem in itself. Finally, the very structures of the political system can help or hinder women's candidacies, with some types of election systems clearly favoring women. Also, once some women gain office, they present a "demonstration effect" that gives a boost to subsequent attempts by other women to run for office. Probably the most serious structural barrier, however, is simply the tremendous electoral advantage that incumbents have. This will almost certainly prevent equal representation for women for several decades even if the other barriers completely vanish, which is all too improbable.

The feminist and modernization approaches would make somewhat different evaluations of the status of women's political representation. Both would view women's tremendous underrepresentation in almost all polities as unjustified and highly undesirable. However, feminists would consider this as a central problem facing society, while the modernization approach would see it as much more peripheral. More importantly, modernizationists would point to the undeniable changes that have occurred in women's social, economic, and political statuses in most developed democracies and claim that modernization will bring women's equality (at least in the long run). Feminists, in contrast, would argue with more than some justification that socialization patterns and overt discrimination have made women second-class citizens in almost every nation on earth and that radical change in this situation does not appear particularly imminent. Whether one sees the glass as half full or half empty (or, more accurately in terms of representation in national legislatures, 10% full and 90% empty) depends upon both temperament and theoretical loyalties.

The position of women politicians in Taiwan has both advantages and disadvantages. Given the patriarchal nature of Chinese society and the island's industrial transformation that has come only recently, socialization and discrimination barriers should be much greater than in Europe and North America. The nature of the election and party system offers more possibilities, though. Taiwan's election districts for both national and local assemblies are fairly large, although the voting system of the single nontransferable vote[78] is the one least favorable to women in multimember districts.[79] The party system seems to be evolving from dominant one-party rule toward intense two-party competition in electoral politics (see Chapter 3), which is normally considered to provide a favorable environment for women. Last and far from least, the Republic of China reserves about a tenth of its legislative seats for women (see Chapter 5), guaranteeing them a level of representation that is only slightly lower than the average for the developed world. An in-depth case study of the status of women in the ROC's politics, therefore, should provide valuable evidence about the various theories of women's underrepresentation.

## Notes

1. Hanna Fenichel Pitkin, *The Concept of Representation* (Berkeley: University of California Press, 1967) Chp. 4.

2. Pitkin, *Representation*, pp. 86–91.

3. Virginia Sapiro, "Research Frontier Essay: When Are Interests Interesting? The Problem of Political Representation of Women," *American Political Science Review* 75:3 (September 1981) p. 703.

4. Sapiro, "Political Representation of Women," pp. 703–704.

5. Peter Bachrach, *The Theory of Democratic Elitism: A Critique* (Boston: Little, Brown, 1967) p. 3.

6. Susan J. Carroll, "Woman Candidates and Support for Feminist Concerns: The Closet Feminist Syndrome," *Western Political Quarterly* 37:2 (June 1984) p. 307.

7. R. Darcy, Susan Welch, and Janet Clark, *Women, Elections, and Representation* (New York: Longman, 1987) p. 14.

8. Mary Lou Kendrigan, *Political Equality in a Democratic Society* (Westport, Conn.: Greenwood, 1984).

9. Emily Stoper, "The Gender Gap Concealed and Revealed: 1936–1984," *Journal of Political Science* 17:1-2 (Spring 1989) pp. 50–62.

10. Maurice Duverger, *The Political Role of Women* (Paris: UNESCO, 1955) pp. 45–73; and Henry C. Kenski, "The Gender Factor in a Changing Electorate," in Carol M. Mueller, ed., *The Politics of the Gender Gap: The Social Construction of Political Influence* (Beverly Hills, Calif.: Sage, 1988) pp. 38–60.

11. Mueller, *The Gender Gap*, especially the Chps. by Julio Borquez, Edie N. Goldenberg, and Kim Fridkin Kahn, "Press Portrayals of the Gender Gap," pp. 124–147; Cynthia Denich, "Sex Differences in Support for Government Spending," pp. 192–216; Kenski, "The Gender Factor," pp. 38–60; Arthur Miller, "Gender and the Vote: 1984," pp. 258–282; and Carol M. Mueller, "The Empowerment of Women: Polling and the Women's Voting Bloc," pp. 16–36. Keith T. Poole and L. Harmon Zeigler, *Women, Public Opinion, and Politics: The Changing Political Attitudes of American Women* (New York: Longman, 1985) Chps. 2 & 3, present more comprehensive data on the gender gap. For an interesting case study of male-female attitudinal differences, see Cal Clark and Janet Clark, "Women's Attitudes Toward the MX: The 'Old' Vs. the 'New' Gender Gap," *Journal of Political Science* 17:1-2 (Spring 1989) pp. 127–140.

12. Pippa Norris, "The Gender Gap: A Cross-National Trend?" in Mueller, *The Gender Gap*, pp. 217–234. For similar findings, see Susan Welch and Sue Thomas, "Explaining the Gender Gap in British Public Opinion," *Women & Politics* 8:3/4 (Fall/Winter 1988) pp. 25–44.

13. Susan J. Carroll, "Women's Autonomy and the Gender Gap," in Mueller, *The Gender Gap*, pp. 236–257.

14. April Carter, *The Politics of Women's Rights* (New York: Longman, 1988); Jennifer Dale and Peggy Foster, *Feminists and State Welfare* (London: Routledge and Kegan Paul, 1986); Barbara Sinclair Deckard, *The Women's Movement: Political, Socioeconomic, and Psychological Issues*, 3rd Ed. (New York: Harper & Row, 1983); Myra Marx Ferree and Beth B. Hess, *Controversy and Coalition: The New Feminist Movement* (Boston: Twayne, 1985); Jo Freeman, *The Politics of Women's Liberation: A Case Study of an Emerging Social Movement and Its Relation to the Policy Process* (New York: David McKay, 1975); Joyce Gelb, *Feminism and Politics: A Comparative Perspective* (Berkeley: University of California Press, 1989); Mary Fainsod Katzenstein and Carol McClarg Mueller, eds., *The Women's Movements of the United States and Western Europe: Consciousness, Political Opportunity, and Public Policy* (Philadelphia: Temple University Press, 1987); Ethel Klein, *Gender Politics: From Consciousness to Mass Politics* (Cambridge: Harvard University Press, 1984); and Joni Lovenduski, *Women and European Politics: Contemporary Feminism and Public Policy* (Amherst: University of Massachusetts Press, 1986) Chps. 2 & 3.

15. Janet K. Boles, *The Politics of the Equal Rights Amendment: Conflict and Decision Process* (New York: Longman, 1979); and Jane M. Mansbridge, *Why We Lost the ERA* (Chicago: University of Chicago Press, 1986).

16. Laura L. Crites and Winifred L. Happerle, eds., *Women, the Courts, and Equality* (Beverly Hills, Calif.: Sage, 1987).

17. Joyce Gelb and Marian Lief Palley, eds., *Women and Public Policies*, Revised and Expanded Ed. (Princeton: Princeton University Press, 1986).

18. Ellen Boneparth and Emily Stoper, eds., *Women, Power, and Policy: Toward the Year 2000*, 2nd Ed. (New York: Pergamon, 1988) Parts II & III; Irene Diamond, ed., *Families, Politics, and Public Policy: A Feminist Dialogue on Women and the State* (New York: Longman, 1983); Steven P. Erie and Martin Rein, "Women and the Welfare State," in Mueller, *The Gender Gap*, pp. 173–191; Gelb and Palley, *Women and Public Policies;* Janet A. Flammang, ed., *Political Women: Current Roles in State and Local Government* (Beverly Hills, Calif.: Sage, 1984) Part IV; Susan M. Hartmann, *From Margin to Mainstream: American Women and Politics Since 1960* (New York: Alfred A. Knopf, 1989); Lovenduski, *Women and European Politics*, Chp. 7; and Vicky Randall, *Women and Politics: An International Perspective*, 2nd Ed. (Chicago: University of Chicago Press, 1987) Chps. 4–6.

19. Anne N. Costain, "Women's Claims As a Special Interest," in Mueller, *The Gender Gap*, pp. 150–172.

20. Irene Tinker, ed., *Women in Washington: Advocates for Public Policy* (Beverly Hills, Calif.: Sage, 1983).

21. Carroll, "Women Candidates," p. 321.

22. Carroll, "Women Candidates," p. 316.

23. Susan J. Carroll and Ella Taylor, "Gender Differences in Policy Priorities," *CAWP News & Notes* 7:2 (Winter 1989) pp. 3–4.

24. Carol Gilligan, *In a Different Voice: Psychological Theory and Women's Development* (Cambridge: Harvard University Press, 1982).

25. Janet A. Flammang, "Introduction: A Reflection on Themes of a Woman's Politics," in Flammang, *Political Women*, pp. 11–15. Parts II and III of the Flammang volume present case studies applying Gilligan's theoretical framework. Also see Gertrude A. Steuernagal, "Reflections on Women and Political Participation," *Women & Politics* 7:4 (Winter 1987) pp. 3–13. For a more recent data analysis showing that the linkage between gender and a "connectedness" perspective on politics is fairly complex and somewhat indirect, see Rita Mae Kelly and Jayne

Burgess, "Gender and the Meaning of Power and Politics," *Women & Politics* 9:1 (Spring 1989) pp. 47–82.

26. Elise Boulding, *Women in the Twentieth-Century World* (Beverly Hills, Calif.: Sage, 1977).

27. Duverger, *The Political Role of Women*, Chp. 1; and Randall, *Women and Politics*, pp. 50–58.

28. Sandra Baxter and Marjorie Lansing, *Women and Politics: The Invisible Majority* (Ann Arbor: University of Michigan Press, 1980); Cal Clark and Janet Clark, "Models of Gender and Political Participation in the United States," *Women & Politics* 6:1 (Spring 1986) pp. 5–25; Poole and Zeigler, *Women, Public Opinion, and Politics*, Chp. 4; and Sidney Verba and Norman H. Nie, *Participation in America: Political Democracy and Social Equality* (New York: Harper & Row, 1976) Chp. 6.

29. Joni Lovenduski and Jill Hill, eds., *The Politics of the Second Electorate: Women and Political Participation* (London: Routledge and Kegan, 1981); and Sidney Verba, Norman H. Nie, Jae-on Kim, and Goldie Shabad, "Men and Women: Sex-Related Differences in Political Activity," in Sidney Verba, Norman H. Nie, and Jae-on Kim, eds., *Participation and Political Equality: A Seven-Nation Comparison* (Cambridge: Cambridge University Press, 1978) pp. 234–268.

30. Lovenduski, *Women and European Politics*, Chp. 4; and Randall, *Women and Politics*, pp. 58–68.

31. Herbert Jacob, "Initial Recruitment of Elected Officials in the U.S.: A Model," *Journal of Politics* 24:4 (November 1962) pp. 703–716.

32. Ronald D. Hedlund, Patricia K. Freeman, Keith E. Hamm, and Robert M. Stein, "The Electability of Women Candidates: The Effects of Sex Role Stereotypes," *Journal of Politics* 41:2 (May 1979) pp. 513–524.

33. Rufus Browning and Herbert Jacob, "Power Motivation and the Political Personality," *Public Opinion Quarterly* 28:1 (Spring 1968) pp. 75–90.

34. Emmy E. Werner and Louise M. Bachtold, "Personality Characteristics of Women in American Politics," in Jane S. Jaquette, ed., *Women in Politics* (New York: Wiley, 1974) p. 83.

35. Deckard, The Women's Movement, Chps 2–4; Irene H. Frieze et al., *Women and Sex Roles: A Social Psychological Perspective* (New York: Norton, 1978); and Robert D. Hess and Judith V. Tourney, *The Development of Political Attitudes in Children* (Chicago: Aldine, 1967) Chp. 8.

36. Jean Bethke Elshtain, *Public Man, Private Woman: Women in Social and Political Theory* (Princeton: Princeton University Press, 1981).

37. Rita Mae Kelly and Mary Boutilier, *The Making of Political Women: A Study of Socialization and Role Conflict* (Chicago: Nelson-Hall, 1978).

38. Virginia Sapiro, *The Political Integration of Women: Roles, Socialization and Politics* (Urbana: University of Illinois Press, 1983).

39. For example, see Diana Owen and Jack Dennis, "Gender Differences in the Politicization of American Children," *Women & Politics* 8:2 (Summer 1988) pp. 23–43.

40. Marianne Githens and Jewel L. Prestage, eds., *A Portrait of Marginality: The Political Behavior of the American Woman* (New York: David McKay, 1977).

41. Claudie Wallis, "Onward Women," *Time* 134:23 (December 4, 1989) pp. 80–89.

42. Irene J. Dabrowski, "The Unnamed Political Woman," in Frank P. Le Veness and Jane P. Sweeney, eds., *Women Leaders in Contemporary U.S. Politics* (Boulder, Colo.: Lynne Rienner, 1987) p. 137.

43. Marianne Githens, "Women and State Politics: An Assessment," in Flammang, *Political Women*, pp. 41–63.

44. Susan J. Carroll, "The Personal Is Political: The Intersection of Private Lives

and Public Roles Among Women and Men in Elective and Appointive Office," *Women & Politics* 9:2 (Summer 1989) p. 57.

45. Janet Clark, Charles D. Hadley, and R. Darcy, "Political Ambition Among Men and Women State Party Leaders: Testing the Countersocialization Perspective," *American Politics Quarterly* 17:2 (April 1989) pp. 194–207; Edmond Costantini and Julie D. Bell, "Women in Political Parties: Gender Differences in Motives Among California Party Activists," in Flammang, *Political Women*, pp. 114–138; Edmond Costantini and Kenneth H. Craik, "Women As Politicians: The Social Background, Personality, and Political Careers of Female Party Leaders," *Journal of Social Issues* 28:1 (No. 2, 1972) pp. 217–236; Diane Fowlkes, Jerry Perkins, and Sue T. Rinehart, "Gender Roles and Party Roles," *American Political Science Review* 73:3 (September 1979) pp. 772–780; and M. Kent Jennings and Norman Thomas, "Men and Women in Party Elites: Social Roles and Political Resources," *Midwest Journal of Political Science* 12:4 (November 1968) pp. 469–492.

46. Jeane J. Kirkpatrick, *Political Woman* (New York: Basic Books, 1974) p. 38.

47. Carol Nechemias, "Changes in the Election of Women to U.S. State Legislative Seats," *Legislative Studies Quarterly* 12:1 (February 1987) pp. 125–142.

48. For applications of this structural approach, see Anthony M. Orum, Robert S. Cohen, Sherri Grasmuck, and Amy W. Orum, "Sex, Socialization, and Politics," *American Sociological Review* 39:2 (April 1974) pp. 197–209; and Susan Welch, "Women As Political Animals? A Test of Some Explanations for Male-Female Participation Differences," *American Journal of Political Science* 21:4 (November 1977) pp. 711–730. For two other studies that link professional occupations to political participation for women, see Kristi Andersen, "Working Women and Political Participation, 1952–1972," *American Journal of Political Science* 19:3 (August 1975) pp. 439–453; and Eileen L. McDonagh, "To Work or Not to Work: The Differential Impact of Achieved and Derived Status upon the Political Participation of Women, 1956–1976," *American Journal of Political Science* 26:2 (May 1982) pp. 280–297.

49. Susan Welch, "Recruitment of Women to Office: A Discriminant Analysis," *Western Political Quarterly* 31:3 (September 1978) pp. 372–380.

50. Harold D. Clarke and Allan Kornberg, "Moving Up the Political Escalator: Women Party Officials in the United States and Canada," *Journal of Politics* 41:2 (May 1979) p. 454.

51. Deckard, *The Women's Movement*, Chp. 14.

52. Peggy Lamson, *Few Are Chosen: American Women in Political Life Today* (Boston: Houghton Mifflin, 1968); Ruth B. Mandel, *In the Running: The New Woman Candidate* (New Haven, Conn.: Ticknor & Fields, 1981); and Susan Tolchin and Martin Tolchin, *Clout: Womanpower and Politics* (New York: Capricorn, 1976).

53. Jean Graves McDonald and Vicky Howell Pierson, "Female County Party Leaders and the Perception of Discrimination: A Test of the Male Conspiracy Theory," *Social Science Journal* 21:1 (January 1984) pp. 13–20.

54. Janet Clark, "Party Leaders and Women's Entrance into the Political Elites," paper presented at the Annual Meeting of the Southwestern Political Science Association, Fort Worth, Texas, March 28–31, 1979.

55. Robert Darcy, Margaret Brewer, and Judy Clay, "Women in the Oklahoma Political System: State Legislative Elections," *Social Science Journal* 21:1 (January 1984) pp. 67–78.

56. Barbara Burrell, "Women's and Men's Campaigns for the U.S. House of Representatives, 1972–1982: A Finance Gap?" *American Politics Quarterly* 13:3 (July 1985) pp. 251–272; Jody Newman, Carrie Costantin, Judie Goetz, and Amy Glosser, *Perceptions and Reality: A Study of Women Candidates and Fundraising* (Washington, D.C.: Women's Campaign Research Fund, 1984); and Carole Uhlaner

and Kay Schlozman, "Candidate Gender and Congressional Campaign Receipts," *Journal of Politics* 48:1 (February 1986) pp. 30–50.

57. Duverger, *The Political Role of Women*, Chp. 2; and Pippa Norris, *Politics and Sexual Equality: The Comparative Position of Women in Western Democracies* (Boulder, Colo.: Lynne Rienner, 1987) Chp. 6.

58. Darcy, Welch, and Clark, *Women, Elections, and Representation*, p. 114.

59. Jorgen Rasmussen, "The Electoral Costs of Being a Woman in the 1979 British General Election," paper presented at the 78th Annual Meeting of the American Political Science Association, Denver, Colorado, September 2–5, 1982; Wilma Rule, "Why Women Don't Run: The Critical Contextual Factors in Women's Legislative Recruitment," *Western Political Quarterly* 34:1 (March 1981) pp. 60–77; and Emmy Werner, "Women in the State Legislatures," *Western Political Quarterly* 21:1 (March 1968) pp. 40–50.

60. Nechemias, "Election of Women," pp. 125–142; and Wilma Rule, "Why Is It Getting Easier to Recruit Women to State Legislatures?" paper presented at the Annual Meeting of the Western Political Science Association, Eugene, Oregon, March 20–22, 1986.

61. David Hill, "Political Culture and Female Political Representation," *Journal of Politics* 43:1 (February 1981) pp. 159–168; Nechemias, "Election of Women," pp. 125–142; Rule, "Why Women Don't Run," pp. 60–77; and Wilma Rule, "Electoral Systems, Contextual Factors, and Women's Opportunity for Election to Parliament in Twenty-three Democracies," *Western Political Quarterly* 40:3 (September 1987) pp. 480–483.

62. Susan Welch and Lee Sigelman, "Changes in Public Attitudes Toward Women in Politics," *Social Science Quarterly* 63:2 (June 1982) pp. 312–322.

63. Susan Welch, Margery M. Ambrosius, Janet Clark, and R. Darcy, "The Effect of Candidate Gender on Electoral Outcomes in State Legislative Races: A Research Note," *Western Political Quarterly* 38:3 (September 1985) pp. 464–475; R. Darcy and Sarah S. Schramm, "When Women Run Against Men," *Public Opinion Quarterly* 41:1 (Spring 1977) pp. 1–12; and Laurie E. Ekstrand and William A. Eckert, "The Impact of Candidate's Sex on Voter Choice," *Western Political Quarterly* 34:1 (March 1981) pp. 78–87.

64. Donley T. Studlar and Susan Welch, "Understanding the Iron Law of Andrarchy: Effects of Candidate Gender on Voting in Scotland," *Comparative Political Studies* 20:2 (July 1987) pp. 174–191; and Susan Welch and Donley T. Studlar, "The Effects of Candidate Gender on Voting for Local Office in England," *British Journal of Political Science* 18:3 (July 1988) pp. 273–281.

65. Darcy, Welch, and Clark, *Women, Elections, and Representation*, p. 115.

66. Kristi Andersen and Stuart Thorson, "Some Structural Barriers to the Election of Women to Congress: A Simulation," *Western Political Quarterly* 37:1 (March 1984) pp. 143–156; R. Darcy and James R. Choike, "A Formal Analysis of Legislative Turnover: Women Candidates and Legislative Representation," *American Journal of Political Science* 30:1 (February 1986) pp. 237–255; and Donley T. Studlar, Ian McAllister, and Alvaro Ascui, "Electing Women to the British Commons: Breakout from the Beleaguered Beachhead?" *Legislative Studies Quarterly* 13:4 (November 1988) pp. 515–528.

67. Irene Diamond, *Sex Roles in the State House* (New Haven: Yale University Press, 1977) pp. 25–28.

68. Each party presents a list of candidates in order of preference. The number of candidates elected from each list is determined by the party's proportion of the vote in the district.

69. Rule, "Women's Opportunity for Election to Parliament," pp. 477–498.

70. Darcy, Welch, and Clark, *Women, Elections, and Representation*, Chp. 6; and

Richard S. Katz, "Intraparty Preference Voting," in Bernard Grofman and Arend Lijphart, eds., *Electoral Laws and Their Political Consequences* (New York: Praeger, 1986) pp. 85–103.

71. Duverger, *The Political Role of Women*, pp. 88–89; and Norris, *Politics and Sexual Equality*, pp. 123–131.

72. Darcy, Welch, and Clark, *Women, Elections, and Representation*, pp. 113–116.

73. Duverger, *Political Role of Women*, p. 79; and Rule, "Why Women Don't Run," p. 77.

74. Rule, "Women's Opportunity for Election to Parliament," p. 494.

75. Diamond, *Sex Roles in the State House*, Chps. 1–3.

76. Richard L. Engstrom, M. D. McDonald, and Bih-Er Chou, "The Election of Women to Central City Councils in the U.S.," paper presented at the Seventh Annual Meeting of the International Society of Political Psychology, Toronto, June 24–27, 1984.

77. R. Darcy, Susan Welch, and Janet Clark, "Women Candidates in Single and Multi-Member Districts: American State Legislative Races," *Social Science Quarterly* 66:4 (December 1985) pp. 945–953.

78. That is, each voter votes for only one candidate; the candidates winning pluralities are elected.

79. Rule, "Women's Opportunity for Election to Parliament," pp. 486–487.

# PART TWO
# THE STATUS OF WOMEN IN TAIWAN

# CHAPTER THREE
# Economic and Political Development in Taiwan

The Republic of China on Taiwan, with one of the most successful economic records in the world during the post–World War II era, has been transformed from a poor agricultural society into a thriving industrial one that is seemingly on the threshold of entering the developed world. Political development and liberalization, while lagging well behind the impressive economic growth for most of this period, have been significant, and the democratization reforms of the late 1980s have wrought considerable change in the previously authoritarian political system. Both economic growth and political development have important implications for the role of women legislators in the ROC. Industrialization provides the opportunity for women to gain employment and move out of complete dependence on the family sector, thereby opening themselves to public life, and the growing salience of political elections and debates in the 1980s transformed the nature of holding a legislative seat.

This chapter, then, provides an overview of economic and political development on Taiwan since the Nationalist regime moved its seat of government to Taipei in 1949. The first section discusses the basic economic changes that have occurred, their implications for the island's social structure, and the major economic strategies that have been employed. The second describes the ROC's central political institutions and the principal changes that have occurred in the political sphere.

## The Economic Development of Taiwan

During the postwar era, the Republic of China has witnessed an "economic miracle," with real growth averaging about 9% a year over the last four decades, one of the highest sustained growth rates in the world. Consequently, the country has been transformed from a rural backwater with a per capita income of $100 in 1950 to a middle-income society with an income per capita of $7,000 in 1989. Taiwan's economic record is all the more remarkable because its prospects in the early 1950s appeared rather dismal, to say the least.

As illustrated by the relief map in Figure 3.1, Taiwan is a large island (about 250 miles long and 100 wide at its widest point) on the Tropic of Cancer; it lies 100 miles from Fujian Province in the People's Republic of China. The ROC also controls several other islands and groups of islands, but they have been unimportant for Taiwan's developmental history (although Quemoy and Matsu certainly made the headlines in foreign policy). Because the main island is quite mountainous, only about a quarter of the land is arable. The tropical island provides an excellent agricultural environment, although intensive farming over the centuries has generally depleted the land and necessitated increasing use of fertilizer. On the other hand, the island is poorly endowed in natural resources, except for some coal deposits that are no longer commercially viable. Thus, Taiwan would not appear a likely candidate for an almost stunning industrialization drive.[1]

The island's historical experience before World War II had both positive and negative implications for its developmental potential. After a brief period of Dutch colonial rule in the seventeenth century, Taiwan was governed by China for the next 200 years. In general, the island remained a frontier of little interest to the central government, with a far from dynamic agricultural economy. An exception to this occurred during the governorship of General Liu Ming-ch'uan (1884–1891), who began a vigorous developmentalist policy, but Liu's dynamism departed with him. Four years later, the island was ceded to Japan at the end of the Sino-Japanese War and remained a Japanese colony for the next fifty years.

Japan had two major goals for its colony: to control the indigenous population and to stimulate agricultural output to help feed the metropole. These goals interacted to provide a mixed legacy. Positively, Japanese investment in infrastructure, education, and agricultural technology stimulated substantial growth, an innovative agricultural sector, some rise in the standard of living, an integrated economy with expanding agriculturally related industry, and the population's development of skills necessary for industrialization. On the other hand, Taiwanese were excluded from significant political and business positions, and Japan's extraction of resources from the island was quite high compared with the practice of other colonial powers.[2]

This mixed colonial heritage was eroded, furthermore, by the way in which the Japanese left Taiwan. U.S. bombing destroyed over half the industrial capacity and infrastructure; the Japanese evacuation took away most of the island's administrators and businessmen; the Chinese Nationalists stripped many of Taiwan's resources to finance their civil war with the Communists; and massive inflation was imported from the mainland. Thus, prewar production levels were not attained until the 1950s. This dismal economic picture was exacerbated by repressive Nationalist rule that stimulated an uprising on February 28, 1947, that embittered relations between the Nationalists and the local population (see the discussion in the next section).[3]

**Figure 3.1 Map of Taiwan**

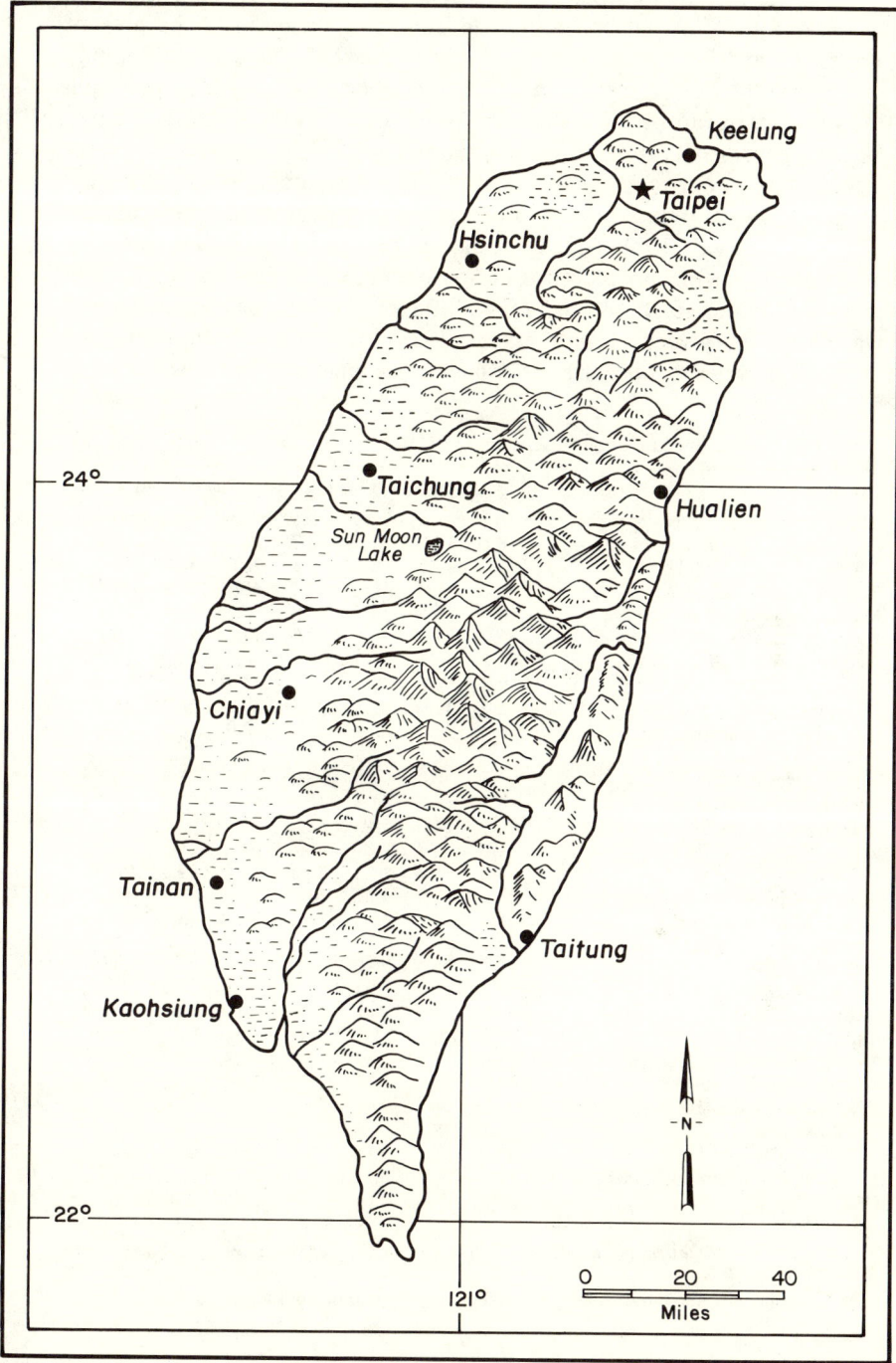

Despite this dubious base for an economic takeoff, rapid growth began in the early 1950s and has continued almost unabated until the present. Tables 3.1 and 3.2 summarize the economic transformation of the Republic of China. Table 3.1 presents data on the level of development (e.g., per capita income, manufacturing's share of total production, investment as a percentage of GNP, income inequality, and food consumption) for seven selected years between 1952 and 1988. These figures indicate Taiwan's progress toward industrialization and prosperity over each approximately six-year interval. Table 3.2, in contrast, contains the annual real (i.e., adjusted for inflation) increase in key economic indicators (e.g., GNP, industrial and agricultural production, inflation, exports, and manufacturing wages) for every year during the 1953–1988 period. These data, then, show the growth cycles that occurred over these three and a half decades.

Table 3.1  Indicators of Development Level

|  | 1952 | 1958 | 1962 | 1968 | 1973 | 1978 | 1988 |
|---|---|---|---|---|---|---|---|
| Population (million) | 8.1 | 10.0 | 11.5 | 13.7 | 15.6 | 17.1 | 19.9 |
| GNP Per Capita (1000 NT$) | 2.0 | 4.3 | 6.5 | 12.1 | 26.6 | 58.3 | 173.1 |
| GNP Per Capita (US$) | 153 | 173 | 162 | 302 | 696 | 1575 | 6055 |
| Manufacturing As % of NDP | 10.8 | 15.5 | 16.9 | 24.0 | 36.2 | 34.1 | 35.1 |
| Agriculture As % of NDP | 36.0 | 31.1 | 29.4 | 22.1 | 14.1 | 11.3 | 6.1 |
| Agriculture As % of Employment | 56.1 | 51.1 | 49.7 | 40.8 | 30.5 | 24.9 | 13.7 |
| Savings As % of GNP | 9.2 | 9.9 | 12.4 | 22.1 | 34.6 | 34.9 | 34.9 |
| Investment As % of GNP | 15.3 | 16.6 | 17.8 | 25.1 | 29.1 | 28.2 | 24.0 |
| US Aid As % of Investment | 45.5 | 37.3 | 20.2 | 0.6 | 0.0 | 0.0 | 0.0 |
| Foreign Investment As % of Investment | 0.5 | 0.8 | 1.5 | 8.4 | 7.9 | 2.8 | 4.2 |
| Exports As % of GDP | 8.5 | 8.6 | 11.3 | 18.6 | 41.6 | 47.4 | 50.5 |
| % Industrial Exports | 8.1 | 14.0 | 50.5 | 68.4 | 84.6 | 89.2 | 94.5 |
| Trade Balance (mil US$) | -71 | -70 | -86 | -114 | 691 | 1660 | 10,929 |
| % Exports to US | 3.5 | 6.2 | 24.4 | 35.3 | 37.4 | 39.5 | 38.7 |
| State % of Industrial Production | 56.6 | 50.0 | 46.2 | 31.1 | 21.1 | 21.5 | 18.1 |
| State % of Investment | 55.7 | 62.6 | 46.8 | 36.6 | 34.7 | 45.0 | 34.6 |
| Government Expenditure As % of GDP | — | 23.8 | 20.0 | 19.5 | 19.5 | 22.9 | 24.0 |
| Unemployment Rate (%) | 4.6 | 4.0 | 4.3 | 1.8 | 1.3 | 1.7 | 1.7 |
| Income Ratio[a] | 20.47[b] | — | — | 5.28 | 4.49[c] | 4.18 | 4.69[d] |
| Caloric Intake (day) | 2078 | 2359 | 2317 | 2545 | 2754 | 2822 | 3017 |
| Food As % of Hshld Spending | 55.6 | 51.7 | 50.1 | 44.8 | 41.3 | 39.8 | 30.1[d] |
| Health Personnel (1000s) | — | 10.8 | 12.7 | 12.5 | 20.4 | 36.2 | 83.0 |
| Communicable Disease Rate/ 100,000 Pop | 14.1 | 22.7 | 8.3 | 6.3 | 1.3 | 0.5 | 1.2 |
| % Primary Grads to Jr HS | 34.9 | 51.1 | 53.8 | 74.2 | 83.7 | 94.1 | 99.1 |
| Expenditure Per Primary Student (1981 NT$) | 3296 | 2784 | 3501 | 4781 | 7861 | 13,002 | 20,224 |

*Source: Taiwan Statistical Data Book, 1989* (Taipei: Council for Economic Planning and Development, 1989).
[a]Ratio of the income of the richest fifth of the population to that of the poorest fifth.
[b]Data for 1953.
[c]Data for 1972.
[d]Data for 1987.

Table 3.2  Real Annual Growth (by percent)

| | GNP | Indus Prod | Ag Prod | Exports | Savgs | Invst | Manf Wages | Consum Prices | Money Supply |
|---|---|---|---|---|---|---|---|---|---|
| 1953 | 9.5 | 25.4 | 15.4 | 11.0 | 5.3 | 13.4 | — | 18.8 | — |
| 1954 | 9.6 | 5.7 | -0.0 | -27.0 | -5.3 | 10.7 | 10.8 | 1.7 | — |
| 1955 | 8.1 | 12.9 | 2.9 | 20.1 | 27.1 | -16.3 | 1.5 | 9.9 | — |
| 1956 | 5.5 | 3.6 | 5.2 | 40.6 | 7.6 | 15.8 | 3.2 | 10.5 | — |
| 1957 | 7.3 | 12.6 | 7.9 | 15.3 | 23.7 | 1.0 | 1.6 | 7.5 | — |
| 1958 | 6.6 | 8.5 | 7.3 | 0.3 | -0.7 | 9.6 | 4.3 | 1.3 | — |
| 1959 | 7.8 | 11.9 | 1.7 | 38.1 | 12.0 | 27.6 | -2.4 | 10.6 | — |
| 1960 | 6.5 | 14.2 | 0.6 | -8.0 | 31.1 | 28.3 | -1.6 | 18.4 | — |
| 1961 | 6.8 | 15.6 | 7.3 | 24.9 | 8.0 | 7.5 | 12.7 | 7.8 | — |
| 1962 | 7.9 | 8.0 | 3.1 | 9.5 | 4.2 | 1.2 | 2.9 | 2.3 | 5.0 |
| 1963 | 9.4 | 9.2 | 1.8 | 47.0 | 50.9 | 18.2 | 1.6 | 2.2 | 28.1 |
| 1964 | 12.3 | 21.1 | 9.5 | 25.4 | 28.5 | 12.6 | 3.7 | -0.2 | 35.0 |
| 1965 | 11.0 | 16.3 | 6.6 | 4.3 | 11.3 | 30.1 | 7.8 | -0.1 | 15.9 |
| 1966 | 9.0 | 15.6 | 3.6 | 16.0 | 19.5 | 4.3 | 4.4 | 2.0 | 12.2 |
| 1967 | 10.6 | 16.7 | 7.1 | 14.4 | 15.5 | 32.7 | 8.6 | 3.4 | 30.1 |
| 1968 | 9.1 | 22.3 | 7.7 | 15.4 | 7.3 | 16.7 | 2.6 | 7.9 | 11.5 |
| 1969 | 9.1 | 19.9 | -1.2 | 25.0 | 17.1 | 8.8 | -3.7 | 5.0 | 15.6 |
| 1970 | 11.3 | 20.1 | 6.9 | 36.5 | 19.1 | 21.3 | 5.2 | 3.6 | 15.0 |
| 1971 | 13.0 | 23.6 | 2.8 | 35.0 | 27.8 | 17.9 | 13.6 | 2.8 | 30.6 |
| 1972 | 13.4 | 21.2 | 4.6 | 37.0 | 26.2 | 11.9 | 4.2 | 3.0 | 34.1 |
| 1973 | 12.8 | 16.2 | 7.0 | 24.2 | 21.7 | 20.5 | 1.1 | 8.2 | 50.4 |
| 1974 | 1.2 | -4.5 | -0.4 | -5.4 | -7.5 | 33.9 | -9.0 | 47.5 | 10.5 |
| 1975 | 4.4 | 9.5 | -1.4 | -7.8 | -11.4 | -14.5 | 14.6 | 5.2 | 28.8 |
| 1976 | 13.7 | 23.3 | 12.7 | 45.9 | 37.2 | 16.1 | 11.9 | 2.5 | 25.1 |
| 1977 | 10.3 | 13.3 | 5.5 | 7.8 | 11.3 | 3.6 | 13.1 | 7.0 | 33.6 |
| 1978 | 14.0 | 22.5 | 0.3 | 25.2 | 20.8 | 13.1 | 5.9 | 5.8 | 37.0 |
| 1979 | 8.5 | 6.4 | 7.9 | 10.9 | 7.2 | 22.8 | 8.6 | 9.8 | 7.7 |
| 1980 | 7.1 | 6.8 | 1.1 | 5.8 | 2.4 | 8.3 | 5.5 | 19.0 | 22.7 |
| 1981 | 5.7 | 3.5 | -1.4 | 4.0 | 2.5 | 0.2 | 5.8 | 16.3 | 13.8 |
| 1982 | 3.4 | -0.9 | 1.8 | 0.7 | -1.8 | -11.1 | 6.0 | 3.0 | 14.6 |
| 1983 | 8.0 | 12.7 | 4.0 | 14.2 | 13.8 | 0.2 | 4.4 | 1.4 | 18.4 |
| 1984 | 10.6 | 11.8 | 3.1 | 18.9 | 16.1 | 3.1 | 14.6 | 0.0 | 9.3 |
| 1985 | 5.1 | 2.7 | 3.1 | 1.3 | 4.5 | -12.7 | -2.0 | -0.2 | 12.2 |
| 1986 | 11.7 | 13.9 | -0.3 | 18.8 | 25.1 | 2.3 | 6.3 | 0.7 | 51.4 |
| 1987 | 11.9 | 10.7 | 8.3 | 12.6 | — | 39.9 | 9.2 | 0.5 | 37.8 |
| 1988 | 7.3 | 4.3 | 1.2 | 0.6 | — | 30.0 | 9.8 | 1.3 | 24.4 |

*Source: Taiwan Statistical Data Book, 1989* (Taipei: Council for Economic Planning and Development, 1989).

In the early 1950s, the government took three major initiatives that helped stimulate the first stage in Taiwan's phoenixlike postwar growth—taming inflation, introducing a radical land reform program, and implementing import-substitution industralization. The regime believed that the raging inflation of the late 1940s had been a major reason for its defeat in the Chinese civil war and moved quickly to stem inflation in Taiwan (which had escalated to a stupendous 30-fold annual rate in early 1949). Interest rates were increased to realistic levels; the New Taiwan dollar (NT$) was depreciated; strict controls were imposed on the financial system to control the growth of money supply and credit; and the government pursued a policy of fiscal conservatism and balanced budgets. These policies proved quite successful in taming inflation—consumer price increases dropped precipitously to 30% in 1951–1952 and 10% or less a year by the mid–1950s, creating an environment for renewed economic growth.[4]

Perhaps the most momentous changes came from the radical land reform that was implemented in three stages between 1949 and 1953: (1) rent reductions of 25%, (2) the sale of public farming land to the peasants, and (3) the "land to the tiller" program that forced sale of all land exceeding approximately three hectares. The land reform itself was supplemented by sizable investments in agriculture and by a large-scale agricultural extension program to stimulate innovation in farming. These various endeavors dovetailed well; the result was a sustained increase in agricultural production averaging 5% a year in the 1950s and 4.5% a year in the 1960s. Agricultural growth, in turn, created enough resources to help finance the initial spurt of industrialization in the ROC. During the 1950s, capital outflows from the agricultural sector through such mechanisms as "the hidden rice tax" (i.e., the forced barter of rice for fertilizer at state-dictated prices) equaled approximately a quarter of total farm production. In addition, agricultural exports (which dominated Taiwan's trade throughout the 1950s) increased rapidly enough to keep the trade deficit tolerable. While agriculture was serving as a major source of capital for the rest of the economy, increased production was sufficient to support a rising standard of living among farmers. The deconcentration of landholdings also produced substantial increases in income equality. Thus, for about two decades, Taiwan's agriculture was quite successful, although it became a lagging sector in the 1970s and 1980s.[5]

In the industrial realm, Taiwan made a conscious effort to promote what is called "import substitution" for light industrial products—that is, to replace previously imported manufactures with domestic production when high tariffs and quotas were adopted to discourage imports. Import substitution proved quite successful, at least in the short run. Real industrial growth, while quite cyclical, averaged over 10% a year during the 1950s; the ratio of imports to total production in manufactured goods fell drastically; Taiwan expanded its industrial base from food processing to other light industries; and total energy consumption, a leading indicator of industrial development, more than doubled between 1952 and 1958.

However, by the late 1950s, the initial surge of import substitution began to subside as the domestic market became saturated with locally produced goods and as increasing imports of capital goods and industrial raw materials boosted the trade deficit. Consequently, overall growth began to decline (from 9% in the early 1950s to 6.5% in the late 1950s), while inflation and unemployment increased.[6] In addition, Taiwan had become highly dependent on U.S. aid, especially for balancing its budget, providing infrastructure and agricultural investment, and paying for the trade deficit. For example, because of this aid, the investment rate averaged 15% of GNP during the

1950s, while the savings rate was only 9%. Thus, it has been estimated that Taiwan's growth rate would have been cut in half during the 1950s and early 1960s without U.S. aid.[7]

As the 1950s ended, therefore, the Republic of China was clearly facing a threat to its continued economic development. It responded with a major change in strategy, shifting its focus to labor-intensive export industries as the nation's engine of growth. This new strategy provoked controversy because many leaders doubted that Taiwan's light industries were internationally competitive and military interests wanted to develop defense-related heavy industry. Yet the top political leadership backed the domestic technocrats and U.S. advisers who urged this reorientation, and comprehensive measures were rapidly implemented to encourage exporting and investment. Exchange rates were made more realistic; cheap credit and rebates on imported components and raw materials were made available to exporters; export processing zones were established; the protectionist trade system was liberalized because most export industries relied on imports; tax reform and decreased regulation were adopted to encourage domestic entrepreneurship; and foreign investment was solicited.[8]

This new economic strategy proved to be phenomenally successful, as illustrated by the aggregate data in Tables 3.1 and 3.2. Real GNP growth accelerated to a very high average of 11% annually during the 1963–1973 period. Furthermore, this rapid growth resulted from a fundamental industrial transformation in the nature of the ROC's economy. For example, between 1958 and 1973, manufacturing's share of net domestic product (NDP) more than doubled from 16% to 36%, while that of agriculture suffered a corresponding decline of 31% to 14%. Energy consumption escalated as well, doubling between 1962 and 1968 and then doubling again between 1968 and 1973.

The export-led nature of this economic growth and structural transformation is also very clear. Exports surged by an average of 15% a year (even in inflation-adjusted terms) for most of the 1960s, and then skyrocketed by 30% annually for the period 1969–1973. Consequently, their share in gross domestic product almost quadrupled from 11% in 1962 to 42% in 1973, indicating that the economy had become extremely export-oriented. Taiwan's export mix became overwhelmingly industrial in composition (industrial goods rose from 14% to 85% of total exports between 1958 and 1973), proving that the island's manufactured products were internationally competitive. Most of these exports went to developed countries, with the U.S. market being by far the largest (rising from 6% in 1958 to 37% in 1973). The export surge also caused a dramatic change in the country's balance of trade—the large deficits of the late 1950s and early 1960s were turned into surpluses by the early 1970s.

The nature of Taiwan's industry changed fundamentally as well. First, the country began to produce a wider range of products that became increasingly sophisticated over time, as the leading domestic production and export sectors advanced from food processing to textiles to electronics assembly and chemicals. Thus, even though labor-intensive industries still dominated the economy, a gradual upgrading occurred in terms of the utilization of capital and technology.[9] Second, the industrialization drive of the 1960s was associated with a privatization and "Taiwanization" of the business elites. Before 1960, state corporations (based mostly on confiscated Japanese assets) accounted for about half of industrial production, and "Mainlanders" who had come to Taiwan in 1949 dominated their management. In contrast, "Islander" entrepreneurs led the business expansion of the 1960s, so that the private sector accounted for over 80% of industrial production in the early 1970s.[10] Finally, because the ROC's industrial structure has been marked by a much greater role for small and medium family-based enterprises than elsewhere in Asia, the structure has spawned complex subcontracting relationships among small entrepreneurs, reflecting what has recently been called "Confucian capitalism." This structure of production allowed businesses to respond quickly to market demand and reduced problems of excess capacity, thus promoting internal competitiveness and external flexibility.[11]

A principal reason for Taiwan's rapid industrial transformation was the country's extremely strong investment record. Savings as a proportion of GNP, which had averaged about 9% in the 1950s, skyrocketed from 12% in 1962 to 22% in 1968 to 35% in 1973—one of the highest savings rates in the world. This great jump permitted the investment rate to rise from 18% of GNP in the early 1960s to 25% over the rest of the decade, despite the termination of U.S. aid that had financed over 40% of the ROC's investment during the import-substitution period. The Republic of China's remarkable record for savings and investment derived from a variety of factors: the popularity of opening small businesses, a cultural emphasis on family advancement, the very low social security net, limited consumer credit, the widespread use of bonus payments, government tax and interest rate incentives, and a loosening of controls over loans to private business.[12]

These increased domestic savings were augmented by the Republic of China's successful measures to stimulate and manage foreign investment. Private foreign investment, which accounted for less than 1% of total investment during the 1950s, rose to just over 4% during the period 1960–1967 and to 9% at the beginning of the 1970s. Multinational corporations (MNCs) are generally credited with a key role in stimulating the export drive, whereas the experience of many other developing nations has been that foreign capital simply displaces domestic businesses. Taiwan's success resulted from the regime's explicit attempts to harness MNCs to the island's developmental objectives. Thus, the government channeled foreign investment into the dynamic export sector, integrated MNCs into the overall economy with domestic content legislation (i.e., requirements to purchase some industrial inputs locally), and maintained state monopolies in the heavy industries usually dominated by foreigners.[13]

Finally, rapid economic growth in Taiwan had a profound effect on improving living standards and reducing socioeconomic inequality for the population at large. The ratio of the income of the richest fifth of the population to the poorest fifth fell rapidly during the 1950s because of the land reform program and then declined further from 5.33 in 1964 to 4.49 in 1972 (a level approximating that of most developed countries) as the rapid growth of labor-intensive industries stimulated real wage increases of over 5% a year during this period.[14] Consequently, many indicators of the standard of living (e.g., caloric intake, percentage of household income spent on nonfood items, the communicable disease rate, real expenditures per primary school student, and the percentage of primary students going on to junior high) showed substantial increases. Taiwan, then, had instituted a takeoff toward becoming a middle-class society.[15]

This dramatic economic expansion was brought to a sudden halt by the oil price explosion of 1973–1974 that disrupted the global economy in general and hit the ROC hard in particular. The inflationary surge was quickly transferred to the domestic economy: Consumer prices jumped by nearly 50% in 1974, and Taiwan's trade performance plummeted. Real exports, which had grown by 30% a year during the period 1970–1973, actually fell by 6.5% a year in 1974–1975, creating a new deficit in the country's balance of trade. As a result, real GNP growth in 1974 slumped to 1.2%; real industrial production fell by 4.5%. Savings also fell by 9% a year in 1974–1975 in inflation-adjusted terms, and this was exacerbated by a precipitous decline in foreign investment from 8% to 2.5% of total investment. Not surprisingly, rapidly deteriorating economic performance hurt the standard of living as well. Real wages in manufacturing grew by a minuscule 1% in 1973 and then fell sharply by 9% the next year. More broadly, while there were only slight dips in the absolute standard of living as measured by most of the indicators in Table 3.1, the previous upward trend was clearly interrupted.

Taiwan responded to this crisis of "stagflation" with an innovative combination of deflationary policies to tame inflation and of state investment to take up the slack of decreased economic activities. Deflationary policies included a sharp increase in interest rates; cutbacks in government spending from 23% to 18% of GNP between 1973 and 1974 that created a budget balance of 22% of total revenues; and a radical drop in the expansion of money supply from 50% in 1973 to 10.5% in 1974. Together, these policies proved highly effective in dampening inflation—the growth rate of consumer prices dropped to 5% in 1975 and 2.5% in 1976.[16]

By 1975, therefore, the economic situation had changed considerably. Inflation had clearly been tamed, but the effects of the crisis were still quite evident in sluggish growth and export performance and in a disastrous drop of 44% in private investment. The government responded by removing the fiscal brake and, additionally, by pressing the accelerator of state investment —the state provided 58% of total investment in 1975. Simply acting to reinvigorate the economy was not enough for a country as trade-dependent as Taiwan, of course. However, Taiwan's rapid taming of inflation meant that its exports became highly attractive on international markets. For example, by Shirley Kuo's calculations, the relative price of Taiwan's exports jumped by 30% between 1972 and 1974 and then declined a bit more gradually over the next three years.[17] This increased export competitiveness finally bore fruit in 1976 when real exports shot up by 46% and ushered in a new period of rapid growth in the late 1970s. During the 1976-1978 period, real GNP growth averaged 13%, real industrial growth 20%, real savings 23%, and real manufacturing wages 11%. With this renewed economic dynamism, in addition, the private sector reasserted its primacy in leading the economic growth.

The second oil price explosion in 1979-1980 again derailed Taiwan's double-digit growth, and the government responded with the same policy mix as before. Both the economic impact of escalating energy prices and the policy response were milder than in the mid-1970s, though, as inflation was tamed fairly easily. Rapid growth did not resume, however, until the economic recovery in the United States in 1983 provided an outlet for another export drive. Real exports leaped by 14% in 1983 and 19% in 1984, stagnated in 1985, and then jumped again by 15% a year in 1986-1987; the centrality of the U.S. market is indicated by the fact that its share of Taiwan's exports jumped from 34% in 1980 to 48% during the period 1984-1986. The ROC's trade surplus burgeoned as well—reaching $15-$20 billion a year in the late 1980s—and by 1988, Taiwan had the second largest foreign reserves in the world, approximately $75 billion. These latter figures, however, were not entirely positive because they helped stimulate trade disputes with the United States that threatened Taiwan's prime marketplace.

Rapid trade expansion, in turn, revved up the economy, which grew by 9% a year during 1983 and 1984, 5% in the "mini-recession" year of 1985, 12% in 1986-1987, and 7% in 1988-1989. Real industrial growth was somewhat higher, indicating the increasingly industrial nature of the island's economy. GNP per capita rose rapidly to $7,000 in 1989, although much of this growth after 1986 was caused by the 40% appreciation of the New Taiwan dollar against the U.S. dollar.[18] Thus, Taiwan appeared to be on the verge of entering the developed world.

This new growth period involved an evolution away from labor-intensive industries because Taiwan was gradually pricing itself out of the low-cost labor niche in the international division of labor. In a structural sense, these emerging industries were diverse. For example, steel was controlled by a state corporation; petrochemicals involved a complex "triple alliance" among state enterprises, MNCs, and domestic private businesses; and much of the high-tech industry was centered on relatively small, innovative firms. This restructuring of Taiwan's economy possesses both advantages and dangers. On the one hand, it represents industrial upgrading and a positive response to international competition from other developing countries. On the other, it threatens the position of small enterprises that have contributed so much to the island's economic flexibility and success in the past.[19] For example, despite a continued savings rate of over 30%, investment as a percentage of GNP fell from 30% to 17% over most of the 1980s before rebounding somewhat to 24% in 1988, as Taiwan businesses began to invest heavily overseas in both the developed and developing worlds.

The standard of living continued to improve as Taiwan's transition toward middle-class status continued apace. Between 1978 and the late 1980s, for example, the number of health personnel per capita and real spending per primary student approximately doubled; and the proportion of household spending devoted to food fell by a fifth.[20] On the other hand, income inequality increased significantly because of the decline of the agricultural sector and the reorientation away from labor-intensive production. (For example, real manufacturing wages grew by only 6% annually from 1980 to 1986 compared with 11% during the period 1975–1979, although they jumped to 9.5% in 1987–1988.) This trend, exacerbated by growing inflation (especially in the price of housing) in the late 1980s, hence, represents a clear threat to the well-being of the bulk of the population.

In sum, Taiwan has experienced very rapid growth and industrial transformation over the last four decades. While it is facing some very real challenges at present, it seems set to enter the developed world as the twenty-first century opens. The ROC's economic success represents a combination of both the state's economic leadership and the entrepreneurial initiatives of Taiwanese businesses to create an extremely flexible economy that has undergone continuous restructuring to retain its competitiveness.[21] Thus, Taiwan's developmental history suggests that "state" and "market" are not necessarily antithetical but can be integrated to stimulate development.[22]

## Political Development in Taiwan

While political development in Taiwan has lagged behind the island's spectacular economic growth, substantial political liberalization has occurred in the authoritarian regime that moved to the island in 1949. This liberalization has involved three major dimensions: First, the composition of the political and economic elites has expanded to include new segments. Second, democratization in terms of competitive elections has gradually expanded from the local to the national level and encompassed an institutionalized opposition to the ruling party. Third, the other two trends have increased the status and power of native Taiwanese Islanders vis-à-vis the Mainlanders who fled to Taiwan at the end of the Chinese civil war. This section, then, describes the ROC's basic political institutions and briefly sketches its political evolution, focusing upon the role of the legislature and legislative elections.

The polity in the Republic of China is structured around the 1947 constitution. The constitution created the institutions for a liberal democracy based on the five branches of government proposed by Dr. Sun Yat-sen in his "Three Principles of the People," the regime's guiding ideology, and on constitutional guarantees of civil rights and liberties. Thus, at the national level, five basic governmental organizations were established: the Executive Yuan, the Legislative Yuan, the Judicial Yuan, the Control Yuan, and the Examination Yuan. An indirectly elected president stood above these five branches of government and served as the top political official in the country. In addition, provisions were made for provincial and local governments. Freedom of speech and other political rights were guaranteed, and universal suffrage and the secret ballot were mandated.

This liberal political edifice was undercut, however, by several important factors. First, the system created the possibility that a strong president could dominate the system even within the constitutional framework—Chiang Kai-shek, the first president under the constitution, used his personal political clout to do so. Second, the extraconstitutional fact that the ROC has been an essentially one-party state meant that many of the democratic elements envisioned by the constitution were drastically curtailed. Third, the constitution contained an "emergency" clause that constitutional provisions could be restricted by law "for reasons of averting an imminent crisis, maintaining social order, or advancing the general welfare" (an admittedly catchall set of categories). Based on this clause, the ROC in 1948 adopted the "Temporary Provisions Effective During the Period of Communist Rebellion" (Temporary Provisions) under which martial law was declared in 1949 and continued until 1987. Finally, the vicious civil war that existed when the constitution was adopted created less than optimum conditions for the exercise of democratic rights.[23]

The keystone of the ROC's government is the president, who is indirectly elected for six-year terms by the National Assembly. The National Assembly itself was originally conceived as a major representative body that, in addition to electing the president and vice-president, was charged with adopting and amending the constitution. Assembly members, originally elected by constituencies of 500,000 for six-year terms, also included representatives of occupational groups, racial minorities, and overseas Chinese.

The power of the president in the ROC derives from both constitutional and extraconstitutional factors. Under the constitution the president appoints the leaders of three of the five branches of government, a power that certainly provides considerable leverage for the position and makes it the focus for coordination among the different branches. More informally, the president has been the focal point for a number of important decisionmaking bodies, such as the somewhat shadowy National Security Council composed of some of the top officials in the regime that was created by Chiang Kai-shek in 1967. In addition, the president has also always been the leader of the Kuomintang Party (with the exception of the three years following the death of Chiang Kai-shek), which provides the most significant power base in Taiwan's politics. Finally, presidential power in Taiwan has also been a function of the personal characteristics and political skills of the position's major incumbents—Chiang Kai-shek (1950–1975), his son Chiang Ching-kuo (1978–1988), and Lee Teng-hui (1988–present).

The most important branch of government has been the executive or administrative. The president appoints a premier to head the Executive Yuan with the consent of the legislature. The premier, in turn, selects a cabinet to administer the eight ministries, ministers without portfolio, and directors of councils and commissions. It is somewhat ambiguous, therefore, whether Taiwan possesses a presidential or cabinet system because the exact division of labor between the president and premier is unclear and depends to a considerable extent upon their personal power positions. For example, although the president has almost always been the supreme leader, Chiang Ching-kuo, who was premier when his father died, assumed the mantle of leadership directly, while Vice President Yen Chia-kan served out the rest of the presidential term.

The Legislative Yuan is a directly elected body, constituted much like the National Assembly. It passes budgets and legislation and exercises oversight of the executive (e.g., the Executive and Legislative Yuans have veto and override powers fairly similar to those exercised by the president and Congress in the United States). In reality, however, the Legislative Yuan has been fairly weak throughout most of its history. While it is probably fair to describe it as a rubber stamp in regard to major policies, at least until recently, legislators do exercise considerable initiative in such important areas as amending legislation, providing constituent service, promoting local development projects, and overseeing the executive in public interpellation sessions.

Traditional Chinese emphasis on administration and the dominant role of the Kuomintang Party in Taiwan's politics explain much of this subservient position, but another key factor has devolved from the ROC's claim to be the sole legitimate government of China. Members of the Legislative Yuan (as well as the National Assembly and Control Yuan) were chosen for three or six year terms in nationwide elections on the mainland (including Taiwan) in 1947 and 1948. With the Communist victory in the civil war, it was obviously impossible to hold new elections at the periods specified in the constitution. Thus, for almost two decades, these bodies basically atrophied, increasingly losing their representative character in relation to the territory actually governed by the ROC. However, to replace them with popularly elected assemblies would have denied the political legitimacy that the regime was desperately seeking to maintain both externally and internally.

The other three branches of government are less salient in Chinese politics. The Control Yuan, whose members are indirectly elected by provincial assemblies for six-year terms, exercises oversight over the other parts of the government (e.g., it holds general auditing powers, must consent to appointments to the Judicial and Examination Yuans, and can censure or, with the approval of the National Assembly, impeach government officials). The Judicial Yuan, whose members are appointed by the president, interprets the constitution and serves as the highest court for the ROC. Finally, the Examination Yuan, which is also appointed by the president, oversees the system of civil service examinations and serves as a personnel agency for the government.

As originally established on the mainland, the governmental structure was a federal one with three levels: national, provincial, and county. The retreat from the mainland left essentially one province (Taiwan) that encompassed almost all of the territory governed by the Republic of China (the offshore islands are under military administration). The provincial administration is directed by the governor, who is appointed by the president. There is a directly elected Provincial Assembly (it was indirectly elected for its first term), whose relationship with the governor and provincial executive parallels that of the Legislative and Executive Yuans. In the past at least, legislative politics at the provincial level has been considerably livelier than in the Legislative Yuan, reflecting the more dynamic nature of the way candidates are selected.[24] Counties and municipalities have elected executives (magistrates and mayors) and councils. In addition, the two largest cities, Taipei in 1967 and Kaohsiung in 1979, were made "special municipalities" directly under the Executive Yuan, ostensibly to give them greater autonomy. Their structure is now fairly similar to the provincial government, with an appointive mayor (which probably provides the real reason for the institutional change, given the rising strength of opposition candidates in mayoral elections) and elected councils. Generally, there has been a gradual devolution of power from the central to the lower levels of government.[25]

Figure 3.2 outlines these basic governmental bodies and their relationship to the electorate (the special municipalities are omitted because they essentially are provinces). Solid arrows indicate the formal power to select; dashed arrows show check-and-balance relationships. The major features suggested by this diagram are that (1) the electorate has substantial powers, but these can be circumscribed in practice by the indirect method of choosing the central and provincial administrations; (2) the institutional structure certainly exists for a strong presidency; (3) the system provides, at least in theory, a significant number of checks and balances, and (4) democracy will probably be strongest at the lowest levels of government.

**Figure 3.2 Government Structure of the ROC**

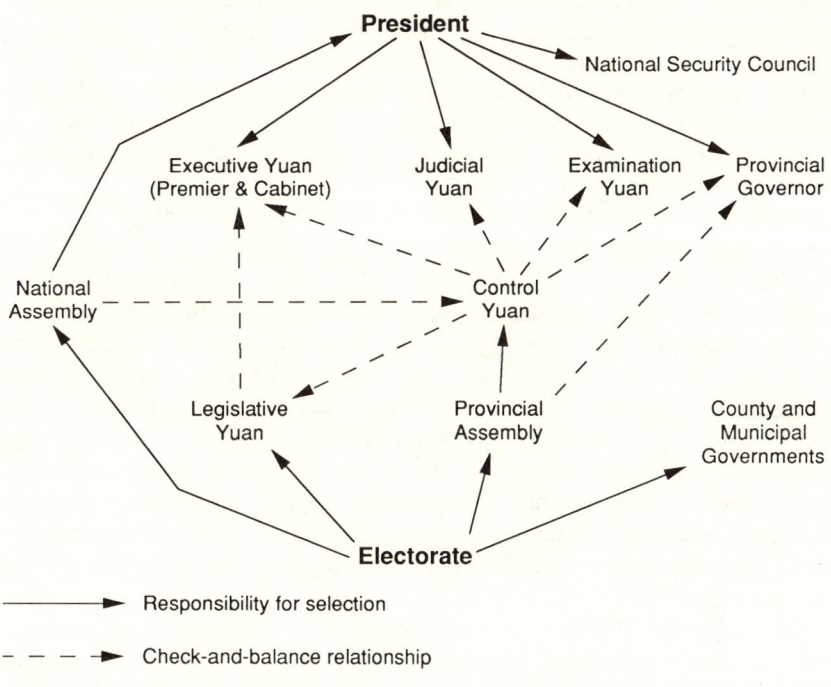

How formal institutions of government operate depends to a large extent, of course, upon the more informal political practices and institutions that exist in a society. The most salient feature of Taiwan's politics has been the dominant position of the Kuomintang (KMT), or Nationalist Party. Not only do KMT members win most of the elections in Taiwan and hold almost all of the significant administrative positions, but the party has exercised the major role in policymaking. Thus, major policy and personnel decisions are approved, if not made, by the top party organs (e.g., the premier formally submits his cabinet choices to the party's Central Standing Committee for approval); at least until recently, the Executive Yuan has been viewed as implementing policy more than initiating it. Furthermore, the most powerful governmental official in the country has maintained the position of party leader as well—Chiang Kai-shek served as director general of the KMT from 1938 until his death in 1975; Chiang Ching-kuo served as party chairman from 1975 until his death in 1988; and President Lee Teng-hui became party chairman as well.

Organizationally, a Nationalist Party Congress is held every five years to elect a Central Committee (which now has 180 members). The Central Committee, in turn, selects a Central Standing Committee (now 31 members plus the party chairman), which serves as the party's highest policymaking body. In the tradition of "democratic centralism," the party chairman usually has a strong role in selecting the membership of these bodies. The KMT chairman also appoints the secretary general of the party, who supervises its extensive administrative structure and is usually one of the most powerful politicians in the country. The KMT falls somewhere between a small tightly organized "cadre" party and a "mass" electoral party. In the early 1980s, it had approximately 2 million members, almost a fifth of the adult population (up from a ninth in 1963). About two-thirds of its members are native Islanders and under the age of 40, reflecting the party's efforts to garner popular support.[26]

The Temporary Provisions and martial law have also affected Taiwan's politics in several very significant ways. First, they permitted the suspension of constitutional rights, giving rise to an extensive security apparatus and censorship activities (e.g., many opposition political journals have been suspended or harassed even in the 1980s). Second, the formation of new political parties, in addition to the KMT and two politically inconsequential parties that came to Taiwan from the mainland, was prohibited, although opposition candidates could run as independents and by the 1980s had formed a quasi-formal party structure. Third, martial law provisions have been used in periodic crackdowns on crime, which have generally proved quite popular.

Initially, KMT rule of Taiwan was clearly authoritarian and sparked substantial strains between Islanders and Mainlanders. Despite the fact that the Taiwanese welcomed Nationalist troops as liberators when the island reverted to China at the end of World War II, the KMT tended to view the Islanders as collaborators with the hated Japanese and, thus, justified the corrupt, brutal, and exploitative policies of the military commander, Ch'en Yi, who administered the island. Ch'en's repression finally sparked a spontaneous uprising on February 28, 1947. A compromise between Ch'en and Taiwanese leaders seemed to settle the crisis, but KMT troops invaded the island in mid-March, killing up to 10,000 people and evidently singling out the intelligentsia and leadership class for slaughter. Although Ch'en was quickly replaced by a more conciliatory administrator and later publicly executed, the trauma had long-lasting effects; and a "Taiwan Independence Movement," headquartered in the United States and Japan and dedicated to overthrowing the KMT sprang up.[27]

In addition to the disaffected majority of Islanders (who constituted 85% of the population), the KMT regime that reestablished itself in Taipei in 1949 faced Communist infiltrators from the mainland and dissident KMT factions. To counter these threats, then, a strong security apparatus was created under Chiang Kai-shek's son, Chiang Ching-kuo, which essentially operated outside the law during the early 1950s and only gradually relaxed over the next two decades. Even in the 1960s, tolerance for political opposition was quite limited, as evidenced by the arrests of Lei Chen in 1960 for trying to organize an opposition party and of Professor Peng Ming-min in 1964 for writing pamphlets that advocated overthrowing the KMT.[28]

Unlike many authoritarian regimes in similar circumstances, however, the KMT did not try to hang onto power simply through repression and terror. Rather, the regime tried to generate popular support in a number of ways. First, the land reform described in the previous section brought greater prosperity and equality to the countryside and allowed new political leaders to emerge in rural regions.[29] Second, the regime moved rapidly to create a system of elections for local governments and the Provincial Assembly. To be sure, the KMT dominated these elections, and the prohibition against forming an opposition party certainly violated the basic tenets of democracy. Still, electoral competition among competing KMT factions was quite intense in many localities, and "independents" were able to win important elections (e.g., they won the mayorships in three of the five largest cities in 1964). Thus, local politicians were forced to become more responsive to their constituencies, and the considerable "Taiwanization" of the lower levels of the party and government occurred because Mainlanders had a hard time winning at the polls.[30] Third, the attempt to gain popular support through promoting economic development entailed a significant broadening of the elite segments included in the regime. The push for rapid growth necessitated bringing technocrats and administrators, many of whom had been educated at leading U.S. universities, into the top levels of government. These technocrats then played the central role in making the much more controversial decision to switch to export-led growth that vitalized the private sector, thereby creating a new elite of Islanders in business.[31]

Significant changes in the authoritarian style of rule began to evolve in the 1970s. On the one hand, the nation's successful modernization and creation of an Islander business community stimulated increasing pressures for more popular participation and government responsiveness. On the other hand, when Chiang Ching-kuo became premier in 1972 he instituted a more liberal program that included bringing younger and better-educated officials into top leadership positions, gradually increasing the power granted to Islanders in the government and party, cracking down on regime corruption, and forcing the government to be more open. These two intersecting trends from both above and below resulted in the gradual liberalization of Taiwan's politics over the 1970s and first half of the 1980s in terms of increasing the scope of freedom of speech and electoral competition and reducing the power of conservatives within the regime. This liberalization was generally cumulative, although setbacks periodically occurred (e.g., a conservative comeback in the KMT following an embarrassing showing at the polls in 1977, a crackdown on dissidents after the Kaohsiung demonstrations in 1979, and the fairly conservative administration of Premier Yu Kuo-hwa in the mid-1980s).

An important component of this liberalization was that the position of the opposition began to improve noticeably. While the formation of an opposition party was still illegal, an informal association of opposition politicians called the *tangwei* (literally, "outside the party") began to grow after the late 1970s and used the more liberal atmosphere of the 1980s to stretch the limits of political discourse. The *tangwei* relied upon three primary techniques: (1) publishing dissident journals that proved fairly successful in avoiding the regime's attempts at censorship (e.g., by changing their names when closed down), (2) conducting vigorous and highly critical election campaigns, and (3) using legislative interpellation sessions to ask embarrassing questions.[32]

The cumulative movement toward political liberalization reached a more dramatic crescendo in 1986–1989. The first step was the open formation of an opposition party. In early 1986, president Chiang Ching-kuo formed a special KMT task force to propose political reforms and directed the party to open negotiations with the *tangwei*. These negotiations broke down, and in September, the opposition proclaimed the formation of the Democratic Progressive Party (DPP). President Chiang then declared that martial law would be ended and that new parties could be formed as long as they supported the ROC constitution and renounced communism and Taiwan independence. The December elections, therefore, marked the first time that the KMT faced an actual opposition party. The ruling party won handily with its normal 70% of the vote, but both the KMT and DPP seemed pleased with the outcome.[33] The next step was the formal abolition of martial law and the "emergency decree" that had been applied to Taiwan ever since the ROC's seat of government had been moved to Taipei. After some evident lobbying of KMT conservatives by the president, the emergency decree was formally repealed in July 1987 and replaced by the National Security Act.

While the abolition of martial law had little direct impact on Taiwan's politics, it marked a symbolic break with the past and opened the way for many of the recent reforms to be institutionalized (e.g., the legalization of new political parties). It also helped create a more open and even raucous style of politics. Street demonstrations that had been unthinkable before 1986 became a common occurrence, and debates in the Legislative Yuan became quite strident, with the regular breaking of microphones.[34] Finally, the balance of power within the KMT appeared to be moving in a more liberal direction. Chiang Ching-kuo's sudden death in January 1988 threw this trend into some question, but the new president, liberal technocrat Lee Teng-hui (who is an Islander), appears to be consolidating power, moving younger and more liberal leaders into top positions, and pushing through innovative domestic and foreign policies.[35]

A central requisite for democracy, of course, is that the winning party can take power. In contemporary Taiwan, however, the continued service of members of the National Assembly and Legislative Yuan who were elected on the mainland in the late 1940s would still prevent a DPP majority. Thus, the nature of "national" representative bodies has certainly become a major issue in Taiwan's politics. Until the late 1960s, no new members were chosen. By then, as shown in Table 3.3, these elected bodies had fallen to about half of their original memberships, and advancing age had made many of the "active members" far from active. When coupled with the pressure to make the elected organs more representative and democratic, these demographic trends led the regime to hold "supplementary" elections beginning in 1969 to rejuvenate the "representative" parts of the national government.

Table 3.3  Composition of Elected Bodies

|  | National Assembly | Legislative Yuan | Control Yuan |
|---|---|---|---|
| Year Original Election | 1947 | 1948 | 1948 |
| Number Original Members | 2,961 | 760 | 180 |
| Original Members Active 1967 | 1,521 | 493 | 84 |
| Original Members Active 1975 | 1,281 | 376 | 57 |
| Members Elected 1969 | 15 | 11 | 2 |
| Members Elected 1972–73 | 53 | 51 | 15 |
| Total Members 1975 | 1,349 | 438 | 74 |
| Directly Elected Members | 5% | 14% | 23% |
| Original Members Active 1986 | 899 | 222 | 35 |
| Members Elected in Supplementary Elections | 91 | 74 | 24 |
| Overseas Chinese Appointed by President | 0 | 27 | 10 |
| Total Members 1986 | 990 | 323 | 69 |
| Directly Elected Members | 9% | 23% | 35% |
| % Members Under Age 70 | 24% | 31% | 39% |
| Average Deaths per Year, 1981–86 | 44 | 14 | 1 |

Sources: Yangsun Chou and Andrew J. Nathan, "Democratizing Transition in Taiwan," Asian Survey 27:3 (March 1987) p. 279; Ralph N. Clough, Island China (Cambridge: Harvard University Press, 1978) p. 35; and Hung-chao Tai, "The Kuomintang and Modernization in Taiwan," in Samuel P. Huntington amd Clement H. Moore, eds., Authoritarian Politics in Modern Society: The Dynamics of Established One-Party Systems (New York: Basic Books, 1970) p. 417.

Gradually, the death of incumbents and the increased number of Taiwan members increased the proportion of directly elected members to about a tenth of the National Assembly, a quarter of the Legislative Yuan, and a third of the Control Yuan (these do not count the replacements appointed by the president to the Legislative and Control Yuans) by the late 1980s. Moreover, given the advanced age of many of the original incumbents, the newly elected members form a much higher percentage of those who actively participate. Consequently, these elective bodies have become reinvigorated over the 1980s, with legislators elected since 1980 being much more active and assertive than older members.[36] By the late 1980s, however, the continued numerical predominance of senior legislators had become highly controversial and an increasing embarrassment to the government. In early 1989, a plan was approved to greatly increase the number of directly elected positions, to end the appointment of replacements, and to try to bribe the senior legislators to retire with huge pensions. By the spring of 1990, the government was even floating a plan that would force the retirement of all the "senior" members of the Legislative Yuan by the end of 1992, although its success was by no means assured.[37]

The elections held in December 1989 for the Legislative Yuan, Provincial Assembly, Taipei and Kaohsiung city councils, and county and city chief executives provided some strong evidence of democratic change. First, it was the first election carried out in Taiwan after opposition parties had been fully legalized. It also included almost complete freedom of speech (i.e., candidates calling for Taiwan independence), although the opposition was denied equal access to the electronic media. Thus, the fact that a vigorous (and quite costly) campaign could be conducted was generally hailed as a big step forward in the island's political development. Second, the DPP did much better than expected (winning about 35% of the vote, up by over 10%), in contrast to the KMT's (58%, down by about 10%). Thus, although the ruling party did better in the local elections in January, the December results were seen as something of a defeat for it and an auger for increasingly competitive electoral politics in the future. This competition, in turn, was believed to have strengthened the hand of president Lee Teng-hui and reformists within the KMT.[38] Thus, the role of freely elected assemblies seems certain to grow in the Republic of China.

## Implications

Taiwan, in sum, has witnessed extremely rapid growth and industrial transformation over the past forty years. Political development has been considerably slower, but significant liberalization has taken place especially since the mid-1980s. Modernization theorists argue that such socioeconomic and political changes should normally enhance the status of women in a society, even if most feminists remain rather skeptical. Industrialization brings opportunities for women to leave the home and enter the workplace. This movement from the private to the public spheres can help wear down traditional socialization patterns that subjugate women to second-class status and can foster more interest in public affairs. Changes in the political system that promote democratization, in turn, create more opportunities for women (as well as men) to participate in public life. Chapter 4, therefore, examines the impact of economic and political change on women's status in Taiwan to determine whether the optimism of modernizationists or the pessimism of feminists is more applicable there.

## Notes

1. Chiao-min Hsieh, *Taiwan—Ilha Formosa: A Geography in Perspective* (Washington, D.C.: Butterworth's, 1964) Part I.

2. Han-yu Chang and Ramon H. Myers, "Japanese Colonial Development Policy in Taiwan," *Journal of Asian Studies* 22:4 (August 1963) pp. 433–449; Thomas B. Gold, *State and Society in the Taiwan Miracle* (Armonk, N.Y.: M. E. Sharpe, 1986) Chps. 2–3; Samuel P.S. Ho, *Economic Development of Taiwan, 1860–1970* (New Haven: Yale University Press, 1978) Chps. 2–5; and Hymen Kublin, "Taiwan's Japanese Interlude, 1895–1945," in Paul K.T. Sih, ed., *Taiwan in Modern Times* (New York: St. John's University Press, 1973) pp. 217–357.

3. Gold, *State and Society*, Chp. 4.

4. Shirley W.Y. Kuo, *The Taiwan Economy in Transition* (Boulder, Colo.: Westview, 1983) Chp. 3; and K. T. Li, *The Evolution of Policy Behind Taiwan's Development Success* (New Haven: Yale University Press, 1988) pp. 119–132.

5. Bernard Gallin, *Hsin Hsing, Taiwan: A Chinese Village in Change* (Berkeley: University of California Press, 1966); Ho, *Economic Development of Taiwan*, pp. 159–174; Teng-hui Lee, *Intersectoral Capital Flows in the Economic Development of Taiwan, 1895–1960* (Ithaca, N.Y.: Cornell University Press, 1971); Erik Thorbecke, "Agricultural Development," in Walter Galenson, ed., *Economic Growth and Structural Change in Taiwan: The Postwar Experience of the Republic of China* (Ithaca, N.Y.: Cornell University Press, 1979) pp. 132–205; Joseph A. Yager, *Transforming Agriculture in Taiwan: The Experience of the Joint Commission on Rural Reconstruction* (Ithaca, N.Y.: Cornell University Press, 1988); and Martin M.C. Yang, *Socioeconomic Results of Land Reform in Taiwan* (Honolulu: East-West Center Press, 1970).

6. Ching-yuan Lin, *Industrialization in Taiwan, 1946–72: Trade and Import-Substitution Policies for Developing Countries* (New York: Praeger, 1973) Chp. 4; and Gustav Ranis, "Industrial Policy," in Galenson, *Economic Growth and Structural Change in Taiwan*, pp. 211–221.

7. Neil H. Jacoby, *U.S. Aid to Taiwan: A Study of Foreign Aid, Self-Help, and Development* (New York: Praeger, 1966).

8. Gold, *State and Society*, pp. 74–78; Lin, *Industrialization in Taiwan*, Chp. 5; Li, *Taiwan's Development Success*, Chp. 4; and Maurice Scott, "Foreign Trade," in Galenson, *Economic Growth and Structural Change in Taiwan*, pp. 321–345.

9. Ho, *Economic Development of Taiwan*, pp. 198–220; Shirley W.Y. Kuo and John C.H. Fei, "Causes and Roles of Export Expansion in the Republic of China," in Walter Galenson, ed., *Foreign Trade and Investment: Economic Development in the Newly Industrializing Asian Countries* (Madison: University of Wisconsin Press, 1985) pp. 66–76; and Chi Shive, "Trade Patterns and Trends of Taiwan," in Colin I. Bradford, Jr., and William H. Branson, eds., *Trade and Structural Change in Pacific Asia* (Chicago: University of Chicago Press, 1987) pp. 316–320, 325–328.

10. Gold, *State and Society*, Chp. 6.

11. John C.H. Fei, "Economic Development and Traditional Chinese Cultural Values," *Journal of Chinese Studies* 3:1 (April 1986) pp. 109–124; Danny Kin Kong Lam, "Guerrilla Capitalism: Export-Oriented Firms and the Economic Miracle in Taiwan (1973–1987)," paper presented at the Annual Meeting of the American Association for Chinese Studies, Stanford University, October 21–23, 1988; Wen Lang Li, "Entrepreneurial Roles and Societal Development in Taiwan," *Journal of Chinese Studies* 3:1 (April 1986) pp. 77–96; and Robert G. Sutter, *Taiwan: Entering the 21st Century* (Lanham, Md.: University Press of America, 1988) Chp. 3.

12. Ramon H. Myers, "The Economic Development of the Republic of China on

Taiwan, 1965–1981," in Lawrence J. Lau, ed., *Models of Development: A Comparative Study of Economic Growth in South Korea and Taiwan* (San Francisco: Institute of Contemporary Studies, 1986) pp. 16–19, 31–34, & 47–49.

13. Thomas B. Gold, "Entrepreneurs, Multinationals, and the State," in Edwin A. Winckler and Susan Greenhalgh, eds., *Contending Approaches to the Political Economy of Taiwan* (Armonk, N.Y.: M. E. Sharpe, 1988) pp. 175–205; Stephan Haggard and Tun-jen Cheng, "State and Foreign Capital in the East Asian NICs," in Frederic C. Deyo, ed., *The Political Economy of the New Asian Industrialism* (Ithaca, N.Y.: Cornell University Press, 1987) pp. 84–135; and Gustav Ranis and Chi Shive, "Direct Foreign Investment in Taiwan's Development," in Galenson, *Newly Industrializing Asian Countries*, pp. 85–137.

14. John C.H. Fei, Gustav Ranis, and Shirley W.Y. Kuo, *Growth with Equity: The Taiwan Case* (New York: Oxford University Press, 1979); and Susan Greenhalgh, "Supranational Processes of Income Distribution," in Winckler and Greenhalgh, *Political Economy of Taiwan*, pp. 67–100.

15. Walter Galenson, "The Labor Force, Wages, and Living Standards," in Galenson, *Economic Growth and Structural Change in Taiwan*, pp. 384–447; and Yung Wei, "Taiwan: A Modernizing Society," in Sih, *Taiwan in Modern Times*, pp. 435–505.

16. Kuo, *Taiwan Economy in Transition*, Chp. 10; and K. T. Li, *Economic Transformation of Taiwan (ROC)* (London: Shepheard-Walwyn, 1988) Chp. 28.

17. Kuo, *Taiwan Economy in Transition*, pp. 206–208.

18. U.S. Department of Commerce, International Trade Administration, *Foreign Economic Trends and Their Implications for the United States: Taiwan* (Washington, D.C.: U.S. Government Printing Office, 1988) p. 2.

19. Gold, *State and Society*, pp. 100–106; Yin-min Ho, "The Production Structure of the Manufacturing Sector and Its Distribution Implications: The Case of Taiwan," *Economic Development and Cultural Change* 28:2 (June 1980) pp. 321–343; Lam, "Guerrilla Capitalism"; and Myers, "Economic Development," pp. 54–58.

20. Wen Lang Li, "Social Development of the Republic of China, 1949–1981," in Hungdah Chiu and Shao-Chuan Leng, eds., *China: Seventy Years After the Hsin Hai Revolution* (Charlottesville: University of Virginia Press, 1984) pp. 478–499, provides a broader analysis of Taiwan's social development. For comparative data on Taiwan's "physical quality of life," see Morris David Morris, *Measuring the Condition of the World's Poor: The Physical Quality of Life Index* (New York: Pergamon, 1979) pp. 68–69 & 75.

21. Ramon H. Myers, "The Economic Transformation of the Republic of China on Taiwan," *China Quarterly* 99 (September 1984) pp. 500–528.

22. Robert Gilpin, *The Political Economy of International Relations* (Princeton: Princeton University Press, 1987) Chps. 1, 3, & 5.

23. The basic political institutions of the ROC are described in Tuan-sheng Ch'ien, *The Government and Politics of China* (Cambridge: Harvard University Press, 1950) Chp. 21; John Franklin Copper, "Political Development in Taiwan," in Hungdah Chiu, ed., *China and the Taiwan Issue* (New York: Praeger, 1979) pp. 40–49; and John F. Copper with George P. Chen, *Taiwan's Elections: Political Development and Democratization in the Republic of China* (Baltimore: School of Law, University of Maryland, 1984) Chp. 2.

24. Arthur J. Lerman, *Taiwan's Politics: The Provincial Assemblyman's World* (Washington, D.C.: University Press of America, 1978).

25. Richard L. Walker, "Taiwan's Movement into Political Modernity, 1945–1972," in Sih, *Taiwan in Modern Times*, pp. 373–378.

26. Robert E. Bedeski, *State-Building in Modern China: The Kuomintang in the Prewar Period* (Berkeley: Institute of East Asian Studies, University of California, 1981) Chp. 7; and Hung-chao Tai, "The *Kuomintang* and Modernization in Taiwan," in Samuel P. Huntington and Clement H. Moore, eds., *Authoritarian Politics in Modern Society: The Dynamics of Established One-party Systems* (New York: Basic Books, 1970) pp. 407–411.

27. Gold, *State and Society*, Chp. 4.

28. Ralph N. Clough, *Island China* (Cambridge: Harvard University Press, 1978) pp. 37–44.

29. Gallin, *Hsin Hsing*, Chps. 3 & 6; Lerman, *Taiwan's Politics*, Part II; and Yang, *Land Reform*, Chps. 9–12.

30. Copper with Chen, *Taiwan's Elections*, Chp. 4; Fred W. Riggs, *Formosa Under Chinese Nationalist Rule* (New York: Octagon Books, 1972) pp. 48–53; and Tai, "*Kuomintang*," pp. 419–430.

31. Allan B. Cole, "Political Roles of Taiwanese Enterprisers," *Asian Survey* 7:9 (September 1967) pp. 645–654; Gold, *State and Society*, pp. 68–72; Samuel P.S. Ho, "Economics, Economic Bureaucracy, and Taiwan's Economic Development," *Pacific Affairs* 60:2 (Summer 1987) pp. 226–247; and Edwin A. Winckler, "Elite Political Struggle, 1945–1985," in Winckler and Greenhalgh, *Political Economy of Taiwan*, pp. 161–168.

32. John F. Copper, *A Quiet Revolution: Political Development in the Republic of China* (Washington, D.C.: Ethics and Public Policy Center, 1988); Copper with Chen, *Taiwan's Elections*, Chps. 5–7; Jurgen Domes, "Political Differentiation in Taiwan: Group Formation Within the Ruling Party and Opposition Circles, 1979–1980," *Asian Survey* 21:10 (October 1981) pp. 1011–1092; Tillman Durdin, "Chiang Ching-kuo and Taiwan," *Orbis* 18:4 (Winter 1975) pp. 1023–1042; Alexander Ya-li Lu, "Future Democratic Developments in the Republic of China on Taiwan," *Asian Survey* 25:11 (November 1985) pp. 1085–1092; Hung-mao Tien, *The Great Transition: Political and Social Change in the Republic of China* (Stanford, Calif.: Hoover Institution Press, 1989); and Edwin A. Winckler, "Institutionalization and Participation on Taiwan: From Hard to Soft Authoritarianism?" *China Quarterly* 99 (September 1984) pp. 481–499.

33. Yangsun Chou and Andrew J. Nathan, "Democratizing Transition in Taiwan," *Asian Survey* 27:3 (March 1987) pp. 284–293; Copper, *Quiet Revolution*, Chp. 4; Ramon H. Myers, "Political Theory and Recent Political Developments in the Republic of China," *Asian Survey* 27:9 (September 1987) pp. 1003–1022; and Sutter, *Taiwan*, pp. 46–51.

34. Susan Chira, "In Taiwan: Change Sweeps Out Taboos," *New York Times* 137:47,495 (May 4, 1988) p. 1; and James D. Seymour, "Taiwan in 1987: A Year of Political Bombshells," *Asian Survey* 28:1 (January 1988) pp. 74–76.

35. Parris H. Chang, "Evolution of Taiwan's Political Leadership After Chiang Ching-kuo," *AEI Foreign Policy and Defense Review* 6:3 (No. 3, 1986) pp. 12–18; Selig S. Harrison, "Taiwan After Chiang Ching-kuo," *Foreign Affairs* 66:4 (Spring 1988) pp. 721–796; and James D. Seymour, "Taiwan in 1988: No More Bandits," *Asian Survey* 29:1 (January 1989) pp. 56–58.

36. Chou and Nathan, "Democratizing Transition," pp. 277–299; Richard L. Engstrom and Chu Chi-hung, "The Impact of the 1980 Supplementary Election on Nationalist China's Legislative Yuan," *Asian Survey* 24:4 (April 1984) pp. 446–458; and Tien, *The Great Transition*, Chp. 6.

37. "The ROC Political Developments in 1989," *Newsletter* (Houston, Tex.: Information & Communications Division, Coordination Council for North American Affairs, 1989) pp. 1–2.

38. I-hsin Chen and Wen-cheng Wu, "Tide Is High for KMT Action," *Free China Journal* 7:8 (February 8, 1990) p. 5; June Tuefel Dreyer, "Taiwan in 1989: Democratization and Economic Growth," *Asian Survey* 30:1 (January 1990) pp. 53–55; Joseph P.L. Jiang, "Rise of a Two-party System," *Free China Review* 40:2 (February 1990) pp. 44–47; and James McGregor, "Bitter Wrangling Seen in Taipei After presidential Vote," *Asian Wall Street Journal Weekly* (March 19, 1990) pp. 1 & 12.

## CHAPTER FOUR
# Development and Women's Status in Taiwan

The Republic of China on Taiwan has clearly undergone a rapid and drastic transformation of its economic and social structure. As detailed in Chapter 3, the socioeconomic structure in Taiwan has developed from a traditional agricultural society to an urban, newly industrializing economy; it has also completed the demographic transition from high to low birth and death rates; the population has experienced massive upward socioeconomic mobility; and the employment structure has made considerable progress from low skill levels toward higher technological occupations. Thus, by the end of the century the ROC will almost certainly have entered the ranks of the industrialized middle-class societies.[1]

Conventionally, such economic development was believed to promote women's progress in upgrading their socioeconomic and political status. Industrialization, it was assumed, brought opportunities to find employment outside the home, which weakened the bonds of socialization into patriarchal norms and increased women's interest in the public sphere. After some time lag, these changes, in turn, led to increased interest and participation in politics by women. Finally, greater interest in public affairs and participation in mass political activities, such as voting, gradually stimulated women's entrance into political leadership positions as they began to act upon their interests and to overcome cultural norms about participating in the public sphere.

This rosy scenario, however, was sharply challenged by Ester Boserup, who argued that development actually was detrimental to women's status.[2] The idea that the relationship between industrialization and women's status might be an inverse one receives support from two different yet somewhat complementary theoretical traditions. First, studies of development in Western industrialized societies have found that despite the rapid increase in women's participation in the labor force, sex segregation in the workplace has been an almost universal phenomenon with women being confined generally to the "secondary labor market"—jobs characterized by low pay, few opportunities for promotion, and no on-the-job training or firm-specific skills. While classical sociological and economic theory explained this gender segregation by individual women's characteristics or employers' tastes, newer "institutional" approaches stress the structure of the labor market within societies dominated by patriarchal social values and capitalist economic values.[3]

Second, studies of developing countries have also found that industrialization generates a considerable gender gap in socioeconomic status. The broader institutional theory for explaining sex segregation in advanced industrial societies is also compatible with the "female marginalization thesis," which holds that industrialization in the developing world results in a diminution of women's status. This perspective argues that capitalist development inherently separates production and reproduction, structures capitalist enterprises hierarchically, requires surplus labor and an industrial reserve army, and engenders a mutual accommodation between capitalism and patriarchy. Thus, it results in women's confinement to the home, to inferior jobs, and to the reserve army of labor.[4] The effects of female marginalization, it has been argued, should be especially severe in Confucian societies, such as Taiwan, where women's subordination within the traditional family is most pronounced.[5]

In particular, capitalist development has three deleterious impacts on the status of women. First, it produces a withdrawal of women from the labor force, especially in the early stages of industrialization. Second, the female labor force is reconstituted as a secondary market, and women are concentrated in inferior positions in the occupational hierarchies. Finally, women's employment is depreciated and destabilized. Empirical tests of the female marginalization thesis have produced inconsistent results, with partial but far from complete support for its hypotheses.[6] One reason for this may be that the impact of development on women's status varies by class. That is, while upper-class women have expanded opportunities, women from poorer and lower classes, especially those in the agricultural sector, suffer at the onset of industrialization.[7]

Taiwan, therefore, should provide an interesting case study for comparing the optimistic and pessimistic perspectives about the impact of development on women's status. On the one hand, traditional Chinese society, strongly patriarchal, placed women in an especially subordinate status. On the other hand, Taiwan's rapid development has produced nearly full employment and substantial upward mobility which should mitigate the problems of female marginalization, and women have been explicitly granted equal rights to participate in politics, education, and employment.[8] This chapter, then, examines the gender gap in Taiwan in employment and in political interest and participation in mass activities. The first section reports occupational data by gender; the second considers political socialization and mass participation.

## Changes in Female Employment Patterns, 1966-1986

The modernization theory—that development should help attack women's gross underrepresentation among political elites—posits a several-stage sequence of improving women's status: first, occupational gains, then greater equality in mass political activities, and finally the beginning of women's competing for leadership positions. Obviously, if this sequence is to succeed, the first step—that industrialization should expand women's occupational horizons—must occur. Thus, if the female marginalization thesis is correct that development actually decreases women's socioeconomic status, the political hypotheses about women's status must fail as well.

This section, hence, examines the impact of industrialization in the Republic of China upon women's employment status. In particular, we investigate the extent of sex segregation along two distinct dimensions of horizontal and vertical segregation.[9] First, horizontal segregation refers to the distribution of women in some sectors of the economy and men in others in disproportion to their overall participation in the labor force. Four general occupational groupings are used to assess horizontal segregation: agriculture, commerce, services (excluding commerce and transportation), and manufacturing. Together, these four sectors have accounted for almost 90% of total employment during the postwar period, and they form a hierarchy of occupational desirability. Manufacturing has been the growth sector, agriculture the declining sector. The tertiary commerce and service sectors fall between the success of manufacturing and the decline of agriculture in terms of employment and production, but commerce would seem the less desirable of the two because of its domination by marginal small-scale units.[10] Thus, our study of horizontal segregation examines whether women were disproportionately concentrated in either the declining or advancing sectors.

The second dimension of occupational sex segregation is the vertical stratification of men and women in an occupational hierarchy. Also termed "rank segregation," this concept means there is a declining proportion of women at successively higher levels of skill, authority, status, and income within a given enterprise or occupation. Two measures of vertical segregation are employed here. First, women's employment in managerial and professional positions at the top of the hierarchy is compared with their participation in lower-status jobs (clerical and sales, production, and agriculture, in declining order). Second, within each of the four major occupational groupings, men and women are compared in terms of their employment status—employer, self-employed, employee, or unpaid family worker, four categories that form a clear hierarchy of prestige and desirability.

The data for this study are taken from the labor surveys that have been conducted by the government's Directorate-General of Budget, Accounting, and Statistics (DGBAS) annually since 1966. While Taiwan had experienced some earlier industrialization (see Chapter 3), the mid-1960s marked the beginning of the rapid industrial transformation of the island based upon labor-intensive production. Thus, an examination of women's changing employment patterns for the 1966–1986 period should provide a good picture of industrialization's impact upon the status of women in the ROC.

A direct measure of horizontal segregation is provided by the percentage of women in total employment reported in Table 4.1. These results indicate that women have benefited from industrialization in Taiwan and that horizontal segregation by basic occupation is not major a problem. Overall, women's share of the labor force increased steadily, from 27% in 1966 to 32% in 1976 to 38% in 1986. Moreover, these employment gains were far from concentrated in the declining agricultural sector. In 1966, women composed 28%–30% of those employed in agriculture, commerce, and manufacturing and a slightly higher 34% in services. By 1986, in contrast, women were 43%–45% of the labor force in the three more desirable sectors, but only 32% of those still working in agriculture. Thus, far from being "marginalized," women scored their biggest employment gains in the more desirable occupations.

Two exceptions to these generally positive trends should be noted, though. First, women's share of the agricultural workforce did increase slightly, although not enough to suggest the "feminization" of agriculture that is part of the agricultural crisis in other developing countries.[11] Second, the growth of women in the labor force in manufacturing, compared with the two tertiary occupations, was higher during the 1966–1976 decade and lower in 1976–1986, implying that women's ability to gain entrance into the most desirable occupation may be declining. Still, in spite of these caveats, these data on gross occupational distribution suggest that women have benefited from the "Taiwan miracle."

Table 4.1  Women's Percentage of Total Employment

|  | 1966 | 1976 | 1986 |
|---|---|---|---|
| Whole Economy | 27.1 | 31.9 | 37.7 |
| Agriculture | 28.7 | 32.3 | 31.6 |
| Commerce | 29.9 | 33.5 | 42.9 |
| Services[a] | 34.0 | 36.1 | 44.6 |
| Manufacturing | 27.9 | 39.7 | 44.1 |

*Source: Annual Report of Labor Statistics, 1966, 1976, & 1986* (Taipei: Directorate-General of Budget, Accounting, and Statistics, Executive Yuan, 1966, 1976, & 1986), in Chinese.
[a]Tertiary sector excluding commerce and transportation.

This positive impression is reinforced by the figures on the proportion of all employed men and women who work in each of these four sectors (Table 4.2). In 1966, almost half of both all employed women and men worked in agriculture, under a fifth were employed in manufacturing. Over the next two decades, women, if anything, led the changes in employment structure that resulted from rapid industrialization. The proportion of women working in agriculture fell faster (from 47% to 14%, as opposed to 43% to 19% for males), while manufacturing's absorption of total employment increased significantly more for women (19% to 40%) than for men (18% to 30%).

Again, a slight negative tendency can be discerned—the share of the less desirable commercial sector in total employment grew somewhat faster for women than for men.

Table 4.2  Percentage of All Employed Men or Women in Specific Industries

|  | 1966 | | 1986 | |
| --- | --- | --- | --- | --- |
|  | Men | Women | Men | Women |
| Agriculture | 43.0 | 46.6 | 18.7 | 14.3 |
| Commerce | 11.2 | 12.9 | 16.4 | 20.4 |
| Service[a] | 13.5 | 18.7 | 13.9 | 18.5 |
| Manufacturing | 17.7 | 18.5 | 30.3 | 39.6 |

*Source: Annual Report of Labor Statistics, 1966 & 1986* (Taipei: Directorate-General of Budget, Accounting, and Statistics, Executive Yuan, 1966 & 1986), in Chinese.
[a]Tertiary sector excluding commerce and transportation.

In terms of horizontal segregation, therefore, these data suggest that there has been an impressive improvement in women's integration into Taiwan's economy. Such data, of course, tell us nothing about vertical segregation or women's status within particular industries. Tables 4.3 and 4.4 provide an initial test of the extent of vertical segregation by comparing the positions of the sexes at different levels of the occupational hierarchy. Table 4.3 presents the percentage of total employed people at different status levels, while Table 4.4 indicates the proportion of all employed women who occupy a given position in the job hierarchy.

Table 4.3  Percentage of All Employed Men or Women at Specific Levels of Occupational Hierarchy

|  | 1966 | | 1986 | |
| --- | --- | --- | --- | --- |
|  | Men | Women | Men | Women |
| Managerial & Administrative | 4.4 | 1.4 | 1.2 | 0.2 |
| Professional | 4.6 | 5.8 | 6.0 | 6.7 |
| Clerical | 7.3 | 6.1 | 11.2 | 18.0 |
| Sales | 10.4 | 12.4 | 13.3 | 13.7 |
| Production | 20.2 | 16.6 | 42.6 | 36.2 |
| Agriculture | 42.4 | 46.6 | 18.5 | 14.2 |

*Source: Annual Report of Labor Statistics 1966 & 1986* (Taipei: Directorate-General of Budget, Accounting, and Statistics, Executive Yuan, 1966 & 1986), in Chinese.

The top of the occupational hierarchy in the ROC, as in almost any nation, is represented by those in administrative and managerial positions; those with professional and technical occupations rank a clear second. Together, people in these occupational strata, who were about 7% of the total workforce in both 1966 and 1986, compose the bulk of the upper and upper-middle classes. Not only do they have the highest status and income in society, but they also form the eligibility pool from which most electoral politicians emerge. Women's ability to gain entrance to managerial and professional positions is important, then, not only as a measure of occupational discrimination, but because entrance into such positions seems a prerequisite for gaining greater representation in the polity.[12]

Table 4.4  Women as a Percentage of Total Employment at Specific Levels of Occupational Hierarchy

|  | 1966 | 1976 | 1986 |
|---|---|---|---|
| Whole Economy | 27.1 | 31.9 | 37.7 |
| Managerial & Administrative | 10.7 | 7.7 | 9.1 |
| Professional | 31.9 | 34.8 | 40.5 |
| Clerical | 23.6 | 41.5 | 49.3 |
| Sales | 30.6 | 31.5 | 38.3 |
| Production | 23.3 | 29.6 | 33.8 |
| Agriculture | 29.0 | 32.4 | 31.7 |

*Source: Annual Report of Labor Statistics, 1966, 1976, & 1986* (Taipei: Directorate-General of Budget, Accounting, and Statistics, Executive Yuan, 1966, 1976 & 1986), in Chinese.

Women's positions in these two occupational groupings differed starkly. They were grossly underrepresented among the top level of managerial and administrative personnel. For example, women were only a third as likely as men (1.4% to 4.4%) to hold managerial jobs in 1966, and while the proportion of people having such positions dropped over the next two decades, the fall was much more precipitous for women (to 0.2%) than for men (to (1.2%). Consequently, women's share of these positions declined from a gross underrepresentation of 11% in 1966 to 8% in 1976 and 9% in 1986. Clearly, there has been at this level very substantial vertical segregation by gender in Taiwan, with no indication whatsoever that the booming economy of the last two decades has led to any improvement.

In fairly sharp contrast, however, women have had relatively equal access to the professional strata. A higher proportion of women than men were employed in these jobs in both 1966 (5.8% to 4.6%) and 1986 (6.7% to 6.0%); and in all three years included in Table 4.4, women's proportion of professional occupations was slightly higher than their share in the total workforce. These figures are at least a little surprising, especially for the earlier years of Taiwan's industrialization, and probably reflect the merit-based access to higher education on the island. Thus, women have gained fairly equal access to many middle-class occupations and even upper-middle-class ones, although the implications for political mobility are not as bright because many of the jobs included in this category (i.e., lower-level management) probably fall below the cutoff point for the electoral eligibility pool.

Clerical and sales jobs come next in the occupational hierarchy. They have considerably lower pay and social status than managerial and professional occupations, and people in these occupations usually do not become ambitious for political office. Yet the economic boom in Taiwan has made many who hold such positions prosperous enough to acquire middle-class tastes, values, and styles of living.[13] The size of these two sectors grew significantly from 18% of total employment in 1966 to 27% in 1986 with almost all the expansion coming in clerical occupations, which doubled their share of the labor force from 7% to 14%.

It is thus quite significant that women did extremely well in gaining clerical positions. Their share of all clerical jobs doubled from 24% in 1966 to 49% in 1986, by far the highest female penetration of any of the major occupational groups. Thus, while women were slightly less likely than men to be employed in clerical jobs in 1966 (6% to 7%), they were over 50% more likely to have clerical positions in 1986 (18% to 11%). In contrast, women were about equally represented with men in the sales sector, both in terms of their proportion of the sales workforce compared with their share in the total labor market and in terms of the percentages of all men and all women employed in sales. Women's ability to gain entrance to these middle-level "white- and pink-collar" positions, especially the rapidly expanding clerical ones, indicates that industrialization did not bring extensive female marginalization in Taiwan. However, it also certainly does not offset the extreme lack of female representation at the top of the occupational ladder.

Agriculture clearly ranks at the bottom of the occupational hierarchy in Taiwan; work in direct production ranks between agriculture and clerical-sales occupations in terms of status and income.[14] In 1966, these two occupational groupings accounted for just over 60% of total employment; this declined to about 55% in 1986. However, industrialization reversed the relative weights of these two sectors in Taiwan's employment—agriculture, twice as high in 1966, was displaced by production by 1986. Throughout these two decades, women were slightly underrepresented among production workers, and their slight overrepresentation in agriculture in 1966 dipped to slight underrepresentation in 1986. Thus, women were clearly not marginalized into the most peripheral economic sectors, although their slight underrepresentation in these two employment categories is probably not enough to be substantively significant.

A second way of measuring vertical segregation is to compare the employment status of men and women within each of the major sectors of the economy. Employment status is divided into four categories: employer, self-employed, employee, and unpaid family worker. Employer is clearly the highest position, and unpaid family helper the lowest. Self-employment is generally considered to bring higher status than working for someone else, although many of the self-employed (especially those in the small-scale "informal sector") do not have very high income or social status. Tables 4.5 through 4.8 present data on the percentage of women and of men in each of the four major occupational groupings (manufacturing, services, commerce, and agriculture) who have the various employment statuses.

It should be noted that there is some bias toward placing women in the lowest status of unpaid family help because of the cultural convention in Taiwan to describe family enterprises (i.e., farms, shops, and small factories) as belonging to husbands, even when wives contribute equal or greater quantities of capital and labor to them, a circumstance that occurs more frequently in commerce than in agriculture. However, since many such farms and shops are run by families assumed to be the most traditional in their value orientations, this assumption probably does not give a false picture of women's status.

Manufacturing and services are fairly similar in that most of their workers are employees and that women are represented about equally with men in the employee category (Tables 4.5 and 4.6). For manufacturing, the proportion of employees in total employment rose from 75% to over 85% between 1966 and 1986, indicating that industry increased in scale somewhat; employees constituted just under 85% of those in service occupations throughout these two decades. Women and men, in addition, were approximately equal in their percentages of employees reported in Tables 4.5 and 4.6, except for manufacturing in 1986, when women were somewhat more likely than men to be employees (93% to 84%). Women's equal representation among employees, however, should not necessarily be taken as proof of an absence of vertical segregation. For example, women form a disproportionate number of the "part-time proletariat" of women who work in factories before marriage. They rank at the bottom of pay and status among manufacturing employees, have almost no opportunity for advancement, and for the most part continue to be subordinated within traditional family structures.[15]

Table 4.5  Percentage of All Men or Women Employed in Manufacturing with Specific Type of Employment Status

|  | 1966 | | 1986 | |
| --- | --- | --- | --- | --- |
|  | Men | Women | Men | Women |
| Employer | 5.4 | 1.7 | 8.2 | 0.6 |
| Self-Employed | 13.7 | 12.8 | 5.5 | 0.9 |
| Employee | 76.4 | 73.4 | 84.4 | 93.2 |
| Unpaid Family Help | 4.4 | 12.1 | 1.9 | 5.3 |

Source: *Annual Report of Labor Statistics, 1966 & 1986* (Taipei: Directorate-General of Budget, Accounting, and Statistics, Executive Yuan, 1966 & 1986), in Chinese.

Table 4.6  Percentage of All Men or Women Employed in Service Industries with Specific Type of Employment Status

|  | 1966 | | 1986 | |
| --- | --- | --- | --- | --- |
|  | Men | Women | Men | Women |
| Employer | 3.7 | 3.0 | 4.8 | 2.0 |
| Self-Employed | 9.9 | 6.3 | 13.8 | 8.9 |
| Employee | 84.5 | 83.6 | 80.1 | 83.3 |
| Unpaid Family Help | 2.0 | 7.2 | 1.4 | 5.8 |

*Source:* *Annual Report of Labor Statistics, 1966 & 1986* (Taipei: Directorate-General of Budget, Accounting, and Statistics, Executive Yuan, 1966 & 1986), in Chinese.
*Note:* Tertiary sector excluding commerce and transportation.

In terms of the other three employment statuses, however, men had a clear advantage that increased somewhat over time. For manufacturing, men were three times more likely than women to be employers in 1966 (5.4% to 1.7%). Over the next two decades, the proportion of men who were employers increased by more than a half, to 8.2%, while the number of women employers dropped to well under 1% of all women in the manufacturing sector. Men and women were about equally likely to be self-employed in 1966 (14% and 13% respectively). Self-employment dropped considerably for both sexes, but the drop was much more precipitous for women. At the lowest end of the spectrum, women were approximately three times as likely as men to be unpaid family workers in both 1966 and 1986; the proportion of workers in this category fell by about a half over these twenty years. Thus, over time there has clearly been a "masculinization" of the "have" and a "feminization" of the "have not" ends of the spectrum in manufacturing.

For services, the gaps between men and women were not as great, but the same pattern of women's disadvantaged position is clear. At the top of the status hierarchy, men were only slightly more likely than women to be employers in 1966 (3.7% to 3.0%), but while the proportion of male employers increased over the next two decades, that of female employers fell (to 4.8% and 2.0% respectively). Likewise, men increased their advantage among the self-employed between 1966 and 1986 (from 9.9% to 13.8%, versus 6.3% to 8.9% for women). At the bottom of the job ladder, women were almost four times as likely as men to be unpaid family workers (7.2% to 2.0% in 1966 and 5.8% to 1.4% in 1986).

In contrast to the situation in manufacturing and services, where the employee category predominated, most of the people in commerce and agriculture fall into the self-employed and unpaid family help category, demonstrating the small-scale and perhaps marginal nature of these activities in the ROC. (See Tables 4.7 and 4.8.) For agriculture, about 80% of the workforce is either self-employed or unpaid family help; for commerce, this percentage decreased a little (68% to 55%) between 1966 and 1986. Since the data on manufacturing and services showed that women are least discriminated against in the employee category, this suggests that women would be especially vulnerable to vertical segregation in these two sectors. The data in Tables 4.7 and 4.8 support this supposition.

Table 4.7  Percentage of All Men or Women Employed in Commerce with Specific Type of Employment Status

|  | 1966 | | 1986 | |
| --- | --- | --- | --- | --- |
|  | Men | Women | Men | Women |
| Employer | 5.6 | 1.5 | 10.6 | 2.4 |
| Self-Employed | 57.7 | 34.6 | 46.6 | 23.1 |
| Employee | 28.4 | 22.3 | 36.2 | 38.3 |
| Unpaid Family Help | 8.3 | 41.6 | 6.6 | 36.3 |

*Source: Annual Report of Labor Statistics, 1966 & 1986* (Taipei: Directorate-General of Budget, Accounting, and Statistics, Executive Yuan, 1966 & 1986), in Chinese.

Table 4.8  Percentage of All Men or Women Employed in Agriculture with Specific Type of Employment Status

|  | 1966 | | 1986 | |
| --- | --- | --- | --- | --- |
|  | Men | Women | Men | Women |
| Employer | 0.9 | 0.3 | 1.8 | 0.5 |
| Self-Employed | 51.8 | 9.4 | 67.6 | 20.4 |
| Employee | 18.6 | 15.5 | 14.1 | 11.8 |
| Unpaid Family Help | 28.7 | 74.9 | 16.5 | 67.3 |

*Source: Annual Report of Labor Statistics, 1966 & 1986* (Taipei: Directorate-General of Budget, Accounting, and Statistics, Executive Yuan, 1966 & 1986), in Chinese.

The strongly disadvantaged position of women in commerce is readily demonstrated by the fact that they were five to six times as likely as men to be unpaid family help (42% versus 8% in 1966 and 36% versus 7% in 1986). Thus, a large proportion of women in this area were in by far the least desirable job status, while only a small percentage of men were. In contrast, men were about four times as likely to be employers and twice as likely to be self-employed in both 1966 and 1986. The only bright spot for women here was that they benefited a little more than men from the growing share of employees in total employment (25% in 1966 to 37% in 1986). Still, it is clear that women face more vertical segregation in commerce than in manufacturing or services.

If anything, Table 4.8 presents an even bleaker picture for women in agriculture. Women were only a third as likely as men to be employers, but since less than 1% of the people involved in agriculture employ others, this is not substantively significant. Likewise, women were only slightly less well represented among employees than men, but this involves only about 13% of the agricultural workforce. The glaring problem of vertical segregation is sharply reflected in the data on the lowest employment status. Three-quarters of the women working in agriculture were unpaid family help in 1966; this decreased only to two-thirds in 1986–approximately three times the percentage for men in the former year and four times in the latter. Superficially, the figures for self-employed farmers look better for women. The percentage of female workers who described themselves as self-employed doubled from 9% to 20% over the 1966–1986 period (while for men this figure rose from 52% to 68%). What this denotes, however, is women running their own small farms. Especially since agriculture is a declining sector,[16] this probably represents an important aspect of the feminization of agriculture in Taiwan that the broader aggregate data discussed here did not uncover.

Thus, women's position in agriculture appears to be particularly disadvantaged. In part, this results from the fact that women in agriculture, especially those who are older and have low levels of formal education, have very restricted mobility into the industrial and urban sectors. Thus, they are left to fill the least desirable roles in a markedly declining economic sector. The implications of these aggregate data, furthermore, are consistent with several broader sociological studies of women's status in Taiwan. These generally show that there are important rural-urban and class differences in how development has affected the status of women in Taiwan. Thus, while rural, uneducated, and older women have suffered a loss of status during industrialization, urban, better-educated, and younger women appear to have benefited from the opportunities generated by economic development.[17]

An examination of the impact of rapid growth and industrialization upon women's employment status in Taiwan, therefore, indicates that women have played an active role in responding to the labor market opportunities generated by the island's fundamental economic transformation. This is clearly illustrated by the growing share of women workers throughout the workforce and by the general absence of horizontal gender segregation (i.e., women workers being concentrated in peripheral and declining sectors). In particular, the ability of women to gain access to professional and lower-level white-collar occupations (clerical and sales jobs) is potentially quite important for promoting socioeconomic mobility, casting off the shackles of traditional culture, and awakening political interest and ambition.

A major reason for women's relatively equal entrance into these more desirable occupations undoubtedly stems from their growing educational achievements. Taiwan's great expansion of primary and secondary schooling and admission to higher education based on competitive entrance examinations has resulted in the considerable narrowing of the huge gender gap in education that existed in the early 1950s. For example, in 1951 men had a decided advantage over women in average years of schooling (3.9 to 1.4), but by 1983 this gap had shrunk considerably in relative terms (8.9 to 7.4); women's share among college students more than doubled from 18.8% in 1958 to 43.6% in 1987; and the tendency for men to have higher literacy rates decreased greatly over time as well (83% versus 57% in 1963 to 96% versus 86% in 1987).[18] Thus, women's increasing educational achievements have been credited for upgrading their economic status.[19]

However, when women's status is measured in terms of their vertical integration into the core of the production system, the picture is much less bright. The aggregate data demonstrate that women generally remain excluded from the top levels of ownership and administrative-managerial positions, while they are grossly overrepresented at the bottom of the occupational ladder as unpaid family helpers. Moreover, many women in agriculture appear trapped in a declining sector by their age and lack of education, and many younger women factory workers still remain within the traditional patriarchal and exploitative system. Thus, the occupational distribution in Taiwan still generates very significant sex segregation.[20] Moreover, women suffer from decided wage discrimination as well. In the mid-1980s, women earned only two-thirds of the salaries paid to men with comparable education, with the gap being inversely related to level of education.[21] Finally, women seemingly face significant discrimination even in the government sector in the sense that the average rank of their positions compared with men's is lower than would be warranted by comparative educational levels or performance on civil service examinations.[22] While seniority in government service explains some of these sex differences, this pattern of discrimination is disturbing in view of the government's ostensible commitment to gender equality and meritocracy.

## Political Socialization, Interest, and Mass Participation

If entrance into the occupational workforce is assumed to be the first step toward promoting women's political representation, the second step is that previously traditional women will become more interested and participate in politics. This section, therefore, explores gender differences in the Republic of China in orientations toward the political system and in basic forms of political participation.

In the advanced industrial society of the United States, for example, women's underrepresentation in political leadership posts has been explained conventionally by their lower levels of interest in politics and voting, characteristics assumed to derive from socialization patterns that inhibited women from entering the public sphere.[23] During the 1970s and 1980s, however, the differences in political interest and mass participatory activities in the United States narrowed and even vanished, although significant preadult gender differences in political orientations continued.[24] This was then explained by women's increased educational achievements and entrance into professional occupations which produced countersocialization,[25] and by the activities of the women's movement, which made politics much more salient for women.[26] Comparative studies, in addition, showed that the gender gap in such areas as political interest and voting was much narrower in the United States than in other developing or even developed nations, implying that both the development processes and indigenous culture have some impact upon sex-role socialization and orientations.[27]

These findings suggest several hypotheses about the nature of male-female differences in socialization experiences and basic political orientations and activities in Taiwan. First, preadult differences in socialization and political orientations between the sexes in Taiwan should be fairly pronounced both because the transformation of the traditional economy is much more recent in the ROC than in the United States and because Chinese culture is particularly patriarchal. Second, the same logic implies that significant overall differences should exist at the adult level as well. Third, for some socioeconomic categories (e.g., those with high levels of education or professional occupation), however, the gender gap should be much narrower. Women's entrance into professional occupations in Taiwan, as described in the previous section, has been associated with changed political orientations among U.S. women.[28] The women's movement that became increasingly active in Taiwan during the 1980s should also increase women's politicization.[29]

Studies of the relationship of gender to political socialization and involvement are much less developed in Taiwan than in the United States and are fairly descriptive in nature. Still, there is sufficient information to provide at least a preliminary test of the preceding hypotheses with both quantitative and qualitative data.

The first hypothesis about gender differences in childhood socialization receives strong support. First, sociological and anthropological analyses of the family in Chinese society in general and Taiwan in particular confirm women's subordinate position within the family, the view that women's primary importance lay in their contributions to the family, and the inhibitions Confucian norms generate against women's venturing beyond the private sphere.[30] Given such a patriarchal socialization context, it would certainly be expected that Chinese boys and girls should differ radically in their political orientations and involvement.

Several studies of high school and college students have found, as expected, that substantial gender differences exist between young men and young women. However, the extent of this gender gap varies significantly in different areas. In particular, while boys and girls have fairly similar "normative" views (i.e., what is good or desired) about the polity and the relationship of the citizenry to the government, they differ quite markedly in the "cognitive" (i.e., political knowledge), "affective" (i.e., interest in politics), and "behavioral" (i.e., actual involvement in political activities) dimensions of political orientations. This pattern, obviously, would be expected to result in women's assuming a passive apolitical stance toward the governmental system.

A national study of the political attitudes of students in junior and senior high school in the early 1980s conforms to this pattern very well, for example. Female students scored much lower (16 below an average of 0) than their male counterparts (13 above 0) on a combined index of the cognitive and affective aspects. In particular, girls had much less knowledge than boys about government policy and the nature of government and politics. There was an even slightly greater difference between the sexes on an index of political behavior as female students (19 below the average score) had much less past participation in political activities and less intention of entering politics in the future than did boys (15 above the average). In contrast, there was no significant gender gap among these students in terms of the normative dimensions of beliefs about citizen duties and feelings of political efficacy.[31]

Several studies of college students have found a similar gender gap in the behavioral, cognitive, and affective dimensions. For example, a survey of nearly 4,000 college students in the early 1960s found that men were much more likely to vote than women.[32] A more extensive study of college students a decade later found sizable gender gaps along several important dimensions. First, male students were twice as likely to participate in politics as were women. For example, 20% of the young men, compared with 10% of the young women, had attended political rallies, speeches, or other campaign activities; and 35% of the males, compared with 16% of the females, expressed an interest in seeking political office in the future. Second, in terms of political interest, men students were almost three times more likely than the women to discuss politics frequently (23.5% versus 8%) and, conversely, less than half as likely never to discuss it at all (4% versus 9.5%). Third, on the cognitive dimension, the male students scored twice as high as females in terms of familiarity with local and international political figures and events. Finally, the young women were significantly less likely to report differences in political views and ideology between themselves and their parents, which implies a lower degree of political independence and assertiveness.[33]

An analysis of the impact of political norms on behavior among college students in the early 1980s provides additional, though more indirect, evidence that young women are less concerned with politics than are young men. Normally, people with self-perceptions of political efficacy (i.e., the belief that one can affect political outcomes) are more participatory.[34] For male students in Taiwan, this clearly held true—their feelings of political efficacy were positively related to a variety of political behaviors, such as voting, handing out information, joining political groups, contacting government officials, and becoming involved in a political party. For female students, in sharp contrast, political efficacy stimulated only voting and spreading political messages. Likewise, college men who held liberal attitudes (which usually include support for democratization) were more participatory on almost all these dimensions, while there was no such relationship for female students. In fact, liberal college women were less likely than others to join political parties.[35] The normal linkage between normative beliefs and political activities, thus, evidently does not exist among female college students in Taiwan, again indicating that their political participation is atypically low.

Another finding from this study is worthy of note: There were no gender differences in the relationship of political alienation and beliefs about citizenship duties to participatory behaviors. Those who felt alienated from the political system were less likely to participate regardless of sex, as might well have been anticipated. However, much more surprisingly, there was no significant relationship at all between feelings of citizen duty and political behavior for either male or female students.[36] These results imply that the rather uniform and depoliticized citizenry-education programs in the schools may have had some success in legitimating the regime and its limited (at least until recently) mechanisms for popular participation.[37] If this is so, it can only reinforce girls' and women's passivity toward the public sphere.

At the preadult level, therefore, there are substantial differences in political knowledge, interest, and participation between the genders, as our first hypothesis predicted. These studies of young adults, moreover, are confirmed by the results from an analysis of the relative impact of six types of political socialization agents experienced by adult Taipei residents. Overall, only educational level had a greater effect than gender on how the political attitudes and behaviors of Taipei residents were influenced by the six sources of socialization (family, educational experiences, peer groups, the mass media, political parties, and foreign culture).[38]

Significant gender differences exist at the adult level as well, but they seem significantly less pronounced than among younger people. Women are clearly less participatory then men, except at the easily accessible level of voting. In 1971, for example, the voting rates for men and women were 76% and 69% respectively, and this modest gap has been closing over time. In contrast, in "harder" behaviors requiring more active involvement, such as membership in political parties and participating in party functions, gender differences have been more substantial and persistent. For example, men are much more likely to attend political rallies and listen to campaign speeches than are female voters. Women, moreover, appear woefully underrepresented in the dominant Nationalist Party. In 1982, 433,184 women belonged to the KMT, constituting only 21% of its total membership and 7% of the adult female population.[39] A major reason for these participatory differences is that women have higher levels of political apathy than men. For example, men claim that their principal reason for not voting is not living in their registered residence (which disqualifies a voter), while the principal reason women cite for not voting is suspicion of the meaning and function of elections.[40]

This research also suggests that women are more cynical about and distrustful of the political system than are men. The evidence here is mixed, but provides another indication of women's comparatively greater political passivity in Taiwan. On the one hand, in the 1983 elections, female voters expressed more serious doubt about the effects of campaign activities and the election's significance for the nation's democratic development.[41] On the other hand, there is little overall difference between men and women in the degree of political alienation or feelings of citizen duty. Furthermore, female voters actually have higher levels of political trust than men do in the government, its officials, and its policies—women are significantly more likely to vote for the dominant KMT Party than are men.[42] Thus, women seem more accepting of political authority and more suspicious of democratization and the increased participatory opportunities that it brings, again suggesting a gender gap in political activity—one, incidentally, that is similar to the situation in Europe and North America before the 1970s (see Chapter 2).

Women's lesser participation is also suggested by findings that motivations for voting differ significantly between the sexes. Men are more "individualistic"—their distinctive motivations include voting as a way to express one's opinion or in response to mobilization by a political party. In contrast, women's voting pattern has been described as more "relational"—it derives from the influence of other people. For example, 42% of the female voters in the 1980 and 1983 elections said that they cast their ballots because of the persuasion or request of family members, relatives, or neighborhood (*li*) heads. Similarly, the tendency, noted in some (but not all) of Taiwan's elections, for party identification to have a stronger impact on men's voting than on women's can be explained by the greater tendency of women to vote in accordance with their families' decisions and desires.[43] Men also appear to be more issue-oriented than women in the way they view political campaigns. Thus, in both the 1980 and 1983 elections, male voters were more concerned with candidates' issue positions and with their past performance in politics, although there was little difference between the sexes in how they evaluated such other candidate characteristics as moral standards, personal conduct, educational achievement, and physical appearance.[44]

Finally, some of these relationships were clearly conditioned by educational level. First, the difference in issue orientation between men and women almost completely vanishes when education is controlled. That is, for those with a high level of education, both men and women are equally oriented to issues, while few voters with low education have much interest in issues regardless of sex.[45] The tendency for women to support the KMT is also conditioned by educational level. Among voters with low- or medium-level education, women are more likely to vote for the KMT than are men, but there is no difference in party voting between the sexes among the highly educated. Thus, the relationship between gender and party voting derives from the fact that women have yet to catch up with men in education (although, as noted earlier, the education gap has decreased substantially in the younger generation).[46] These findings imply that as more women receive higher education, female citizens should become more active and issue-oriented and less passive toward political authority.

In sum, a considerable gender gap continues among children in terms of political interest and participation. Among adults, this gap is significant, but seemingly of a lesser magnitude than for children, paralleling the relationship that has been found in the United States. This supports the "adult role socialization" perspective (see Chapter 2) and also suggests at least a semi-optimistic prognostication. While Taiwan's gender gap in political participation is considerably wider than in the United States, as expected by our second hypothesis, the conditions that eradicated this gap there (women's entrance into higher education and professional occupations, the women's movement, etc.) can be found in the ROC. In particular, higher education does much to equalize the political orientations and behaviors of the sexes, as predicted by our third hypothesis.

## Implications

The manner in which the socioeconomic transformation away from a traditional society can attack the underrepresentation and near-exclusion of women in political leadership posts has been conceptualized here as a three-step process. First, women's entrance into the labor market, especially into jobs at the top of the occupational hierarchy, gives them greater freedom and control over material resources and challenges the monopoly previously exercised over their lives by patriarchal kinship systems. Second, these factors of greater freedom and contact with the public sphere gradually increase feelings of political interest and efficacy in women that stimulate their participation in mass political activities. Finally, mass participation is transferred—after a substantial time lag—into more aggressive competition for positions among the political elites.

This chapter has examined the first two steps: women's occupational status in Taiwan's rapidly industrializing society and women's political interest and mass participation relative to men's. On both these dimensions, women in Taiwan have made impressive gains, but still fall far short of equality. Occupationally, women have participated almost equally in the expanding industrial production sector and have had significant success in gaining entrance to the more desirable clerical and even professional jobs. However, they still remain largely excluded from the top of the occupational hierarchy, and many older and less-educated women are trapped in marginal agricultural work. Thus, Taiwan may be beginning to follow the pattern found in the United States where considerable mobility opportunities for individual women coexist with a continuing structure of sex segregation derived from the operation of what Jerry Jacobs terms informal processes of "social control." This further implies that women may become increasingly divided into those with "high-status careers" and those "more marginally connected to the labor force."[47]

Increased occupational status and the greater education that accompanies it have also reduced the gender gap in mass political participation somewhat. Moreover, the fact that this gap seems to be narrower among adults than children shows that Confucian culture does not inevitably continue patriarchal subjugation. The experience of the United States, though, suggests that simply entering the labor force does not revolutionize women's political attitudes. Rather, political changes occur primarily among those who are highly educated and employed in professional or managerial jobs. As in the case of employment status, therefore, it seems probable that women may become divided into a minority who receive a participatory stimulus and the majority who do not because of informal social controls, especially in a recently industrializing country like Taiwan. One's evaluation of women's political status on Taiwan, then, depends upon whether one sees the glass as half empty or half full. Still, the data presented here imply that there should be a significant number of women ready to take the third step of running for office.

## Notes

1. P. K. Liu and K. S. Hwang, *Relationships Between Changes in Population, Employment, and Economic Structure in Taiwan* (Taipei: Institute of Economics, Academia Sinica, Studies of Modern Economy Series, #8, 1987), in Chinese.
2. Ester Boserup, *Women's Role in Economic Development* (London: Allen & Unwin, 1970).
3. Martha Blaxall and Barbara Reagan, eds., *Women and the Workplace: The Implications of Occupational Segregation* (Chicago: University of Chicago Press, 1976), especially the Chps. by Francine D. Blau and Carol L. Jusenius, "Economists' Approaches to Sex Segregation in the Labor Market: An Appraisal," pp. 181–199; Heidi Hartmann, "Capitalism, Patriarchy, and Job Segregation by Sex," pp. 137–170; and Sandra S. Tangri, "Comment IV," pp. 84–86. William A. Bridges, "Industry Marginality and Female Employment: A New Appraisal," *American Sociological Review* 45:1 (February 1980) pp. 58–75; William Gross, "Plus Ça Change . . .? The Sexual Structure of Occupations Over Time," *Social Problems* 16:2 (Fall 1968) pp. 198–208. Barbara F. Reskin, ed., *Sex Segregation in the Workplace* (Washington, D.C.: National Academy Press, 1984), especially the Chps. by Andrea H. Beller, "Trends in Occupational Segregation by Sex and Race, 1960–1981," pp. 11–26; William T. Bielby and James N. Baron, "A Women's Place Is With Other Women: Sex Segregation Within Organizations," pp. 27–55; Francine D. Blau, "Occupational

Segregation and Labor Market Discrimination," pp. 117–143; and Myra H. Strober, "Toward a General Theory of Sex Segregation," pp. 144–156. Patricia A. Roos, *Gender and Work: A Comparative Analysis of Industrial Societies* (Albany: State University of New York Press, 1985); Donald J. Treiman and Heidi Hartmann, eds., *Women, Work, and Wages: Equal Pay for Jobs of Equal Value* (Washington, D.C.: National Academy Press, 1981); and Gregory Williams, "The Changing U.S. Labor Force and Occupational Differentiation by Sex," *Demography* 16:1 (February 1979) pp. 73–88.

4. Boserup, *Women's Role in Economic Development*; Carolyn M. Elliott, "Theories of Development: An Assessment," in Wellesley Editorial Committee, *Women and National Development: The Complexities of Change* (Chicago: University of Chicago Press, 1977) pp. 1–8; Susan Tiano, "Gender, Work, and World Capitalism: Third World Women's Role in Development," in Beth B. Hess and Myra Marx Ferree, eds., *Analyzing Gender: A Handbook of Social Science Research* (Beverly Hills, Calif.: Sage, 1987) pp. 216–243; and Irene Tinker, "The Adverse Impact of Development on Women," in Irene Tinker and Michele Bo Bramsen, eds., *Women and World Development* (Washington, D.C.: Overseas Development Council, 1976) pp. 22–34.

5. Susan Greenhalgh, "Sexual Stratification: The Other Side of 'Growth with Equity' in East Asia," *Population and Development Review* 11:2 (June 1985) pp. 265–314.

6. Uhn Cho and Hagen Koo, *Capital Accumulation, Women's Work, and Informal Economies in Korea* (East Lansing: Michigan State University, Women in International Development Program, Working Paper #21, 1983); John Humphrey, "The Growth of Female Employment in Brazilian Manufacturing Industry in the 1970s," *Journal of Development Studies* 20:4 (July 1984) pp. 224–247; and Alison MacEwan Scott, "Women and Industrialization: Examining the 'Female Marginalization' Thesis," *Journal of Development Studies* 22:4 (July 1986) pp. 649–680.

7. Heleieth I.B. Saffioti, *The Impact of Industrialization on the Structure of Female Employment* (East Lansing: Michigan State University, Women in International Development Program, Working Paper #15, 1983). Wellesley Editorial Committee, *Women and National Development*, especially the Chps. by Lourdes Arizpe, "Women in the Informal Labor Sector: The Case of Mexico City," pp. 25–37; Norma S. Chincilla, "Industrialization, Monopoly Capitalism, and Women's Work in Guatemala," pp. 57–73; and Ann Stoler, "Class Structure and Social Change: A Comparative Appraisal of Turkey's Women," pp. 74–89.

8. Lan-hung Nora Chiang and Yenlin Ku, *Past and Current Status of Women in Taiwan* (Taipei: National Taiwan University, Population Studies Center, Women's Research Program, Monograph #1, 1985) pp. 12–25, provide a good overview of women's constitutional and legal status in the ROC.

9. Gail Warshofsky Lapidus, "Occupational Segregation and Public Policy: A Comparative Analysis of American and Soviet Patterns," in Blaxall and Reagan, *Women and the Workplace*, pp. 119–136; and Joanne Miller and Howard H. Garrison, "Sex Roles: The Division of Labor at Home and in the Workplace," *Annual Review of Sociology* 8 (1982) pp. 237–262.

10. *Taiwan Statistical Data Book, 1989* (Taipei: Council for Economic Planning and Development, 1989), pp. 16 and 41 provide data on sectoral shares of employment and GNP respectively. Between 1952 and 1988, manufacturing's share of GNP more than tripled from 11% to 38%, while agriculture's plummeted from 36% to 6%. Commerce's share of GNP fell slightly from 19% to 16% (although its share in total employment actually increased from 11% to 19%, denoting a substantial fall in relative productivity); the share of other services (excluding transportation and

communications) increased slightly from 23% to 26%. Data showing the small-scale nature of commercial establishments are presented later in the chapter (see Table 4.8).

11. Elsa M. Chaney, *Scenarios of Hunger in the Caribbean: Migration, Decline of Smallholder Agriculture, and the Feminization of Farming* (East Lansing: Michigan State University, Women in Development Program, Working Paper #18, 1983).

12. Susan Welch, "Recruitment of Women to Office: A Discriminant Analysis," *Western Political Quarterly* 31:3 (September 1978) pp. 372–380.

13. Tun-jen Cheng, "Is the Dog Barking? The Middle Class and Democratic Movements in East Asian NICs," *International Studies Notes* 15:1 (Winter 1990) pp. 10–16.

14. For data on the comparative wage and salary levels in these occupations, see *Annual Report of Labor Statistics, 1966 & 1986* (Taipei: Directorate-General of Budget, Accounting, and Statistics, 1966 & 1986), in Chinese.

15. Hill Gates, "Dependency and the Part-time Proletariat in Taiwan," *Modern China* 5:3 (July 1979) pp. 381–407; Greenhalgh, "Sexual Stratification," pp. 265–314; and Lydia Kung, *Factory Women in Taiwan* (Ann Arbor, Mich.: UMI Research Press, 1983).

16. Shu-min Huang, *Agricultural Degradation: Changing Community Systems in Rural Taiwan* (Lanham, Md.: University Press of America, 1981); and Eldon L. Johnson, Frederick C. Fliegel, John L. Woods, and Mel C. Chu, *The Agricultural Technology System of Taiwan* (Urbana: University of Illinois, Office of International Agriculture, 1987).

17. Catherine S. Farris, *The Sociocultural Construction of Femininity in Contemporary Urban Taiwan* (East Lansing: Michigan State University, Women in International Development Program, Working Paper #131, 1986); Rita S. Gallin, "Women, Family, and the Political Economy of Taiwan," *Journal of Peasant Studies* 12:1 (October 1984) pp. 76–92; Lydia Kung, "Perceptions of Work Among Factory Women," in Emily Martin Ahern and Hill Gates, eds., *The Anthropology of Taiwanese Society* (Stanford, Calif.: Stanford University Press, 1981) pp. 184–211; and E. Y. Tsui, *Are Married Daughters "Spilled Water"?—A Study of Working Women in Urban Taiwan* (Taipei: National Taiwan University, Population Studies Center, Women's Research Program, Monograph #4, 1987).

18. Chiang and Ku, *Status of Women in Taiwan*, p. 5; and *Statistical Yearbook of the Republic of China, 1988* (Taipei: Directorate-General of Budget, Accounting, and Statistics, 1988) pp. 228 & 237–240.

19. Chiang and Ku, *Status of Women in Taiwan*, pp. 4–6; Ching-lung Tsay, "Sex Differentials in Educational Attainment and Labor Force Development in Taiwan," paper presented at the Conference on the Role of Women in the National Development Process in Taiwan, National Taiwan University, Taipei, March 1985; Ching-lung Tsay, "Status of Women in Taiwan: Educational Attainment and Labor Force Development, 1951–1983," *Academia Economic Papers* 15:1 (No. 1, 1987) pp. 153–182; and Esther Lee Yao, "Successful Professional Women in Taiwan," *Cornell Journal of Social Relations* 16:1 (Spring 1981) pp. 39–55.

20. S. L. Tsai, "Gender and Social Stratification in a Changing Society: The Case of Taiwan," paper presented at the Annual Meeting of the American Association for Chinese Studies, University of California, Berkeley, October 21–23, 1988.

21. Chiang and Ku, *Status of Women in Taiwan*, pp. 10–11. For those with graduate education, women's salaries are 88% of men's, but the gender gap in salaries drops drastically to 66% for college graduates and to 50% for those with primary education.

22. Chiang and Ku, *Status of Women in Taiwan*, pp. 30–31.

23. Angus Campbell, Philip E. Converse, Warren E. Miller, and Donald E. Stokes, *The American Voter* (New York: John Wiley, 1964) pp. 255–261; Barbara Sinclair Deckard, *The Women's Movement: Political, Socioeconomic, and Psychological Issues*, 3rd Ed. (New York: Harper & Row, 1983) Chps. 2–4; Fred I. Greenstein, *Children and Politics* (New Haven: Yale University Press, 1965) Chp. 6; and Robert D. Hess and Judith V. Tourney, *The Development of Political Attitudes in Children* (Chicago: Aldine, 1967) Chp. 8.

24. Diana Owen and Jack Dennis, "Gender Differences in the Politicization of American Children," *Women & Politics* 8:2 (Summer 1988) pp. 23–43. Two explanations for the eradication of the participation gap despite the continuation of childhood socialization differences have been adduced. First, David Easton and Jack Dennis, *Children in the Political System: Origins of Political Legitimacy* (New York: McGraw-Hill, 1969) pp. 335–343; and M. Kent Jennings and Richard G. Niemi, *Generations and Politics: A Panel Study of Young Adults and Their Parents* (Princeton: Princeton University Press, 1981) pp. 281–285, concluded that while preadult differences between boys and girls were significant, they were much more muted than the original socialization theory believed. Thus, they did not constitute such an obstacle to women's later participation in politics. Second, Virginia Sapiro, *The Political Integration of Women: Roles, Socialization, and Politics* (Urbana: University of Illinois Press, 1983), argued that childhood socialization experiences are mediated and reinforced by the adult roles that women assume, especially family and occupational ones. Thus, women with some adult roles can overcome the inhibitions against political participation transmitted by childhood socialization.

25. Kristi Anderson, "Working Women and Political Participation, 1952–1972," *American Journal of Political Science* 19:3 (August 1975) pp. 439–453; Sandra Baxter and Marjorie Lansing, *Women and Politics: The Invisible Majority* (Ann Arbor: University of Michigan Press, 1980); Cal Clark and Janet Clark, "Models of Gender and Political Participation in the United States," *Women & Politics* 6:1 (Spring 1986) pp. 5–25; Janet Clark, Charles D. Hadley, and R. Darcy, "Political Ambition Among Men and Women State Party Leaders: Testing the Countersocialization Perspective," *American Politics Quarterly* 17:2 (April 1989) pp. 194–207; Diane Fowlkes, "Ambitious Political Women: Countersocialization and Political Party Context," *Women & Politics* 4:4 (Winter 1984) pp. 5–32; Wilma Rule Krauss, "Political Implications of Gender Roles: A Review of the Literature," *American Political Science Review* 68:4 (December 1974) pp. 1706–1723; Eileen L. McDonaugh, "To Work or Not to Work: The Differential Impact of Achieved and Derived Status upon the Political Participation of Women, 1956–1976," *American Journal of Political Science* 26:2 (May 1982) pp. 280–297; Anthony M. Orum, Roberta S. Cohen, Sherri Grasmuck, and Amy W. Orum, "Sex, Socialization, and Politics," *American Sociological Review* 39:2 (April 1974) pp. 197–209; and Susan Welch, "Women As Political Animals? A Test of Some Explanations for Male-Female Participation Differences," *American Journal of Political Science* 21:4 (November 1977) pp. 711–730.

26. Deckard, *The Women's Movement*; Ethel Klein, *Gender Politics: From Consciousness to Mass Politics* (Cambridge: Harvard University Press, 1984); Mary Fainsod Katzenstein and Carol McClarg Mueller, eds., *The Women's Movements of the United States and Western Europe: Consciousness, Political Opportunity, and Public Policy* (Philadelphia: Temple University Press, 1987); and Vicky Randall, *Women and Politics: An International Perspective*, 2nd Ed. (Chicago: University of Chicago Press, 1987) Chps. 5 & 6.

27. Sidney Verba, Norman H. Nie, Jae-on Kim, and Goldie Shabad, "Men and Women: Sex-Related Differences in Political Activity," pp. 234–268 in Sidney Verba,

Norman H. Nie, and Jae-on Kim, eds., *Participation and Political Equality: A Seven-Nation Comparison* (Cambridge: Cambridge University Press, 1978); and Randall, *Women and Politics*, Chp. 2.

28. Anderson, "Working Women," pp. 439–453.

29. Chiang and Ku, *Status of Women in Taiwan*, pp. 38–45.

30. Greenhalgh, "Sexual Stratification," pp. 265–314; Kung, *Factory Women in Taiwan*, especially Chp. 2; Margery Wolf, *Women and the Family in Rural Taiwan* (Stanford, Calif.: Stanford University Press, 1972); and Margery Wolf and Roxane Witke, eds., *Women in Chinese Society* (Stanford, Calif.: Stanford University Press, 1975).

31. Wen-jen Chen, "The Formation of Political Attitudes of High School Students in Taiwan" (Taipei: Unpublished Ph.D. Dissertation, National Chengchi University, 1982) pp. 90–148, in Chinese.

32. Wen-hai Tsou, *Local Elections in Taiwan* (Taipei, Universe Publishing, 1964), cited in Yih-yen Chen, "Voting Behavior in Taiwan: Review and Prospects," *Shei Yu Yen* 23:6 (March 1986) pp. 569–585, in Chinese.

33. Shiou-hong Woon, "A Study of the Political Culture of College Students in Taiwan" (Taipei: Unpublished Master's Thesis, National Taiwan University, 1973) pp. 94–99 & 134–141, in Chinese.

34. Sidney Verba and Norman H. Nie, *Participation in America: Political Democracy and Social Equality* (New York: Harper & Row, 1972) Chp. 5.

35. Chia-cheng Lin, "The Political Attitudes and Political Participation of Taipei University Students," *Cheng Chi Hsueh Pao* [Journal of politics] 9 (December 1981) pp. 353–419, in Chinese.

36. Lin, "Taipei University Students," pp. 353–419.

37. Sheldon Appleton, "The Social and Political Impact of Education on Taiwan," *Asian Survey* 16:8 (August 1976) pp. 703–720; and Gerald A. McBeath, "Roots of Regime Stability in the Taiwanese Family," *Journal of Chinese Studies* 4:1 (April 1987) pp. 1–18.

38. Shu-chin Koo, "The Effect of Selected Socialization Agents on the Formation of Political Attitudes: An Analysis of the Residents of Song-San Chu, Taipei" (Taipei: Unpublished Master's Thesis, Soochow University, 1986), in Chinese.

39. Shu-huei Huang, "The Political Participation and Intentions of Female College and High School Students in Taiwan" (Taipei: Unpublished Master's Thesis, National Taiwan University, 1985), in Chinese; and Chia-chen Lin, "Voting Behavior in the 1983 Election," *Cheng Chi Hsueh Pao* [Journal of politics] 12 (June 1984) pp. 123–183, in Chinese.

40. Fu Hu, Teh-yu Chen, Ming-tong Chen, and Ying-lung Yu, *Voting Behavior of Taiwan Residents* (Taipei: Central Election Committee, Ministry of Interior, 1987) pp. 79–98, in Chinese.

41. Hu et al., *Voting Behavior of Taiwan's Residents*, pp. 193–194.

42. Koo, "Formation of Political Attitudes," pp. 112–120; and Lin, "The 1983 Election," pp. 123–183.

43. Hu et al., *Voting Behavior of Taiwan's Residents*, pp. 60–62 & 112–120; Fu Hu and Ying-lung Yu, "The Party Choice of Voters: An Analysis of Voters' Attitudes and Backgrounds," *Cheng Chi Hsueh Pao* [Journal of politics] 12 (June 1984) pp. 1–59, in Chinese; Lin, "The 1983 Election," pp. 123–183; and Ying-lung Yu, "System Orientation and Voting Behavior" (Taipei: Unpublished Master's Thesis, National Taiwan University, 1982) pp. 206–210, in Chinese.

44. Hu et al., *Voting Behavior of Taiwan's Residents*; and Hu and Yu, "Party Choice of Voters," pp. 1–59.

45. Hu et al., *Voting Behavior of Taiwan's Residents*; Hu and Yu, "Party Choice of Voters," pp. 22–24; and Yu, "Voting Behavior," pp. 203–217.
46. Lin, "The 1983 Election," pp. 123–183.
47. Jerry A. Jacobs, *Revolving Doors: Sex Segregation and Women's Careers* (Stanford, Calif.: Stanford University Press, 1989).

CHAPTER FIVE

# The Reserved-Seats System and Women's Political Representation in the Republic of China

The Republic of China guarantees a minimum level of representation of about 10% for women in its legislative bodies. This chapter discusses this reserved-seats system and its impact upon women's representation in some detail because its unique method for enforcing the recruitment of women into political leadership positions should be of interest to anyone concerned with promoting greater political equality for women. The first section discusses the general principles of the reserved-seats system; the second one describes the statutes implementing the system at the national and local levels of government; the third presents data on how many women have sought and won office in the ROC; and the conclusion evaluates the efficacy of this electoral system in light of recent socioeconomic and political changes on Taiwan.

## General Principles

Women are guaranteed some representation in the Republic of China's legislative assemblies by article 136 of the 1947 constitution.[1] While the exact number of guaranteed seats and the mechanisms for selecting women to hold them were left to statutory law, this assurance of female representation in the political leadership is a unique and impressive contribution of the constitution. The inclusion of this article, along with article 7 of the constitution, which provides for equality before the law,[2] has been hailed by many as an important milestone in feminist striving for political equality in the early history of modern China. However, contrary to general belief, the inclusion of article 136 did not come about easily or naturally. Instead, it required persistent and at times serious struggle on the part of many women and their male supporters between 1912 and 1936, as the principles underlying the 1947 constitution evolved through several drafts.[3]

Thus, the reserved-seats system was included in the constitution during the early stage of the republic because women as a group were severely disadvantaged in their social and economic status by the traditional Confucian culture and, thus, could not compete on an equal footing with men in the political arena. In order to compensate for their lower competitiveness, the quota system was designed to ensure that women would receive at least a minimal level of political representation in line with the commitment of Sun Yat-sen, the founder of the republic, to help women assume a more equal position in Chinese society.

Two aspects of the reserved-seats system deserve special mention. One is the principle that a number of legislative seats should be reserved for women. In addition, since the purpose of the quota system is to promote political equality between the sexes, the number of assemblywomen fixed by law should be interpreted as a minimum guarantee rather than as a final representative ratio. Although there were disputes over this principle among scholars and in actual practice in the past, the conclusion that the reserved seats form a minimum for women's representation is now well accepted.[4] Indeed, in the past forty years of election history in Taiwan, women candidates have almost always won slightly more than the number of seats guaranteed them by election laws (see the data presented later in this chapter).

The other vital aspect is how the women are selected for these reserved seats, which are filled in two ways. First, when a sufficient number of female candidates win election, they are viewed as fulfilling the quota reserved for women. However, when no or not enough female candidates gain a plurality in Taiwan's multimember assembly districts, then the votes of all the women candidates are tallied separately.[5] The female candidates with the most votes are then elected to fulfill the seats reserved for women. Thus, only in the second method (i.e., when women candidates would normally be declared losers) does the reserved-seats system serve its function of promoting women's political representation. However, since the women, who are elected on the basis of this quota system, can and often do have considerably fewer votes than male candidates who lose the election, this mechanism often leads to antagonism between candidates of different sexes. It also occasionally calls attention to what really constitutes political equality.

It should also be noted that women are not the only category of people for whom the constitution has reserved a fixed number of seats to guarantee their representation in government. Articles 26, 64, and 135 provide that racial minority groups, "overseas Chinese" who live outside the country, and members of "occupational groups" (e.g., farmers' associations, commercial and industrial groups, and labor unions) shall receive representation in the National Assembly and Legislative Yuan.[6] However, the reservation of legislative seats for these categories of people is operative only for the national elections to the National Assembly and Legislative Yuan, rather than across all levels of legislative elections as in the case of women's reserved seats. Thus, the scope of the quota system for other groups is considerably more limited than is the reserved-seats system for women.

Additionally, the quota system for women operates only in elections for legislative bodies; there are no reserved seats in the various executive positions. In practice, executive elections in the ROC are limited to local government below the provincial level, including county magistrates, city (of county status) mayors, township/village chiefs, and track and neighborhood (*li* or *lin*) chiefs.[7] At the national level, the president is indirectly elected by the National Assembly, and the premier is appointed by the president with the consent of the Legislative Yuan. Although the constitution (article 113) prescribes that provincial governors should be directly elected,[8] the governor of Taiwan Province is appointed by the president on the recommendation of the Executive Yuan and with the consent of the Legislative Yuan under the Temporary Provisions.[9] Similarly, the mayors of the two cities with provincial status, Taipei and Kaohsiung, are appointed by the Executive Yuan and approved by the Legislative Yuan.[10]

Seats are reserved for women, therefore, only in elections to Taiwan's legislative bodies. At the level of central government, this includes elections for delegates of the National Assembly and members of the Legislative Yuan. In addition, while members of the Control Yuan are indirectly elected by the provincial and special municipality assemblies, the original election law for this body did prescribe one seat for women among the five seats allotted to each province. At the level of local government, the election of legislative representatives includes delegates to the provincial (and municipalities of provincial status) assemblies, county (and city) councils, and township councils.

In all these elections, multimember districts are used, usually with between five and ten seats per district (the number varies by the level of election). Voters can only vote for one of the candidates running for office in one of these legislative districts (i.e., the single nontransferable vote system). The candidates who receive the most votes are elected unless there is a need to fill one or more reserved seats. In addition to the general territorial constituencies, there are special constituencies (e.g., occupational groups) that vote in the national-level elections for the National Assembly and Legislative Yuan. Only members of officially approved groups can vote in these elections.

## Specific Legal Mechanisms for Women's Quota

The elections for the two national-level representative bodies, the National Assembly and Legislative Yuan, are similar to each other and different from local elections in several important respects. First, the inability to hold new elections on the Chinese mainland led to supplementary elections for additional members of these bodies from Taiwan to serve with the surviving members elected throughout China in 1947–1948. Second, representation is provided for occupational groups, national minorities, and overseas Chinese. However, the National Assembly and Legislative Yuan differ fundamentally in the way in which they provide for the representation of women.

The method of reserving seats for women in the election of National Assembly delegates differs fundamentally from that used in other types of elections. For the National Assembly, seats are reserved for women by allowing approved women's groups to act as a special constituency and directly elect delegates. In all other elections, in contrast, women run in the general constituencies, and female candidates are guaranteed a certain minimum number (usually one) of the seats being contested in each election district.

As noted, women's representation in the National Assembly is provided for by articles 26, 34, and 134 of the constitution. These articles require that a number of delegates elected by women's groups be included in the National Assembly in addition to the delegates selected by the general population, Tibetan special racial and religious groups, overseas Chinese citizens, and occupational groups.[11] Legislation (the Statute and Implementation Rules of the Election and Recall of the Delegates of the National Assembly, 1947) then specified the technical procedures for implementing the quota system for women.[12] These included the exact number of the seats reserved for women's groups under the quota system,[13] the distribution of these seats among the women's groups and across provinces,[14] the eligibility of voters for this category,[15] the constituency for this category of voters,[16] and the election procedures, including the ballot counting for female candidates and the fulfillment of the women's quota.[17]

Because the Communist victory on the Chinese mainland precluded holding elections for the National Assembly and Legislative Yuan, these "representative" bodies began to atrophy. Thus, beginning in 1969, Taiwan began to hold supplementary elections to permit the direct election of at least some members of these assemblies. The laws passed to regulate them are now the ones that define the representation of women's groups in the elections that actually continue to be held. The laws have lengthy titles: Statute and Implementation Rules on the Election and Recall of Supplementary Legislative Representatives of the Central Government in the Free Area for the Duration of Mobilization to Suppress the Communist Rebellion, 1969 and 1972;[18] and Statute and Implementation Rules on the Election and Recall of Public Officials for the Duration of Mobilization to Suppress the Communist Rebellion, 1980, 1983, and 1989.[19]

The number of delegates to the first National Assembly reserved for election by women's groups as specified in the 1947 statute was 168, distributed proportionally among women's organizations at the provincial level. For the National Assembly seats currently subjected to election, seven were reserved for women's groups in the last election in 1986. Among them, five were for Taiwan Province and one each for the Taipei and Kaohsiung special municipalities. For the upcoming 1992 National Assembly elections, the total number of delegates reserved for women's groups will be increased to eight, with Taiwan Province gaining one seat. When there are no women candidates or fewer female candidates than the quota reserved, these seats remain vacant.[20] In practice, however, women's groups have always elected their full complement of candidates in past elections in Taiwan.

Because the seats reserved for women in the National Assembly are elected only by members of women's organization, the nature of these women's groups is very important. In terms of the qualifications of the women's organizations to be eligible for participating as a constituency for the National Assembly, the original legislation specified that only those women's organizations lawfully registered with the appropriate government agencies could participate in this type of election. Under the Temporary Provisions, the election law specifies that *Fu Nu Huei* (Women's Association) is the only women's organization qualified as the constituency for the election of candidates to fill the women's quota. This is because *Fu Nu Huei* is the only women's organization approved by the codes on civic organizations under the Temporary Provisions to be a lawfully organized women's group. Accordingly, only the members of *Fu Nu Huei* can register as the voters for these women's reserved seats. However, *Fu Nu Huei's* members have to choose between voting in general constituencies or in the women's group constituency in elections for the National Assembly.

Several points should be emphasized about how the reserved-seats system works for selecting delegates to the National Assembly. The most obvious one is that the reservation of women's seats does not involve fixing a level or a proportion of the total number of delegates elected by general voters to represent women. Rather, it restricts the selection of women's representatives to the members of certain women's organizations that meet the criteria stipulated by law. Thus, this provision of the women's quota seems to assume that women, like occupational groups, have a special interest in selecting the president and the vice-president and need to have their own representatives to the National Assembly. However, this system also implicitly assumes that women's organizations necessarily (or automatically) represent the interest of all female electors. Conceivably, this latter assumption is fallacious. In most societies, especially developing ones, most women do not belong to any civic or voluntary organization. Only a small proportion of women, usually drawn almost exclusively from the socioeconomic elite, join associations of any kind. Consequently, by allocating the selection of women's reserved seats to only the members of women's organizations, the quota system puts the representation of women's interests into the hands of a small and unrepresentative minority.

This turns our attention to the second point—the nature of the officially recognized women's organization in Taiwan. Since the election law sets the conditions that a women's organization must meet in order to qualify as a constituency for the National Assembly, this quota system leaves a good deal of room for manipulation by the regime that interprets and implements the law. For example, the dominant Nationalist Party could systematically exclude those women's organizations it did not like. This was especially true under martial law and the Temporary Provisions, which curtailed the right of the people to form civic associations freely.

Although *Fu Nu Huei*, which has local chapters throughout the island, is registered as a civic organization, it has operated under the auspices of and maintained a close relationship with the Women's Department of the Kuomintang. In short, by designating women's representation to women's organizations (which in practice has been limited to one group) and by further imposing certain constraints on the qualifications of the women's organizations, the prescriptions of the constitution and the election law have raised serious questions about the fairness and representativeness of the women's reserved-seats system for the National Assembly and about the power of the ruling party to manipulate these elections.

The basic principle for reserving representation for women in the Legislative Yuan and other assemblies at the provincial and local level differs fundamentally from the procedures used in the election of National Assembly delegates. Rather than having women's groups form a special constituency, a certain proportion of seats elected by the general public are reserved for women candidates. The legal provisions relevant to elections for the Legislative Yuan come from sources similar to those for the National Assembly. The only different source is the 1947 Original Statute on the Election and Recall of Members of the Legislative Yuan.[21]

The number of seats to be reserved for women is defined by article 5 of that statute. One seat was reserved for women when a constituency elected up to ten members of the Legislative Yuan; one more seat was reserved for women each time the size of the electoral district increased by ten seats. In practice, this meant that an electoral district had to elect twenty members before a second reserved seat was designated for female candidates.[22] Originally, this women's quota was applicable to all constituencies for the Legislative Yuan, including both the general population and the special groups (i.e., racial minorities, occupational groups, and overseas Chinese). However, this across-the-board quota system was revised in the law about electing supplementary members to the Legislative Yuan in the "free area" of Taiwan that was enacted under the Temporary Provisions in 1972. The accompanying implementation rules applied the quota system only to the popular election of the directly elected members of the Legislative Yuan from Taiwan Province and the two special municipalities of provincial status. In other words, there were no reserved seats for women in the constituencies for occupational groups and Chinese residing overseas. In terms of number of reserved seats in the supplementary elections for the Legislative Yuan carried out in Taiwan, one seat was reserved in constituencies of five to ten members and another reserved seat was added whenever the constituency size increased by ten.[23] In practice, this means that there is one reserved seat in almost every district.

The original election law of 1947 stipulated that if enough women candidates were not elected to fill the reserved seats in the initial counting of ballots, the votes for women should be counted separately to determine who should win these seats. If there were not enough female candidates to fill the reserved seats, these seats should remain vacant rather than going to a male candidate.[24] There is some ambiguity now because the latter provision about seats remaining vacant was not included in the legislation governing supplementary elections for the Legislative Yuan on Taiwan. However, there have always been enough women candidates to fill the reserved seats in elections held thus far.

In comparison with the quota system used for the election of National Assembly delegates, the women's quota system in elections of Legislative Yuan members has two distinctive characteristics. The first is that it is an across-the-board reservation of seats. That is, it does not limit or restrict the women's quota only to certain special groups (i.e. approved women's groups). Overall, therefore, the Legislative Yuan's quota system appears to be more reasonable. On the one hand, it recognizes that women as a part of the electorate may have their own special needs or views differing from those of men. On the other hand, though, it does not assume that these different views in the legislative process have to be represented or expressed by women who belong to certain organizations (especially by those organizations approved by special laws). Consequently, it can avoid the ambivalences and problems implicit in the quota system for the National Assembly.

The second point concerns the level of the representation provided by a women's quota. Although the rationale for reserving a specific number of seats for female candidates is unclear, the current formula for calculating the quota possesses a markedly "U-curve" distribution. That is, when the total number of seats to be elected is small, say five or six, the level of women's guaranteed representation appears to be high (i.e., 20% or 17%). However, as the total number increases (from 5 to 19), the average level of women's reserved representation decreases to 5% before it increases again. Only when the total number of seats reaches 20 will the level of women's reserved representation increase again to a maximum of 10%. In actual practice, the number of seats reserved for women has never exceeded one.

The constitution places lower levels of government—provinces and special municipalities—directly under the jurisdiction of the central government. Provinces are divided into *hsiens* (counties) and *shihs* (cities). In 1950, after the Nationalist government moved to Taiwan, it set up a self-government system for Taiwan Province through legislation (General Rules for Provincial, *Hsien*, and *Shih* Self-Government in Taiwan Province). According to this law, the *hsien* is the basic administrative unit of Taiwan

Province and is divided into *hsiangs* (villages), *chengs* (townships), and *shihs* (cities). (*Shihs* under a *hsien* are of lower status than the *shihs* under the province.)[25]

The provincial government includes a governor to direct and supervise the overall administrative affairs and a Provincial Assembly as the legislative body. The Provincial Assembly consists of 77 members (as of the 1989 election) elected by popular vote for four-year terms.[26] In addition, since Taipei and Kaohsiung were upgraded into special municipalities directly under the jurisdiction of the central government, their city assemblies have been given provincial status. The organization and the function of these two city assemblies (alternatively called city councils) are equivalent to that of the Provincial Assembly.

At the county level, every *hsien* has a county government and a county council; every *shih* has a city government and a city council. The government is the executive body directed by the county magistrate or city mayor, and the council is the legislative body. Both the county magistrate (or city mayor) and the councilmen/women are elected by popular votes every four years. Similarly, at the township or village level, every *hsiang/cheng* has an office and a representative council. Their division of functions is similar to that at the county level.

The three provincial-level legislatures (the Provincial Assembly and the Taipei and Kaohsiung City Councils) are similar in that elections are held in districts whose number of members is determined by their population size. Representation in the Taiwan Provincial Assembly is based on the county, with each *hsien* being given a number of seats proportionate to its population (one seat per 150,000 population before 1981 and one per 180,000 after that year). No county, however, can have more than ten seats.[27] Similarly, the size of the city assemblies in Taipei and Kaohsiung is determined by total city population (now 40 members for the first million plus one more member for each additional 100,000). This total membership (now 51 in Taipei and 43 in Kaohsiung) is then distributed proportionally among five (in Taipei) or six (in Kaohsiung) election districts in accordance to their proportion of total city population.[28]

One seat is reserved for a woman in every Provincial Assembly district (i.e., *hsien*) that has at least four seats and in every Taipei or Kaohsiung City Council district that has at least five seats (seven before 1981).[29] The criteria by which a district could gain a second seat are not clear; in fact, for these three provincial-level legislatures, only one district (for the Taipei City Assembly, which now has 14 seats) has been granted two reserved seats for women. Among the *hsien*, 9 of 16 meet the requirement of having at least four representatives in the Provincial Assembly, while there are six reserved seats for the Taipei City Council and five for the Kaohsiung City Council. Consequently, women are reserved 12% of the seats in these three assemblies.

With regard to the procedures for fulfilling the women's quota, when a woman wins a plurality in a district with a reserved seat (only one district has two seats reserved for women), the quota is considered satisfied. However, when there are no women among the winners as determined by conventional counting, the woman who receives the most votes wins the reserved seat. Unlike in the national-level elections, though, if there is no female candidate in a district, then the reserved seat reverts to the remaining male candidate with the highest number of votes.[30]

The procedures for electing councilmen and councilwomen for local governments (counties, cities, townships, and villages) have changed somewhat over time, but have generally aimed at reserving about a tenth of the seats for female candidates. Over time, changes in laws regulating local elections have become more precise and less confusing about reserving seats for female candidates, thus making it easier to ensure the representation of women in local government.[31] The size of these councils is determined by population, and members are elected by the general population and special constituencies of aborigines.[32] Now, one seat is reserved for women in city and county election districts (except those in aboriginal villages) that have five or more members; a second reserved seat is added when the district size reaches 16. The same formula applies in township and village elections, except that the minimum size for an election district in order to attain a reserved seat is four.[33] Finally, the procedures for counting ballots and selecting women for these reserved seats are the same as at the provincial level.[34]

## Women's Representation: Election Statistics

An examination of how many women run for and are elected to office is essential for evaluating the effects of the reserved-seats system. These basic data are presented in Tables 5.1 through 5.3. The first table describes women's representation in the two national bodies (the National Assembly and Legislative Yuan); the second focuses upon the three provincial legislatures (the Provincial Assembly and the Taipei and Kaohsiung City Councils); and the final one presents summary data for all county/city and township/village councils, as well as for county magistrates and city mayors for the last two elections, when women were finally able to achieve an electoral breakthrough and win a few of these executive positions.

The general impression from all three tables is that women win a low but significant proportion of legislative seats in Taiwan; their success has increased slightly but not dramatically over time. From the local to the national levels, women generally won between 10% and 15% of the total seats throughout the postwar period (although elections for the two national bodies were not held in Taiwan until 1969). For almost all of these bodies, moreover, women have slightly increased their office-holding from the 1950s and 1960s to the 1980s. There is also a slight tendency for women to have better representation at the provincial and county/city levels than in the two national bodies. However, these differences are fairly small (2%–4% at most), and women's representation in township and village councils is somewhat lower than at the provincial and county/city levels.

Table 5.1  Women's Representation in National Legislative Bodies

|      | Candidates | | | Seats | | | |
|------|-------|-------|---------|-------|----------------------|-------|---------|
|      | Total | Women | % Women | Total | Reserved for Women | Women | % Women |
| NATIONAL ASSEMBLY | | | | | | | |
| 1969 | 29  | 2  | 6.9  | 15  | 2 | 2  | 13.3 |
| 1972 | 78  | 10 | 12.8 | 53  | 5 | 8  | 15.1 |
| 1980 | 185 | 17 | 9.2  | 76  | 7 | 12 | 15.8 |
| 1986 | 169 | 25 | 14.8 | 84  | 8 | 16 | 19.0 |
| LEGISLATIVE YUAN | | | | | | | |
| 1969 | 25  | 4  | 16.0 | 11  | 0 | 1  | 9.1  |
| 1972 | 55  | 6  | 10.9 | 36  | 3 | 4  | 11.1 |
| 1975 | 61  | 4  | 6.6  | 37  | 3 | 4  | 10.8 |
| 1980 | 218 | 17 | 7.8  | 70  | 5 | 7  | 10.0 |
| 1983 | 171 | 22 | 12.9 | 71  | 5 | 8  | 11.3 |
| 1986 | 137 | 12 | 8.8  | 100 | 6 | 8  | 8.0  |
| 1989 | 302 | 26 | 8.7  | 101 | 7 | 13 | 12.9 |

*Source: Statistical Abstracts of Elections in the Republic of China, 1946-1982* (Taipei: Central Election Committee, Ministry of Interior, 1982); *Records of Elections, 1985-1986* (Taipei: Central Election Committee, Ministry of Interior, 1987); and *Official Voting Returns of the 1989 Elections* (Taipei: Central Election Committee, Ministry of Interior, 1990), all in Chinese.

These overall figures indicate that the reserved-seats system has promoted women's representation from several perspectives. First, women's representation in these legislative assemblies can be contrasted with their near-exclusion from top decisionmaking positions in the executive branch and the dominant Kuomintang Party. For example, before the summer of 1988, when a new and more liberal government cabinet and party leadership were named, no woman had ever held a cabinet post or been a member of the KMT's Central Standing Committee (the highest party body, now with 31 members). The selection of Shirley Kuo both as a member of the Central Standing Committee and as minister of finance was certainly a breakthrough for women, through it also underlined their previous total exclusion from powerful posts.[35] In addition, women's inability to win elective executive positions was underlined by the fact that no woman ever won an election as a county magistrate or city mayor before 1985. Even at the local level, there were only three women among the 312 township supervisors in the mid-

1980s. Finally, women appear to be discriminated against in the government bureaucracy—they hold lower ranks, on average, than men with comparable attainments in education and on civil service exams.[36]

Table 5.2  Women's Representation in Provincial-Level Legislative Bodies

|  | Candidates | | | Seats | | | |
|---|---|---|---|---|---|---|---|
|  | Total | Women | % Women | Total | Reserved for Women | Women | % Women |
| *PROVINCIAL ASSEMBLY* | | | | | | | |
| 1951 | 140 | 12 | 8.6 | 55 | 5 | 5 | 9.0 |
| 1954 | 110 | 18 | 16.4 | 57 | 6 | 6 | 10.5 |
| 1957 | 118 | 22 | 18.6 | 66 | 9 | 9 | 13.6 |
| 1960 | 126 | 18 | 14.3 | 73 | 9 | 10 | 13.7 |
| 1963 | 137 | 14 | 10.2 | 74 | 9 | 10 | 13.5 |
| 1968 | 129 | 19 | 14.7 | 71 | 10 | 11 | 15.5 |
| 1972 | 121 | 21 | 17.4 | 73 | 10 | 12 | 16.4 |
| 1977 | 125 | 23 | 18.4 | 77 | 10 | 13 | 16.9 |
| 1981 | 199 | 34 | 17.1 | 77 | 9 | 10 | 13.0 |
| 1985 | 158 | 28 | 17.7 | 77 | 9 | 13 | 16.9 |
| 1989 | 157 | 30 | 19.1 | 77 | 9 | 14 | 18.2 |
| *TAIPEI CITY COUNCIL* | | | | | | | |
| 1969 | 77 | 8 | 10.4 | 48 | 4 | 7 | 14.6 |
| 1973 | 63 | 8 | 12.7 | 49 | 4 | 7 | 14.3 |
| 1977 | 61 | 8 | 13.1 | 51 | 5 | 8 | 15.7 |
| 1981 | 83 | 11 | 13.3 | 51 | 5 | 7 | 13.7 |
| 1985 | 74 | 10 | 13.5 | 51 | 5 | 9 | 17.6 |
| 1989 | 100 | 24 | 24.0 | 51 | 6 | 10 | 19.6 |
| *KAOHSIUNG CITY COUNCIL* | | | | | | | |
| 1981 | 81 | 15 | 18.5 | 42 | 5 | 6 | 14.3 |
| 1985 | 71 | 13 | 18.3 | 42 | 5 | 6 | 14.3 |
| 1989 | 94 | 14 | 14.9 | 43 | 5 | 6 | 14.0 |

*Source:* *Statistical Abstracts of Elections in the Republic of China, 1946-1982* (Taipei: Central Election Committee, Ministry of Interior, 1982); *Records of Elections, 1985-1986.* (Taipei: Central Election Committee, Ministry of Interior, 1987); and *Official Voting Returns of the 1989 Elections* (Taipei: Central Election Committee, Ministry of Interior, 1990), all in Chinese.

Second, the representation of women in Taiwan is fairly good in comparative terms, low as it may be in absolute percentage terms. It is significantly above the worldwide average for national legislatures, at least three times greater than for nonsocialist developing countries, and approximately equal to the average for Western Europe, the region with the highest level of women's office-holding in the noncommunist world (see Table 1.1). Given the moderate development level and strongly patriarchal society in the ROC —factors that should inhibit women's entrance into public life—the record depicted in Tables 5.1–5.3 appears quite good, if not remarkable. On the other hand, Taiwan deviates from the pattern of such countries as the United States, where women's level of office-holding increases dramatically at lower levels of government.[37] Since lower-level legislators form a principal element in the eligibility pool for higher office, the absence of this relationship in Taiwan constitutes something of a disadvantage for prospective women candidates.

Table 5.3  Women's Representation at County/Township Level

| | Candidates | | | Seats | | | |
| --- | --- | --- | --- | --- | --- | --- | --- |
| | Total | Women | % Women | Total | Reserved for Women | Women | % Women |
| *COUNTY MAGISTRATES/CITY MAYORS*[a] | | | | | | | |
| 1985 | 54 | 4 | 7.4 | 21 | 0 | 2 | 9.5 |
| 1989 | 69 | 6 | 8.7 | 21 | 0 | 3 | 14.3 |
| *COUNTY/CITY ASSEMBLIES* | | | | | | | |
| 1950 | 1827 | 116 | 6.3 | 814 | 70 | 69 | 8.5 |
| 1952 | 1844 | 224 | 12.1 | 860 | 74 | 74 | 8.6 |
| 1954 | 1579 | 142 | 9.0 | 928 | 94 | 94 | 10.1 |
| 1958 | 1621 | 168 | 10.4 | 1025 | 102 | 101 | 9.9 |
| 1961 | 1629 | 162 | 9.9 | 929 | 91 | 95 | 10.2 |
| 1964 | 1563 | 230 | 14.7 | 907 | 108 | 123 | 13.6 |
| 1968 | 1262 | 208 | 16.5 | 847 | 100 | 123 | 14.5 |
| 1973 | 1480 | 206 | 13.9 | 850 | 99 | 119 | 14.0 |
| 1977 | 1271 | 190 | 14.9 | 857 | 93 | 121 | 14.1 |
| 1982 | 1683 | 226 | 13.4 | 799 | 89 | 115 | 14.4 |
| 1986 | 1472 | 209 | 14.2 | 837 | 97 | 127 | 15.2 |
| 1990 | 1743 | 265 | 15.2 | 842 | NA | 128 | 15.2 |
| *TOWNSHIP/VILLAGE COUNCILS* | | | | | | | |
| 1952 | NA | NA | NA | 5695 | NA | 11 | 0.2 |
| 1954 | NA | NA | NA | 6397 | NA | 550 | 8.6 |
| 1958 | NA | NA | NA | 6834 | NA | 629 | 9.2 |
| 1961 | 8833 | 1068 | 12.0 | 5260 | NA | 660 | 12.5 |
| 1964 | 8510 | 668 | 7.8 | 4776 | NA | 385 | 8.1 |
| 1968 | 7769 | 736 | 9.5 | 4709 | NA | 497 | 10.6 |
| 1973 | 5575 | 516 | 9.3 | 3757 | NA | 378 | 10.1 |
| 1977 | 6460 | 872 | 13.5 | 3793 | NA | 488 | 12.9 |
| 1982 | 6717 | 878 | 13.1 | 3699 | 397 | 490 | 13.2 |
| 1986 | 6066 | 901 | 14.9 | 3754 | 417 | 560 | 14.9 |

*Source: Statistical Abstracts of Elections in the Republic of China, 1946-1982* (Taipei: Central Election Committee, Ministry of Interior, 1982); *Records of Elections, 1985-1986* (Taipei: Central Election Committee, Ministry of Interior, 1987); and *Official Voting Returns of the 1989 Elections* (Taipei: Central Election Committee, Ministry of Interior, 1990), all in Chinese.

[a]No women ran for these executive positions before 1985.

Third, there are several clear indications that women would have fared much worse at the hands of the electorate, especially in the 1950s and 1960s, without the reserved-seats system. For example, there are several indications that women initially won many, if not most, of their seats because of their quota. Only one of the assembly elections included in these tables did not involve the application of the reserved-seats system for women—the 1952 elections for township and village councils. In these elections, women could win only 11 of 5,685 council seats, a meager representation of 0.2%. Only two years later, however, after the quota system was introduced, women won almost 9% of the seats on the township and village councils. Unfortunately, data on the number of seats reserved for women at these levels are not available, so it is impossible to specify how much of this increase derived from the women's quota per se. It seems reasonable, though, to assume that most of these victories were for reserved seats. At the county/city level, for instance, women never won more than their assigned minimum quota throughout the 1950s. At the national and provincial levels, moreover, the number of seats won by women did not exceed their minimum reservation significantly until the 1980s, except for the Taipei City Council and the National Assembly.

The reserved-seats system in the Republic of China, hence, has increased women's representation in legislative assemblies at all levels of government to slightly over 10%. If women in Taiwan are to achieve more equitable representation in Taiwan, however, they will have to win a much larger share of assembly contests in the future. This raises the question of whether women have been able to build upon the minimum of representation guaranteed them to become more competitive in electoral politics.

Probably the most direct measure of women's competitiveness is whether they are able to win more than their minimum quota of seats. Here the news is fairly good, though certainly not spectacularly so. At the local level, women have clearly done much better over time. During the 1950s, for example, women could not exceed their minimum quota in county and city councils by even one seat. During the 1970s and 1980s, in sharp contrast, they consistently won between a fifth and a third more council positions than they had been guaranteed. Thus, women clearly had become significant actors in local politics—quite a feat in itself because politics at this level is dominated by traditional faction and kinship groups that would normally be expected to be fairly unreceptive to women.[38] Similarly, the first victories by two women in the 21 races for county magistrate and city mayor in 1985 showed their growing acceptance as local political leaders. For example, the DPP woman magistrate of Kaohsiung County (which surrounds the island's second-largest city) has a family with extensive political ties (including a daughter who was then in the Provincial Assembly) and initiated significant expansions in the county's social services.[39]

Women's ability to win more than their minimum quota was much slower to develop at the provincial and national levels, except in the Taipei City Council and the National Assembly. Women have generally won a third or more than their minimum reserved seats for both these bodies since elections began to be held for them in 1969. The reasons for this success probably differ. As the urban center and political capital of the ROC, Taipei would be expected to provide the most conducive context for women candidates according to the normal tenets of modernization theory. Conversely, the greater representation of women in the National Assembly can be explained by findings from other countries that women do better in elections for less-desirable offices.[40] The National Assembly, despite its prestige, might not be considered particularly attractive to ambitious politicians because it does not participate in policymaking and because it has been heavily dominated by senior legislators elected on the Chinese mainland (see Table 3.3).

In almost all the other bodies as well, women were finally able to exceed their minimum quota by a significant extent in the last half of the 1980s. The December 1989 elections, in particular, clearly stand out in several respects: the number of women candidates who ran, their ability to attract the attention of both the domestic mass media and foreign observers of the election, and (most important, of course) their capabilities for getting voters to support them. For example, almost a quarter of the candidates and a fifth of the winners for the Taipei assembly were women, and women had their highest proportion of winners ever for most of the elections summarized in Tables 5.1–5.3. Even in the Legislative Yuan and Provincial Assembly, where women's representation had traditionally lagged, women won, respectively, almost twice and half as many seats as their reserved minimums. In addition, the increase of women county magistrates and city mayors from two to three gave them 14% of these elected executive positions, almost on par with their assembly representation rates. Two political factors have been advanced to explain the political success: First, the growing strength of the women's movement in Taiwan, led by the feminist group Awakening and other similar organizations, has stimulated both women's aspirations for political participation and public sympathy for these ambitions, developments that parallel the Western experience of the 1970s. Second, the growing electoral competition between the KMT and DPP made both parties more sensitive to appealing to female voters through slating attractive women candidates.

Thus, women seem to be increasing their competitiveness in Taiwan's legislative elections. Another way of assessing this is to measure the relative electability of male and female candidates.[41] While there are insufficient data to introduce statistical controls for such important factors in electoral outcomes as incumbency and party affiliation,[42] a crude measure of electability can be made by simply comparing the percentage of women candidates with the percentage of women winners. If considerable discrimination against women exists in voting in Taiwan, there should be a much higher percentage of women candidates than winners. In fact, for almost all of the elections covered by Tables 5.1–5.3, there was no systematic difference between the proportions of women who ran for office and who were elected.

This perhaps surprising lack of bias against women candidates by the ROC's electorate raises the last question of how many women run for office. If men and women can compete fairly evenly in Taiwan's elections, more women could presumably be elected if more chose to offer themselves as candidates. Here, the data are both pessimistic and optimistic. On the one hand, women's candidacy rates remain quite low—under 20% of all candidates (except for the 1989 Taipei city elections)—and the percentage of women candidates for most of these offices has increased only marginally since about the mid-1970s. Still, a few hopeful signs can be discerned. In the last election, women composed 20%–25% of the candidates for the Provincial Assembly and the Taipei City Council; the percentage of female candidates generally has increased slightly from one decade to the next; and in several instances, the number of women candidates increased significantly even if their percentage of all candidacies did not (e.g., for the Legislative Yuan and city/county assemblies).

## Implications

The reserved-seats system has clearly been beneficial for promoting women's political representation in the Republic of China. Because of the quota for women, the proportion of women serving in Taiwan's assemblies is quite high in comparative terms, especially in light of the island's patriarchal society and development level. Furthermore, women politicians have evidently built upon their assured representation to increasingly transform themselves from mere "tokens" elected because of the quota into competitive candidates who win significantly more than their reserved minimum. While assemblywomen in the ROC fall far short of providing equal or equitable representation for their gender, the more than modest progress that has been made certainly should not be gainsaid. Thus, the legal framework for the reserved-seats system described in this chapter should be of interest to other nations, particularly developing ones, that wish to stimulate political participation by women.

However, somewhat ironically, the need for the reserved-seats system in Taiwan is coming under question even by many women voters and politicians. There are two basic reasons for this. First, despite the progressive language and spirit of the 1947 constitution, the quota is fairly low (e.g., a district would be given a second reserved-seat only if it were to become impossibly large), usually between 8% and 12% of the seats in a specific assembly. Theoretically, this low level of representation for women prescribed by law should provide a floor for guaranteeing them an opportunity to enter electoral politics. However, because of actual political practice, the implementation of the quota system has had the effect of turning the floor into a ceiling. Thus, before the 1989 elections, the major political parties (both KMT and non-KMT) were quite reluctant to nominate and support more women candidates than the number prescribed by the quota. However, as noted in the previous section, greater electoral competition for women's votes may be undermining this conservative bias.

Second, as the socioeconomic status of women in the society has improved, the rationale for this protective provision has increasingly come under suspicion and scrutiny. Thus, women political activists (and many women voters as well) do not favor the reserved-seats system because it reinforces the stereotype of women as a secondary class in politics who need protection. By being protective, the quota system can help perpetuate the notion that women are weaker and less competitive in politics, thereby reinforcing the idea of gender inequality. Furthermore, the stigma of being elected for reserved seats can create serious barriers for many women politicians who are elected in their own right and are striving for equal recognition within assemblies.

In conclusion, as Taiwan's society enters a new stage of socioeconomic development and a new era of political culture, more and more women—younger women in particular—aspire to enter the public sphere and possess the socioeconomic, educational, and political resources to compete equally with men. Consequently, such protective provisions as the quota system do not appear to be necessary any longer. On the contrary, women's primary demand will be for equality, putting the existing reserved-seats system into a new context. The irony, in view of the theoretical clash between feminist and modernization theory, is that Taiwan's modernization has seemingly provided a better basis for a feminist movement to emerge and flourish.

## Notes

1. Article 134 of the ROC constitution states: "In the various kinds of elections, the number of women to be elected shall be fixed, and measures pertaining thereto shall be prescribed by law." See Hung-mao Tien, *The Great Transition: Political and Social Change in the Republic of China* (Stanford, Calif.: Hoover Institution Press, 1989) p. 269.

2. Article 7 of the constitution states: "All citizens of the Republic of China, irrespective of sex, religion, race, class, or party affiliation, shall be equal before the law." Furthermore, article 17 specifies that one of the rights of the people is the freedom to participate in elections.

3. Robert Bedeski, *State-Building in Modern China: The Kuomintang in the Prewar Period* (Berkeley: Institute of East Asian Studies, University of California 1981); and Tuan-sheng Ch'ien, *The Government and Politics of China* (Cambridge: Harvard University Press, 1950) Chps. 10–19.

4. Shiou-fong Li, "A Reconsideration of the Women's Quota System," in *Monograph on Election and Recall Laws* (Taipei: Legislative Bulletin #5, Library of the Legislative Yuan, 1986) pp. 15–17, in Chinese; Moong-wu Sa, *The Chinese Constitution: A New Look* (Taipei: San Min Publishing, 1973) pp. 181–185, 244–247,

& 302–305, in Chinese; and Song-sih Yan et al., eds., *The Election and Recall System of the R.O.C.* (Taipei: Central Election Committee, 1985) pp. 61–63, in Chinese.

5. *The Public Officials Election and Recall Law, Republic of China* (POER), 1989, article 65 (Taipei: Central Election Committee, Ministry of Interior, 1989), prescribes: "In an election of public officials when there is a women's quota and when the women elected are less than the quota, the ballots obtained by the female candidates shall be separated from those obtained by male candidates and shall also be counted separately. The female candidate(s) who has (have) won a plurality of ballots shall be declared elected."

6. *Republic of China, 1988: A Reference Book* (Taipei: Hilit, 1988), pp. 119–120 & 132; and Tien, *The Great Transition*, pp. 257, 261–262, & 269.

7. *Annual Review of Government Administration, Republic of China* (Taipei: Research, Development, and Evaluation Commission, Executive Yuan, 1988) pp. 16–17, in Chinese.

8. Tien, *The Great Transition*, p. 267.

9. Tien, *The Great Transition*, pp. 273–275.

10. *Annual Review of Government Administration*, pp. 15–16.

11. Tien, *The Great Transition*, pp. 257–258 & 269.

12. Pao-tsin Tsu, ed., *Statutes and Rules of the Election Laws of the Republic of China*, Vol. 2 (Taipei: Central Election Committee, 1985) pp. 158–172 & 190–226, in Chinese.

13. *Original Statute of Election and Recall of Delegates of the National Assembly* (ERODNA), 1947, article 4, item 7. See Tsu, Election Laws, Vol. 2, p. 158.

14. *Executive Order on the Distribution of the Election of the Delegates of the National Assembly*, July 10, 1947; and *Executive Order of Temporary Provisions of the Election and Recall of Public Officials* (EROPO), article 6, item 4. See Pao-tsin Tsu, ed., *Statutes and Rules of the Election Laws of the Republic of China*, Vol. 3 (Taipei: Central Election Committee, 1987) pp. 190–226.

15. *Implementation Rules of the Original ERODNA*, article 6; *Temporary Implementation Rules of EROPO*, article 9, item 7; and *Temporary Statute of EROPO*, article 24. See Tsu, *Election Laws*, Vol. 2, p. 168; and *POER*, 1989, pp. 22 & 68.

16. *Temporary Statute of EROPO*, article 40. See *POER*, 1989, p. 22.

17. *Original ERODNA*, articles 32 & 33; and *Temporary Statute of EROPO*, article 65. See Tsu, *Election Laws*, Vol. 2, p. 162; and *POER*, 1989, p. 41.

18. Tsu, *Election Laws*, Vol. 3, pp. 11–21, 88–141, & 237–282.

19. *The Public Officials Election and Recall Law, Republic of China* (POER), 1980, 1983, & 1989 (Taipei: Central Election Committee, Ministry of Interior, 1980, 1983, & 1989).

20. *Original ERODNA*, article 33. See Tsu, *Election Laws*, Vol. 2, p. 162.

21. Tsu, *Election Laws*, Vol. 2, pp. 232–275.

22. *Original Statute on the Election and Recall of Members of the Legislative Yuan* (EROMLY), 1947, article 5. See Tsu, *Election Laws*, Vol. 2, p. 233.

23. *Implementation Rules, POER*, 1980, article 12.

24. *Original EROMLY*, article 30. See Tsu, *Election Laws*, Vol. 2, p. 237.

25. *Annual Review of Government Administration*, pp. 15–18.

26. Arthur J. Lerman, *Taiwan's Politics: The Provincial Assemblyman's World* (Washington, D.C.: University Press of America, 1978), presents a fascinating portrait of both the formal and informal characteristics of the Provincial Assembly.

27. *Rules on the Election and Recall of Members of the Provincial Assembly*, 1960, article 2; and *Revised Regulations on the Organization of the Taiwan Provincial Assembly*. See, respectively, Pao-tsin Tsu, *Statutes and Rules of the*

*Election Laws of the Republic of China*, Vol. 4 (Taipei: Central Election Committee, 1987) p. 486; and Tsu, *Election Laws*, Vol. 4, p. 446.

28. Tsu, *Election Laws*, Vol. 4, pp. 1004 & 1012.
29. Tsu, *Election Laws*, Vol. 4, p. 1012.
30. Tsu, *Election Laws*, Vol. 4, p. 1029.
31. Article 4 of the *Organization Regulations of County/City Council*, 1950, and Article 13 of the *Rules of Implementing County/City Self-government*, 1950, initially provided that in election districts for county and city councils (i.e., those involving the general population and aborigines not living in aboriginal villages), the women's quota should be not less than one-tenth of the total seats. Perhaps because of the confusion in determining the exact number of the women's quota, this one-tenth formula was revised in 1952 to reserve one seat for women when the district size reached 10, two seats for districts of 20, etc. In the 1954 revision of the *Rules of Implementing County/City Self-government* (article 14), the formula was slightly liberalized: A second reserved seat was mandated for districts with 16 representatives, and for "plains aboriginal" constituencies, districts of seven were given a reserved seat. Finally, the 1967 revision of the *Rules of Implementing County/City Self-government* (article 2) created the present system described in the text. See Tsu, *Election Laws*, Vol. 4, pp. 110, 116, & 125.
32. The county/city council is composed of councilmen and councilwomen of three different groups elected by the citizens of a county/city—those elected by the general population, those by aboriginal villages, and those by aborigines living outside of specific aboriginal villages. For the councilmen and women elected by the general population of a county or city, the number of seats to be elected is determined as follows (with the exception of the two smallest counties on the island): one council member for the first 10,000 residents, another member for every additional 5,000 residents. For council members from aboriginal settlements, one member is chosen by each aboriginal village (*hsiang*). For the council members elected by the aborigines residing in the plains areas outside their designated settlements, one council member is selected by a constituency of between 500 and 5,000, with another member added for each increment of 5,000 population. *The Organization Regulations of County/City Councils*, 1950, article 4. See Tsu, *Election Laws*, Vol. 4, p. 209.
33. *The Rules of Implementing Self-government of Counties/Cities*, 1967, article 2; and *The Organization Rules of Township/Village Councils*, 1967, article 2. See Tsu, *Election Laws*, Vol. 4, pp. 156 & 640. Before 1964, the statutes for deriving the women's quota in the election of county/city council members also applied in the elections at the township (*cheng*)/village (*hsiang*) level.
34. *Regulations on the Election and Recall of Public Officials of Counties/Cities, Taiwan Province*, 1967, article 53; and *Regulations on the Election and Recall of Public Officials of Counties/Cities, Taiwan Province*, 1971, article 54. See Tsu, *Election Laws*, Vol. 4, pp. 773 & 813.
35. Selig S. Harrison, "Taiwan After Chiang Ching-kuo," *Foreign Affairs* 66:4 (Spring 1988) pp. 791–796; and James D. Seymour, "Taiwan in 1987: A Year of Political Bombshells," *Asian Survey* 28:1 (January 1988) pp. 56–58.
36. Lan-hung Nora Chiang and Yenlin Ku, *Past and Current Status of Women in Taiwan* (Taipei: National Taiwan University, Population Studies Center, Women's Research Program, Monograph #1, 1985) pp. 30–31; and Suan-laine Liang, "Women and Political Participation," in Suan-laine Liang, ed., *Women and Political Participation* (Taipei: Awakening Foundation, 1989) pp. 5–34.
37. Ruth B. Mandel, "The Political Woman," in Sara E. Rix, ed., *The American Woman, 1988–1989* (New York: Norton, 1988) pp. 88–100.
38. Teh-fu Huang, "Grassroots Organizers," *Free China Review* 39:12

(December 1989) pp. 24–29; J. Bruce Jacobs, "A Preliminary Model of Particularistic Ties in Chinese Political Alliances: *Kan-ch'ing* and *Kuan-hsi* in a Rural Taiwanese Township," *China Quarterly* 78 (June 1979) pp. 237–273; Lerman, *Taiwan's Politics*, Part II; and Edwin A. Winckler, "Roles Linking State and Society," in Emily Martin Ahern and Hill Gates, eds., *The Anthropology of Taiwanese Society* (Stanford, Calif.: Stanford University Press, 1981) pp. 50–86.

39. Carl Chang, "Detailed Platform," *Free China Review* 39:12 (December 1989) p. 21.

40. Irene Diamond, *Sex Roles in the State House* (New Haven: Yale University Press, 1977) Chps. 2 & 3; and Richard L. Engstrom, Michael D. McDonald, and Biher Chou, "The Desirability Hypothesis and the Election of Women to City Councils," *State and Local Government Review* 20:1 (Winter 1988) pp. 38–40.

41. Albert K. Karnig and B. Oliver Walter, "Election of Women to City Councils," *Social Science Quarterly* 56:1 (March 1976) pp. 605–613.

42. R. Darcy, Susan Welch, and Janet Clark, *Women, Elections, and Representation* (New York: Longman, 1987) Part II.

# PART THREE
# ASSEMBLYWOMEN IN THE REPUBLIC OF CHINA

## CHAPTER SIX
# The Study and Research Methodology

The reserved-seats system has guaranteed that a minimal but significant number of women are serving in all of the legislative assemblies in the Republic of China at any particular moment. These assemblywomen (with the exception of the senior legislators elected on the mainland in the late 1940s) face increasingly competitive elections every three to six years. Thus, they form a pool of successful women politicians whose experiences should be quite instructive for considering how women can overcome the institutional and cultural barriers against their political participation in modernizing societies. This chapter, then, provides an overview of our case study of women legislators in Taiwan. The first section describes the study itself; the second presents a conceptual model for structuring women's political roles and orientations; and the third discusses the methodology employed in analyzing the data.

### A Study of Women Legislators in Taiwan

The overall goal of this study is to find the social traits, attitudes, and activities of women in the rapidly modernizing Chinese society on Taiwan that help promote their entrance into the political elites. The basic data for this assessment come from in-depth interviews of assemblywomen aimed at discovering the special characteristics stimulating their political activism in a hostile social and cultural context. In particular, questions were asked concerning seven major areas relating to political participation and legislative activities and to the factors generally believed to influence them: (1) childhood socialization experiences, (2) adult socioeconomic roles and socialization, (3) political resources, (4) ideology, (5) views about women in politics, (6) basic orientations about legislative activities, and (7) a legislator's effectiveness and success within the assemblies.

The interview schedule was based on a modification of a biographical questionnaire developed by the Center for the American Woman and Politics of Rutgers University that has been used extensively in the study of the career patterns of women politicians in the United States.[1] It was modified slightly to include political conditions and issues in Taiwan and to exclude U.S.-specific materials. It was then translated into Chinese and pretested both on women politicians and academics. There appears little reason, therefore, to question the validity of the survey instrument. While the basic questionnaire has been used primarily in the United States, many of the items included in it have been used in cross-national studies, and the pretests indicated no apparent biases in applying the modified survey to the Chinese society on Taiwan.

An evaluation of the attitudes and characteristics of women politicians, of course, rests not just upon what they are but also upon how they compare with those of other significant groups. In the case of assemblies in the Republic of China, three other such comparator groups may be discerned. First, women politicians should be compared with their male counterparts. This comparison raises such questions as, Do women pursue similar legislative careers as their male colleagues? If differences emerge, are they caused by greater role conflicts? Are their political attitudes the same or different? Do women need the help of special resources, such as greater socioeconomic status and wealth or atypical socialization experiences, to become active in politics? In short, the answers to these questions should highlight the barriers politically active women have to overcome in Taiwan that are not faced by male leaders.

Second, it should also be instructive to compare winning women candidates with women who ran for assembly posts but lost. What types of factors account for the fact that some women are successful in the electoral arena while others are not—background resources, support from party leaders and interest groups, a conducive family context and lack of role conflicts, issue positions, or representative role orientations? By analyzing what contributes to successful women's candidacies, such a study should suggest strategies for increasing women's political representation in the ROC.

Society and politics in Taiwan have changed radically in a relatively short time, as sketched in Chapter 3, and the data in Chapter 4 suggest that this social change has affected the roles and status of women as well. Thus, a third important comparison would be between generational cohorts of women politicians in Taiwan. Here, both differences in generational norms and the much less competitive and democratic system of the earlier period should create significant differences in political attitudes and activities. This raises the question of whether the presumably more favorable conditions in the 1980s have created a more assertive and aggressive type of female political leader or, conversely, whether the greater social and cultural obstacles to women's political participation earlier meant that only very special "pioneer" women entered the political arena.

To permit these comparisons, the study included four specific subsamples. The first group was composed of all women serving in the ROC's major legislative bodies: the Legislative Yuan, the National Assembly, the

Provincial Assembly, and the Taipei and Kaohsiung City Councils. In 1985 when the research was conducted, these assemblies had a total of 43 women members who had not held their positions in 1969–1970. Comparable male legislators formed the second group. A sample of 43 assemblymen was selected randomly from the five legislative bodies. This sample matched up well with the women legislators on such key characteristics as social origin (Islander versus Mainlander), party (Kuomintang versus non-KMT), and legislative service (i.e., length of office-holding). The third group included all 56 women who had run for but lost seats in these legislative bodies in the previous election for each. Finally, the last group consisted of the 21 women who had served in these bodies in 1969–1970 and were still living. This last group, incidentally, included five assemblywomen who were still serving in the same office, bringing the total number of active women legislators to 48.

The actual interviewing was conducted during the spring of 1985 by the staff of Academia Sinica (one professor and several graduate assistants), who were matched by gender to the interviewees. The survey instrument contained both open- and closed-ended questions and took between one and two hours to complete. In a few instances, people in the samples could not be found or refused to be interviewed, but the overall response rate was a very high 91%. Table 6.1 shows the number and percentage of completed interviews for each group. All exceeded 90% except for losing female candidates, who were the hardest to locate because they did not hold official positions. Even for them, though, 84% of the interviews were completed. After the administration of the questionnaires, they were coded and keypunched by the staff of Academia Sinica. The many open-ended questions in the survey (those for which precoded response categories were not provided for the interviewees), were coded inductively, with each separate response being counted as an individual category.

Table 6.1 Samples and Completed Interviews

|  | Sample Size | Completed Interviews | Response Rate (%) |
|---|---|---|---|
| Assemblywomen | 43 | 39 | 91 |
| Assemblymen | 43 | 43 | 100 |
| Losing Women | 56 | 47 | 84 |
| 1969 Assemblywomen | 21 | 20 | 95 |

## Conceptual Research Design

As noted, the politicians included in this study were asked questions about seven areas related to women's success in the legislative arena in the Republic of China. These seven areas, in turn, can be divided into three broader blocks of variables: (1) social factors that affect a political career, (2) general political characteristics and orientations, and (3) legislative activities. This section outlines our basic research design by briefly discussing each of these three blocks and indicating how the groups of variables within them should be related to one another. Our general hypotheses about how these factors are connected are summarized in Figure 6.1. In general, social background (i.e., childhood socialization and adult roles) is expected to have a fairly strong impact upon political orientations (i.e., politicial resources, ideology, and attitudes about women in politics). In turn, political orientations should have a major influence upon legislative activities (i.e., orientations toward the assembly and legislative effectiveness), while the impact of social background factors on legislative activities should occur primarily through their effects on political orientations.

**Figure 6.1 Relationships Among Central Blocks of Factors**

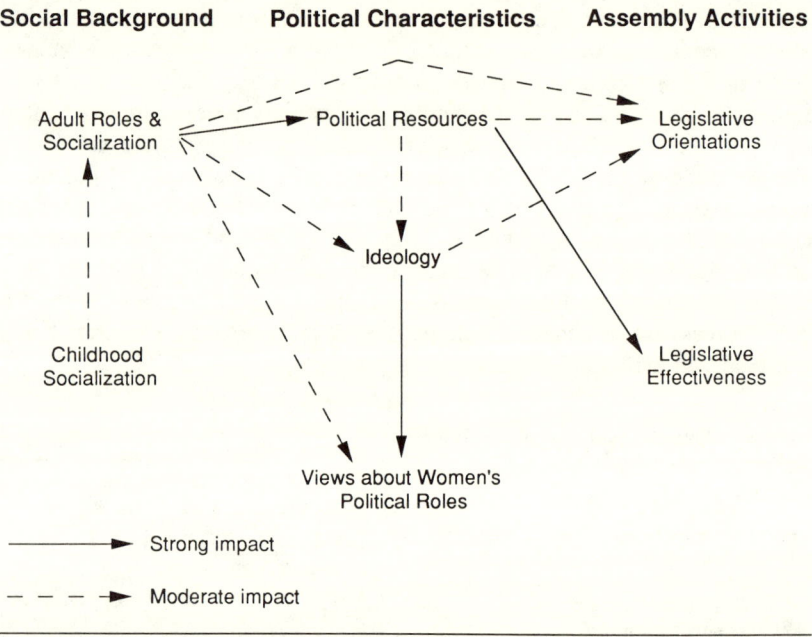

The modernization and feminist approaches suggest somewhat divergent perspectives about how these characteristics and attitudes should differ between male and female politicians. Taken to its logical extreme, modernization theory implies what may be termed the "gender-neutral" model. That is, as the social values in traditional society that form a barrier to women's political participation erode during industrialization and modernization, women come to participate in politics on approximately the same basis as men. Thus, few systematic gender differences would be predicted. Conversely, taking feminist theory to its logical extreme suggests the "disadvantaged-status" model. That is, women are treated as inferiors in both traditional and modern industrial societies—thus, they should rank well below men in terms of socioeconomic status, political resources and participation, and legislative effectiveness. Finally, a less extreme form of feminism (which is also consistent with less Panglossian modernization theory) adduces the "countersocialization" model, which assumes that most women must overcome stong cultural norms to enter public life. Thus, having countersocialization experiences that help to break down these norms is an important determinant of political participation for women but not for men, who do not need countersocialization.[2]

Childhood socialization and adult roles are the two major types of social background variables considered here. Some of the principal childhood socialization factors in this study include class background (as indicated by father's education), generation, family political involvement, and mother's education. These are the factors that countersocialization theory emphasizes. For example, countersocialization for girls would be expected to occur most often in upper-class and more politicized families, among the younger generation, and where the mother provides a positive role model in terms of educational achievement and political interest. The disadvantaged-status model would probably concur that some of these variables, such as class and family politicization, help promote women's participation but would give this relationship another interpretation—that they constitute "status advantages" for both men and women.

The major factors relating to adult roles and socialization include current class position (as indicated by education and occupation), spouse politicization, role conflicts between public and private life, and personal self-confidence. On these factors, a clear divergence occurs between the countersocialization and disadvantaged-status approaches. The former looks for countersocialization that would stimulate women's participation (e.g., high socioeconomic status, the absence of role conflicts, or high self-esteem and confidence), while the latter predicts that men will rate well above women on all these dimensions. Thus, the disadvantaged-status perspective explains women's gross underrepresentation in the political arena as attributable to the disparity in distribution of power resources and advocates social change that would more equally distribute between the sexes the opportunity to enter the political eligibility pools.

Although substantial intergenerational social mobility has occurred in rapidly developing Taiwan,[3] several of the childhood socialization factors (e.g., class, generation, and perhaps mother's role model) should influence the adult roles and socioeconomic resources (e.g., education, occupation, and income) attained by an individual. These resources, in turn, should be an important determinant of the personal self-confidence and of the role conflicts facing legislators, especially female ones, between their public careers and the responsibilities of their private lives. Thus, a fairly strong relationship is posited between childhood socialization and adult role characteristics in Figure 6.1.

There are three sets of variables within the second block of general political orientations. First, ties with organized groups, membership in the dominant Kuomintang Party, and past political office-holding are considered to be political resources that can certainly help a politician's career. The disadvantaged-status model, of course, would predict that male politicians would hold many more of these political resources than would their female counterparts. Countersocialization theory would not necessarily disagree with this hypothesis, but it is also consistent with the gender-neutral model in the sense that women who have experienced successful countersocialization, especially in the form of obtaining socioeconomic resources, might not differ too greatly in their political careers from comparable men. This implies, moreover, that adult roles should have a strong impact on the possession of political resources.

The other two sets of factors focus upon political attitudes—general ideological position (as indicated by a respondent's self-placement on a liberal-conservative scale)[4] and views about women in Taiwan's politics (i.e., whether women make a positive contribution to political life and whether they suffer from political discrimination). Both the countersocialization and disadvantaged-status perspectives suggest that women politicians would be more liberal and supportive of women's political roles than their male counterparts in view of the cultural obstacles that they must overcome to enter politics. In terms of the relationships among specific sets of variables, political resources and adult roles should have a moderate influence on ideology, with more resources and higher socioeconomic status inducing conservative pro-establishment beliefs; liberals should be much more supportive than conservatives of women in politics; and countersocialization at both the childhood and adult levels should stimulate greater consciousness about women's political roles.

The final subject of analysis is activity within the assemblies. One important aspect involves the area of legislative activity (i.e., primary role definitions and the substantive fields of committee service and resolutions drafted). A second dimension measures legislative effectiveness in terms of activism (i.e., amount of time devoted to official work, introduction of resolutions, and holding committee chairs) and success (i.e., resolution success rate, perceived influence, enjoyment of office, and ambition for future office). The disadvantaged-status model would predict that women would be less active and effective within assemblies and that they should primarily focus their activities upon women's issues. Countersocialization theory would agree with the latter hypothesis but, as in the case of political resources, does not necessarily imply that women politicians should be inferior to men once they become politically active.

These variables should be influenced by a variety of factors in the other blocks, such as socialization context, adult roles and socioeconomic status, political resources, and perhaps ideology. In particular, political resources should have a strong impact on legislative effectiveness. The impact of the social background factors should be fairly indirect, though, and operate through their influence on the intermediate political items (e.g., political resources). In addition, legislative orientations should have some impact on effectiveness within the assemblies, although it is difficult to deduce specific hypotheses about these relationships.

## Analysis Methodology

Our analysis here of each set of factors (e.g., childhood socialization, legislative effectiveness, etc.) moves through three tasks or stages. The first compares the four subsamples in terms of how many of their members possess a certain characteristic or attitude and employs simple cross-tabulations and measures of association (Cramer's V). The second explores the possible causal influences on a particular item and is based on multiple regression analysis. Finally, we examine the extent to which the variables in a particular set can distinguish between the three "analytic categorizations" described in the first section (female versus male legislators; winning versus losing female candidates; and older- versus younger-generation women) using discriminant analysis.

For the purpose of these statistical analyses, all the variables being studied were converted into dichotomies (i.e., variables with two categories denoting the presence or absence of a characteristic), with respondents having the characteristic (e.g., a college education, children under 12, the introduction of over 15 resolutions or amendments per assembly session) being coded as 1 and those not having it as 0. Using such dichotomies has the disadvantage of ignoring information (e.g., differences between respondents with high school and grade school educations) that might be analytically useful. There are several important advantages, however. First, it results in easily interpretable tables; second, it conforms to the requirements that multiple regression and discriminant analysis use "interval data;"[5] third, as will be seen, it makes the statistics produced by the regression analysis more substantively meaningful; and fourth, preliminary analysis indicated that using dichotomies does not distort our results.

The remainder of this section provides an illustrative demonstration of these techniques using nine variables on which women and men might be expected to differ significantly. Thus, it is intended both as a methodological introduction for readers unfamiliar with these statistical techniques and as a brief overview of some of the principal themes that will be developed in the next three chapters.

The specific variables to be considered here are whether the respondent (1) had a mother interested in politics, (2) attended an elite university, (3) first became interested in politics through family, (4) had a spouse who held political office, (5) believed that family obligations impede the performance of official duties, (6) considered himself or herself a liberal, (7) introduced over 15 resolutions and amendments in an average legislative session, (8) devoted more than 50 hours a week to official duties, and (9) believed that constituent service should be an important function for assembly members. Thus, these variables cover most of the sets to be studied here and should provide at least a preliminary idea of what women legislators in the Republic of China are like.

Table 6.2 contains the cross-tabulation of whether the spouse had held political office (elected, bureaucratic, or party) by the four categories of respondents (female legislator, male legislator, female losing candidate, and 1969 assemblywoman). By convention, the respondent group is placed in columns that go down the table because it is assumed to affect the characteristics of politicians; spouse activity is placed in the rows across the table. The numbers within the table represent how many people share two characteristics. For example, there were 10 women legislators whose husbands had held political office, while 42 male legislators had wives who never had had an official position. The totals of the rows and columns represent how many people in the entire sample had a specific characteristic, and the percentages below these totals are their proportion of the entire sample of 149. For example, 27 (or 18%) had spouses who had held some official post, and 47 (or 32%) were losing women candidates.

Table 6.2  Cross-Tabulation of Spouse-Held Political Office by Respondent Group

| Spouse Held Political Office | Female Legislator | Male Legislator | Female Loser | Female 1969 Legislator | TOTAL |
|---|---|---|---|---|---|
| No | 29 | 42 | 39 | 12 | 122 |
|    | 74% | 98% | 83% | 60% | 82% |
| Yes | 10 | 1 | 8 | 8 | 27 |
|     | 26% | 2% | 17% | 40% | 18% |
| TOTAL | 39 | 43 | 47 | 20 | 149 |
|       | 26% | 29% | 32% | 13% | |

*Note:* Cramer's V = .32; statistically significant at .002 level.

In analyzing the cross-tabulation, we are primarily concerned with comparing the tendencies of each of these four groups to have politically involved spouses. Our basic hypothesis is that this would constitute countersocialization that might overcome women's reluctance to enter the political arena. Thus, more women than men should have spouses who had held a political post. This expectation can be tested by comparing the percentage of respondent type having active spouses. Consequently, the percentages within Table 6.2 are computed down each column. For example, for current assemblywomen, 26% had office-holding husbands, while 74% did not.

Finally in the substantive interpretation of this cross-tabulation, our basic hypothesis receives quite strong support. Only 2% of the male legislators had wives who had filled an official position at some time. In sharp contrast, each of the three groups of women was much more likely to have husbands who were so involved in political affairs, ranging from 40% for the 1969 legislators to 26% for current assemblywomen and 17% for losing female candidates. In addition, the fact that this percentage was much higher for the 1969 assemblywomen than for the other two groups suggests that the political system in Taiwan may have opened up for women significantly over time, making the "spouse connection" somewhat less important in the 1980s than it had been in the 1960s.

Comparing the percentages certainly gives us some idea of the degree of difference among the four subsamples. In addition, statisticians have provided two more precise and standardized measurements of how strong such a relationship is. The first is the use of correlation coefficients, or measures of association. Generally, a correlation coefficient can vary between 0 when the two variables in question are completely unrelated to 1 when a "perfect" relationship exists (i.e., knowing the value of the predictor variable for any case allows the exact prediction of the value of the other variable). As a very crude indicator of the strength of a correlation, those under .15 indicate no or weak association; those between .15 and .30 moderate association; those between .30 and .50 fairly strong association; and those over .50 very strong association.

Different correlation coefficients are appropriate for variables based on different measurement techniques. In Table 6.2, the variable of respondent group is a "nominal" categorization without inherent numerical order (i.e., giving male legislators a higher or lower coding score than female losing candidates is completely arbitrary). For such a cross-tabulation, Cramer's V probably represents the best measure of association.[6] The V in Table 6.2 is .32, indicating a moderate to fairly strong degree of association and confirming that there are marked differences among the four types of legislators and legislative candidates in terms of their spouses' political activities.

The second measure of a relationship is its degree of statistical significance. Technically, statistical significance applies only to random samples drawn from some larger population. It is the probability that the degree of association found in the sample could occur if there was actually no relationship in the population that the sample represents. When this probability is small, conventionally 5% (the .05 level) or less, the relationship in the sample is said to be "statistically significant." The probability is determined by two factors: (1) the strength of the correlation in the sample (the higher the correlation, the more significant it is) and (2) the size of the sample (the larger the sample, the more confidence can be placed in the results).[7]

In cases such as this study that are not based on random samples, it is not really appropriate to use measures of statistical significance. However, they are used in such instances quite frequently in social science research. Especially when the number of cases is small, as here, statistical significance provides an additional indicator of how much confidence can be placed in a specific correlation. Thus, we report statistical significance for our various data. For the relationship described in Table 6.2, the significance level is .002—that is, a 0.2% probability of a "null relationship." Note that lower significance levels denote stronger relationships (the opposite of correlation coefficients). Substantively, this means we can be quite confident that the four subsamples vary significantly in terms of the degree of office-holding by their husbands and wives.

After this methodological overview, the relationship between respondent type and the other eight illustrative items can be conducted fairly quickly. It might well be expected (eclectically combining the countersocialization and disadvantaged-status models for the moment) that women politicians, as opposed to their male counterparts, would be more dependent upon countersocialization experiences, less likely to gain entrance to elite institutions, more subject to role conflicts, more liberal, less enthusiastic about interacting with their constituents, and less active and ambitious within assemblies.

Table 6.3 tests these hypotheses. Note that the data presentation is much more compact than in the full cross-tabulation in Table 6.2, but the same information is still essentially there. Each line in the table contains the percentage of respondents in each group exhibiting a particular characteristic or attitude. Then Cramer's V is listed, with its statistical significance at either the .05 or .15 level indicated by notes to the table.

The data in Table 6.3 support most but not all of our initial hypotheses. First, women were quite likely to have become interested in politics for family-related reasons (between 38% and 49% of each of the three female subsamples did so), while family stimulation was important only for 9% of the men, producing a fairly strong V of .33. Family support and encouragement, hence, appear to provide an important countersocialization effect for women in Taiwan. In contrast, current women legislators were more likely to have had mothers interested in politics (24%) than their male counterparts had (14%), as expected. However, this difference did not exist for the other two groups. In fact, none of 1969 assemblywomen had politically interested mothers, perhaps suggesting a generational difference among the mothers in the sample, with the older ones being almost completely docile regarding the political system. Thus, this relationship appears fairly marginal.

The next hypotheses are that women would have less access to the institutions of power and would face greater role conflicts. First, men were about three times as likely (26%) as women to have attended elite universities in Taiwan (top-ranked National Taiwan University or politically oriented National Chengchi University), producing a moderate to fairly strong V of .29. Second, about a third of the women in each of the subsamples reported that family obligations had hurt their legislative performance (for the losing candidates, these percentages are based on the 14 who had held previous assembly seats), while not one of the men had such a conflict between public and private responsibilities. The resulting V is a fairly strong .42, giving a good deal of credence to the argument that role conflicts constitute a significant barrier to women that men do not face.

Table 6.3  Social and Political Differences Among Respondent Groups

|  | Female Legislator (%) | Male Legislator (%) | Female Loser (%) | Female 1969 Legislator (%) | V |
|---|---|---|---|---|---|
| Mother Politically Interested | 24 | 14 | 16 | 0 | .20[a] |
| Family-related 1st Political Interest | 49 | 9 | 38 | 40 | .33[b] |
| Elite University | 8 | 26 | 4 | 5 | .29[b] |
| Family Obligations Hurt Office-holding[c] | 39 | 0 | 29 | 35 | .42[b] |
| Liberal | 56 | 47 | 72 | 75 | .24[b] |
| Constituent Service Important | 92 | 70 | 81 | 90 | .23[b] |
| Over 15 Resolutions per Session[c] | 34 | 52 | 17 | 41 | .24[a] |
| 50+ Hrs Legislative Work/Wk[c] | 49 | 59 | 60 | 47 | .11 |

[a]Statistically significant at .15 level.
[b]Statistically significant at .05 level.
[c]Percentages for female losers based on 14 women who had held a legislative office earlier.

Current female legislators were also somewhat more liberal (56%) than their male colleagues (47%), as predicted; the other two groups of women were much more liberal (about 75%). The liberalism of losing candidates was not unexpected, but the strong liberalism of women representatives from the 1960s is rather surprising, especially given the conservative nature of Taiwan's politics at that time. Perhaps, only quite nontraditional women sought and won public office then. Furthermore, the degree of liberalism among all the respondents is interesting given the generally conservative image of the Republic of China. To some extent, these results probably reflect the respondents' placing themselves on the political spectrum within Taiwan where a relative liberal might be conservative by the standards of other societies, but they also suggest that assembly members may view themselves as something of outsiders vis-à-vis the stronger executive branch of government.

Finally, our anticipation that women would be less active and ambitious receives only partial support. On the one hand, men were clearly more active than women in terms of introducing legislation. Just over half the men averaged over 15 resolutions and amendments per session, compared with about 40% of the 1969 women legislators, a third of the current assemblywomen, and 17% of the previous women seat holders who had lost office (suggesting that the wages for inactivity are loss of public recognition and confidence). These data also suggest a high level of legislative activity that is somewhat surprising given the executive-dominated nature of the government. On the other hand, almost 90% of the women, compared with 70% of the men, believed that constituent service was important, and although the difference was not statistically significant, women worked slightly longer hours than men at their official duties.

Thus far, we have examined the differences among the four subsamples on the nine variables under consideration. A second task is to develop explanations for why some politicians are more liberal, subject to role conflicts, or active than others. Tables 6.2 and 6.3 indicate that significant gender differences exist on all these items, but other explanatory items might be posited as well. For example, a person's class (as indicated by education and social origin), political orientations (as indicated by party and experience in elected posts), and socialization context (as indicated by generation) could well influence these attitudes and behaviors also. To test such possible effects, then, we developed statistical models explaining three of the variables analyzed here (family obligations as a role conflict, liberalism, and introducing resolutions in the assembly) by gender and the five other explanatory factors just noted.

Multiple regression is the best technique for assessing how a group of explanatory factors affect another item that is often termed the "dependent variable" because its values are assumed to depend upon the values of the explanatory factors (called "independent variables" because the regression makes no attempt to explain them). Multiple regression analysis produces two major types of statistics. First, an overall correlation coefficient, Multiple R, measures the combined impact of all the predictor items upon the dependent variable. Like V, its values vary between 0 and 1, and measures of its statistical significance are available.

The regression results for each of the three dependent variables are presented in Table 6.4. The correlation coefficients show that the six explanatory variables taken together have a fairly strong impact on perceived role conflicts between family obligations and official duties ($R = .47$) but only moderate ones on liberalism ($R = .30$) and sponsoring resolutions ($R = .37$). Note that because we now have six independent variables working together, somewhat higher correlations would be expected than in the simple association between just two variables. Thus, the independent variables do exercise a quite significant influence over each of the dependent items, but they clearly fall short of providing a complete explanation of why some politicians rather than others in Taiwan feel subject to role conflicts, espouse liberalism, or introduce many resolutions. Either we have left out important explanatory factors, or these traits are subject to a good deal of idiosyncratic variation among sample members. (The more complete analysis in the following chapters suggests that the latter is the case, which incidentally is generally true of most social science research.)

Table 6.4  Regression Explanations of Role Conflicts, Liberalism, and Assembly Activism

|  | Family Obligations Hurt Legislative Work | Liberalism | Over 15 Resolutions per Session |
|---|---|---|---|
| Multiple R | .47[a] | .30[a] | .37[a] |
| *Regression Coefficients* | | | |
| Female | .50[a] | .19[a] | -.15[b] |
| Over 45 | .02 | -.20[a] | .05 |
| College Education | .0006 | .06 | .22[a] |
| Mainlander | -.10 | .03 | .01 |
| KMT | .04 | -.07 | -.19[b] |
| Substantial Electoral Experience | .19[b] | .03 | .14[b] |

[a]Statistically significant at .05 level.
[b]Statistically significant at .15 level.

The overall Multiple R, however, tells us nothing about the individual effects of the six independent variables. These effects also represent the independent influence of a specific predictor after the impact attributable to the other independent variables in the regression analysis is statistically controlled. Such an effect for each of the explanatory items is indicated by its regression (or $b$) coefficient, a technical measurement of how much change is produced in the dependent variable by an increase of one unit in the predictor item. Unlike the V and Multiple R correlation coefficients, which have only positive values, these regression coefficients can be either positive or negative. A positive one indicates that possessing a particular trait makes a respondent more likely to have the characteristic denoted by the dependent variable, while a negative one shows that it makes the respondent less likely to have the trait. Finally, measures of statistical significance can be computed for each regression coefficient.

When all the variables in a multiple regression analysis are dichotomies coded either 0 or 1, as they are here, the regression coefficients have a valuable substantive meaning. An increase of one unit in the independent variable can obviously be only from 0 to 1, that is, from not having to having a particular characteristic. The amount of change that this produces in the dependent variable, therefore, can be interpreted as the increased probability of possessing the trait denoted by the dependent variable that results from having the characteristic measured by the explanatory one.[8]

The regression coefficients in Table 6.4 demonstrate that only a few of the independent variables exercise a significant effect in each of the regressions and that the causal pattern of their influences differs for each of the three dependent variables. Except for gender, there is little a priori reason to believe that role conflicts would be related to the other explanatory factors, and this turns out to be the case. Gender has a strong impact on perceptions that family obligations detract from official duties—being a woman increased the probability of holding this view by 50%. Among the other independent variables, only having substantial experience in elected posts ($b = .19$) had any influence whatsoever. Evidently, experience makes one more cognizant of the strains of office-holding.

The pattern is much different for introducing resolutions. While Table 6.3 showed that men were much more likely than any of the groups of women to score highly on this dimension, gender's regression coefficient (Table 6.4) is a fairly modest -.15. This suggests that other factors are at work. Education, which is highly valued in Taiwan, has the greatest impact, as those with a college education were 22% more likely to be active than those without one. Experience in elected posts also has some positive impact ($b = .14$) as might be expected, but it is rather surprising that being a member of the majority Kuomintang Party made an assembly member 19% less likely to sponsor a large number of resolutions and amendments. Evidently, the opposition used aggressive activity in legislative bodies to get its message across and generate political support.[9] For ideology, both being a woman and being younger than 45 increased the probability of a politician's being a liberal by about a fifth, as would be expected. Surprisingly, the anticipated greater conservatism of KMT members and Mainlanders turns out not to exist. Just as for the high level of liberalism in the sample, this implies that even assembly members associated with the "ins" may feel somewhat on the "outs" in the executive-dominated system of government in the ROC.

Our third analytic goal is to see how well sets of variables distinguish female from male legislators, winning from losing women candidates, and older- from younger-generation women. Here, we provide an illustration using the nine variables discussed in this section to differentiate male and female legislators. The cross-tabulations in Tables 6.2 and 6.3 showed that assemblywomen and men differed significantly on all these items. More sophisticated statistics, however, can estimate the combined ability of these variables to distinguish between male and female legislators and the relative contribution of each explanatory factor to this relationship. A statistical technique called "discriminant analysis" provides such results. In particular, it calculates a "discriminant function" from an additive combination of the discriminating variables that maximizes the distinctiveness between cases falling into two categories—in this instance, assemblywomen and men.

Three different discriminant results are discussed from the data presented in Table 6.5. First, the "canonical correlation" (which is analogous to R or V) between the discriminant function and the categorization of men and women legislators measures the combined power of the explanatory variables to predict whether an assembly member is male or female. Here, the canonical correlation is a very high .78, indicating that taken together the nine variables have a high degree of predictive power. Second, the "centroids" for the two groups show whether each group scores high or low on the discriminating function. In this case, women were high (centroid = 1.39) and men were low (centroid = -1.12).

Table 6.5  Discriminant Analysis for Women Versus Men Legislators

| | |
|---|---|
| *Canonical Correlation* | .78[a] |
| *Group Centroids* | |
| Assemblywomen | 1.39 |
| Assemblymen | -1.12 |
| *Discriminant Function Coefficients* | |
| Family Obligations Hurt Legislative Duties | .65[b] |
| Family-Related 1st Political Interest | .64[b] |
| Over 15 Resolutions per Session | -.51[b] |
| Constituent Service Important | .49[b] |
| Spouse Held Political Office | .32[b] |
| Mother Interested in Politics | .25[b] |
| Attended Elite University | -.19 |
| Over 50 Hrs Legislative Work/Wk | .12 |
| Liberal | -.04 |

[a]Statistically significant at .0000 level.
[b]Statistical significance of individual discriminant coefficients cannot be computed, but these variables entered the discriminant equation at the .05 level.

Finally, "standardized discriminant function coefficients" (which are analogous to the $b$'s in regression analysis) are computed for each of the discriminating variables. These coefficients indicate the relative contribution that each variable makes to the discriminant function and whether this influence is positive or negative. This explains, incidentally, the importance of the group centroids. Knowing that women legislators have high scores on the discriminant function, thus, tells us that variables with positive discriminant function coefficients are associated with assemblywomen, while characteristics with negative coefficients tend to be held by their male colleagues.[10]

Substantively, the discriminant coefficients indicate that becoming interested in politics for family-related reasons and having family obligations interfere with official duties are the factors providing the most powerful differentiation between male and female legislators, as indicated by their discriminant coefficients of about .65. Because these coefficients are both positive, they also show that women were more likely to hold these attitudes than men. In addition, there is a moderate tendency for women to have had politically active spouses and politically interested mothers ($dc = .32$ and $.25$ respectively). Thus, these results confirm the importance for women of countersocialization within the family and of role conflicts between their private and public lives. As predicted, women were much less likely to have sponsored legislation ($dc = -.51$), but contrary to the original hypothesis, they were much more likely to stress constituent service ($dc = .49$). Finally, after these other factors are taken into account, the other three variables did not add any significant ability to discriminate between assemblywomen and assemblymen.

## Plan of the Study

To summarize this introductory chapter, we plan to study the barriers facing women's entrance into the political arena in Taiwan by comparing the attitudes, characteristics, and behaviors of women legislators—an important political elite group—with those of their male colleagues and of female candidates who ran for office but lost. Consequently, we conducted an extensive interview survey with the relevant groups in the spring of 1985. Our research design follows the sequential impact of three blocks of variables upon each other: (1) social background, (2) political characteristics, and (3) assembly activities. As a preliminary illustration of our methodological techniques, this chapter discussed a few representative items from these broad blocks. In general, this preliminary analysis found considerable support for the basic propositions that women politicians, compared with men, would be more dependent upon experiencing countersocialization, less able to gain entrance into the society's elite institutions, more subject to role conflicts, more liberal in political orientation, and less active within the assemblies (although the evidence on the last proposition was mixed). The next three chapters, then, discuss each of these blocks of variables in more detail and build upon these initial hypotheses and results to evaluate how women can overcome barriers against their participation in elite politics in Taiwan.

## Notes

1. Susan J. Carroll, *Women As Candidates in American Politics* (Bloomington: Indiana University Press, 1985); and Marilyn Johnson and Susan Carroll, *Profile of Women Holding Office II* (New Brunswick, N.J.: Center for the American Woman and Politics, Rutgers University, 1978).

2. Diane L. Fowlkes, "Developing a Theory of Countersocialization: Gender, Race, and Politics in the Lives of Women Activists," *Micropolitics* 3:2 (No. 2, 1983) pp. 181–225; Diane L. Fowlkes, "Ambitious Political Women: Countersocialization and Political Party Context," *Women & Politics* 4:4 (Winter 1984) pp. 5–32; and Sue Tolleson Rinehart, "Toward Women's Political Resocialization: Patterns of Predisposition and the Learning of Feminist Attitudes," *Women & Politics* 5:4 (Winter 1985/86) pp. 11–26.

3. David C. Shack, "Socioeconomic Mobility and the Urban Poor in Taiwan," *Modern China* 15:3 (July 1989) pp. 346–373; and Charlotte Shiang-yun Wang, "Social Mobility in Taiwan," in James C. Hsiung, ed., *Contemporary Republic of China: The Taiwan Experience, 1950–1980* (New York: Praeger, 1981) pp. 246–257.

4. It would certainly be expected that party affiliation, treated here as a political resource, would also measure ideology, with KMT members being more conservative than independents. However, as will be seen in Chapter 8, party membership is almost completely uncorrelated with ideological position.

5. An "interval level" of measurement exists when the scale measures the exact difference between items. For example, a basket of 10 apples has exactly 10 fewer than a basket of 20. In contrast, the scale on which a college education is scored 4 and a high school education is scored 3 is an "ordinal" one in which higher numbers denote more of the quantity (i.e., education), but the interval between them is arbitrary. See Hubert M. Blalock, *Social Statistics*, 2nd Ed. (New York: McGraw-Hill, 1972) Chp. 2. Technically, regression and discriminant analysis can only be applied to interval data (although this requirement is often violated in social science research). Most of the variables used in our study are such "ordinal" ones. However, dichotomies are considered to represent an "interval" level of measurement.

6. Blalock, *Social Statistics*, Chp. 15, discusses measures of association for nominal data.

7. Blalock, *Social Statistics*, Chps. 8 & 15.

8. Blalock, *Social Statistics*, Chps. 17–19, provides an excellent description of correlation and regression techniques.

9. Yangsun Chou and Andrew J. Nathan, "Democratizing Transition in Taiwan," *Asian Survey* 27:3 (March 1987) pp. 280–282; Richard L. Engstrom and Chu Chi-hung, "The Impact of the 1980 Supplementary Election on Nationalist China's Legislative Yuan," *Asian Survey* 24:4 (April 1984) pp. 446–458; and Alexander Ya-li Lu, "Future Democratic Developments in the Republic of China on Taiwan," *Asian Survey* 25:11 (November 1985) pp. 1085–1092.

10. William Klecka, "Discriminant Analysis," in Norman H. Nie, C. Hadlai Hull, Jean K. Jenkins, Karin Steinbrenner, and Dale H. Bent, *SPSS: Statistical Package for the Social Sciences*, 2nd Ed. (New York: McGraw-Hill, 1975) pp. 434–467, provides an excellent introductory description of this statistical technique.

CHAPTER SEVEN

# The Roots of Participation: Selective Countersocialization

A prominent strand of theory concerning women's political participation focuses upon countersocialization experiences as the primary means for motivating women to challenge and overcome cultural barriers against their participation in the political process. In addition, many studies of women in elite political positions have found them to suffer from distinct status and resource disadvantages vis-à-vis their male counterparts. This chapter, then, begins our analysis of women legislators in the Republic of China with an exploration of several central countersocialization and disadvantaged-status factors in the social backgrounds of Taiwan legislators, both to see how well they distinguish various groups of legislators and candidates from one another and to set a foundation for modeling the impact of these socialization variables on the other factors considered in later chapters.

In particular, eight types of socialization contexts are examined here. The first three—family class and group affiliation, mother's role model, and family politicization—relate to childhood socialization. The latter five—spouse politicization, factors involved in starting a political career, socioeconomic resources, self-confidence, and role conflicts—are part of adult socialization. As will be seen, the importance of these different types of socialization factors varies widely, with adult socialization generally having the larger impact. The chapter then concludes with an analysis of how well these socialization factors differentiate between the three sets of analytic groups on which this study is centered—current male and female legislators, women legislators and losing candidates, and older- and younger-generation women.

## Childhood Socialization Background

The theory of countersocialization hypothesizes that certain experiences make women more willing to challenge the conventional norms against their political activity and, thus, more likely to seek political office.[1] This section examines this assumption with data about three types of childhood socialization factors: whether a respondent grew up in an upper-class or nontraditional family environment, whether his or her mother provided an activist role model, and whether the family was involved in politics. If the basic countersocialization hypothesis holds true, such socialization experiences should be much more important for stimulating the political careers of women than of men. Consequently, considerably more female than male politicians should have had them. The data for testing this are presented in Table 7.1, which compares the percentages of each of the four subsamples (current assemblymen, current assemblywomen, 1969 assemblywomen, and losing women assembly candidates in 1983) having particular family backgrounds.

Table 7.1 Childhood Socialization Differences Among Respondent Groups

|  | Male Legislator (%) | Female Legislator (%) | Female Loser (%) | Female 1969 Legislator (%) | V |
|---|---|---|---|---|---|
| Family Class |  |  |  |  |  |
| Father College Education | 12 | 23 | 33 | 15 | .21[a] |
| Mainlander | 5 | 10 | 23 | 30 | .26[b] |
| Traditional Family |  |  |  |  |  |
| Over 45 | 56 | 56 | 43 | 85 | .26[b] |
| Urban Life | 49 | 70 | 68 | 65 | .19[a] |
| Buddhist | 47 | 46 | 45 | 55 | .07 |
| Christian | 7 | 10 | 21 | 20 | .18[a] |
| Mother Role Model |  |  |  |  |  |
| Mother HS Education | 15 | 23 | 15 | 5 | .15 |
| Mother Political Interest | 14 | 24 | 16 | 0 | .20[a] |
| Political Family |  |  |  |  |  |
| Father Political Interest | 37 | 47 | 42 | 24 | .15 |
| Parents Held Office | 21 | 33 | 28 | 20 | .12 |
| Other Relatives Held Office | 9 | 44 | 23 | 45 | .32[b] |

[a]Statistically significant at .15 level.
[b]Statistically significant at .05 level.

Two indicators of elite status are used here. These are having a father who graduated from college and being of Mainlander descent—the first because of the centrality of education to status in Chinese society, the second because of Mainlander domination of Taiwan's politics until quite recently.[2] As hypothesized, women were significantly more likely than men to possess both types of elite characteristics. More than twice as many current assemblywomen and losing women candidates had fathers with college educations (28%) than did the assemblymen (12%). While the 1969 assemblywomen were much lower than the other female samples (15%), this probably reflects the facts that they were by far the oldest group and that the opportunity for a college education has expanded over time. Similarly, while only 5% of the current assemblymen were Mainlanders, 10% of the current assemblywomen, 23% of the losing candidates, and 30% of the 1969 assemblywomen came from Mainlander families. These figures also indicate the general disadvantage that Mainlanders face at the polls and their much greater dominance in the National Assembly and Legislative Yuan before the supplementary elections began. Thus, elite family background appears more important for women than for men in the ROC, as predicted. On the other hand, more than two-thirds of the women came from nonelite backgrounds on both measures, showing that neither was a prerequisite for political success. In addition, the correlation coefficients were only moderate (.21 and .26 respectively), indicating that stark differences between the sexes did not exist on these variables.

The evidence concerning traditional family backgrounds is more mixed, however. One would expect that respondents from the older generation, rural backgrounds, and the Buddhist religion would be more traditional, while Christians would be less traditional. Buddhism was unrelated to gender, and there was little real generational difference. The 1969 assemblywomen were understandably the oldest group and the 1983 losing candidates the youngest, but current assemblywomen and men had the same average age. On the other hand, women were more likely than men to have spent most of their life in urban areas (68% to 49%) and to be Christians (16% to 7%). Still, the correlations for these two relationships were fairly low (just under .20); in particular, Christianity was far less related to women's office-seeking than has been shown in Korea, where it has been credited with breaking down cultural restraints against women's entering public life.[3]

Perhaps most surprising is the absence of a significant relationship between gender and mother's role model as measured by having a mother who was interested in politics or had graduated from high school (the percentage of mothers graduating from college was too minuscule to use). Female legislators did have somewhat more active mothers in terms of these two dimensions than did their male colleagues (24% to 15%), but the other two groups of women did not. Thus, mother's role model, which is usually assumed to provide a major force for countersocialization, was clearly limited as a childhood socialization factor.

The indicators of family political involvement suggest a more complex picture than simply support for or disconfirmation of the countersocialization theory. For the two other indicators of politicization in the nuclear family (besides mother's political interest)—father's political interest and parents' having held a political office—the same pattern is repeated. Women were slightly more likely to come from politically involved families, but the relationship was not large enough to be really significant. In addition, for the whole sample, more than twice as many fathers (40%) as mothers (15%) were interested in politics, betokening a substantial gender gap. However, the conclusion that family political involvement did not provide countersocialization is clearly unwarranted, because a substantial difference existed between the sexes in terms of having other relatives who had served in an official position. About 45% of current and 1969 women legislators and 23% of losing women candidates came from such families, in contrast to less than 10% of the assemblymen, producing a V of .32. Thus, while political involvement by the nuclear family may not have been sufficient to engender new participatory norms in women, being part of politically active extended families clearly was a significant countersocialization experience.

These findings concerning family politicization are confirmed by more complex multiple regression analysis reported in Table 7.2, which explains the four family involvement items by gender and by the family background items (in addition, mother's education and father's political interest were added to the regression for mother's political interest). As explained in more detail in Chapter 6, the Multiple R measures the combined impact of the independent variables; the regression coefficients (the $b$'s) estimate the independent influence of each predictor variable. In the special type of analysis used here, the $b$'s can be interpreted as the increased or decreased probability that a respondent will have the trait denoted by the dependent variable given that the person possesses the characteristic tapped by the independent variable. Unlike the sample regressions in Table 6.4, though, with the exception of gender, only independent variables that are statistically significant at the .15 level are included in the final analyses.

Table 7.2   Regression Explanations of Family Politicization

|  | Mother Political Interest | Father Political Interest | Parents Held Office | Other Relatives Held Office |
|---|---|---|---|---|
| Multiple R | .65[b] | .35[b] | .44[b] | .38[b] |
| *Regression Coefficients* | | | | |
| Female | .01 | -.01 | .01 | .32[b] |
| Father College Education | .12[a] | .41[b] | .47[b] | — |
| Mainlander | -.15[b] | — | — | -.21[b] |
| Mother HS Education | .31[b] | — | — | — |
| Father Political Interest | .28[b] | — | — | — |
| Urban Life | — | — | — | -.18[b] |

[a]Statistically significant at .15 level.
[b]Statistically significant at .05 level.

The results in Table 7.2 show an even starker difference between politicization in nuclear and extended families than appeared in the cross-tabulations in Table 7.1. Gender itself is completely unrelated to the three items concerning the nuclear family. Father's political interest and parents' office-holding were primarily a function of father's education, indicating social class had a constraining effect on becoming involved in politics a generation ago in Taiwan. A mother's political interest was almost equally influenced by her own educational achievement ($b = .31$) and having a husband interested in politics (.28). In addition, there was a marginal tendency for Islanders and for those with higher social class to be the more politically active women of the previous generation.

In contrast, gender had the strongest impact on whether a respondent came from a politically involved extended family—women were 32% more likely to do so than men. Thus, it is clear that while a politically active nuclear family was not enough to generate countersocialization, the existence of a politicized extended family did indeed make women more likely to go into politics. In addition, political office-holding by other relatives was also more likely among Islanders ($b = -.21$) and rural residents ($b = -.18$). In conjunction with similar findings in the next section concerning adult socialization, this suggests that while the image of politics in Taiwan generally focuses on Mainlander-dominated national-level events, there is also a vibrant local politics with traditional rural roots that can serve as the base for political careers.[4]

The ability of these childhood experiences to produce countersocialization, therefore, is clearly discernible but far from universal. In particular, coming from an elite family, having a politically involved extended family, and having some nontraditional characteristics seemingly led to significant countersocialization for women in Taiwan. On the other hand, the expected impact of mother's role model was completely absent, and politically active families were unable by themselves to stimulate above-average political participation among their daughters. Still, in the aggregate, these findings seem strong enough to reject the gender-neutral model and to conclude that countersocialization has played a significant role in the political activation of women in Taiwan.

## Adult Socialization

This section examines five aspects of adult socialization—the political involvement and support of a respondent's spouse, the role of the family (as opposed to political factors) in stimulating a legislator's career, the person's socioeconomic achievements and resources, his or her self-confidence, and the role conflicts a politician faces. The first two of these factors should be subject to the countersocialization hypothesis. That is, having an active and supportive spouse and family should provide countersocialization. Thus, women politicians should be much more likely than their male counterparts to come from such a currently politicized family, and family factors should be more important in stimulating the political careers of women than of men. The explanatory logic for the other three is more ambiguous, though. On the one hand, the possession of socioeconomic resources and strong self-confidence and the avoidance of role conflicts can provide countersocialization, implying that women should score higher than men. On the other hand, all these dimensions could also reflect a continuing disadvantage for most women politicians, implying that men should rank higher on them in terms of the disadvantaged-status theory.

The cross-tabulations testing these hypotheses are summarized in Table 7.3. Women politicians in Taiwan clearly had more politically involved adult families than their male counterparts. While almost no assemblymen had spouses or in-laws who had served in official capacities, about a quarter of the women were married to political activists and about a tenth had in-laws who had held some office. Spouse support was also much more important for the activation of women's than men's political careers. At their entrance into politics, women were more than twice as likely than men to have spouses interested in politics (62% to 28%) and considerably more likely to have spouses who encouraged them to run for office (64% to 46%), although these differences narrowed to insignificance with the passage of time.

This conclusion is confirmed by regressions for the three key variables concerning spouse influence on political career (see Table 7.4). Even after other relevant explanatory factors are statistically controlled, women were considerably more likely than men to have had an activist and supportive spouse—24% for a spouse holding office, 35% for a spouse being intitially interested in politics, and 13% for a spouse encouraging their political career. Gender, in fact, was the most important independent variable for the first two items. Thus, the countersocialization perspective receives strong support from these data, supporting Virginia Sapiro's argument about the importance of adult socialization.[5]

The influence of the other independent variables produced some interesting results too. The socialization impact of having an extended family active in politics is strongly indicated by the fact that other relatives having held official positions had a significant impact on all three items concerning spouse politicization (which also indicates that "other relatives" can refer to the spouse's as well as the respondent's family). Islander political activism was again indicated, since Islander spouses were considerably more likely than Mainlander ones to be interested in politics and supportive of the respondent's political career when it began. In addition, younger politicians were more likely to have politically interested spouses when their careers began, perhaps in response to the gradual liberalization of Taiwan's politics over time. Spouses also were more likely to encourage political careers in urban than in rural settings. While this finding is consistent with modernization theory, it is a little surprising in the Taiwan context, given the greater prevalence of political involvement by extended families in rural areas that was discussed in the last section. Finally and also surprisingly, something of a negative relationship existed between childhood and family politicization: Having politically active parents and a father with a college education were negatively related, respectively, to spouse office-holding and political interest. That is, even among people who later developed political careers, children from politicized families seemed more repelled by than attracted to politically connected mates.

Table 7.3 Adult Socialization Differences Among Respondent Groups

|  | Male Legislator (%) | Female Legislator (%) | Female Loser (%) | Female 1969 Legislator (%) | V |
|---|---|---|---|---|---|
| *Political Family* | | | | | |
| Spouse Held Office | 2 | 26 | 17 | 40 | .32[a] |
| In-laws Held Office | 0 | 10 | 9 | 10 | .17 |
| *Spouse Political Support* | | | | | |
| Initial Interest in Political Career | 28 | 56 | 61 | 71 | .31[a] |
| Initial Encouragement for Political Career | 46 | 64 | 64 | 61 | .16 |
| Now Interested | 56 | 61 | 63 | 68 | .08 |
| Now Supports | 67 | 64 | 70 | 60 | .07 |
| *Political Activation* | | | | | |
| Family 1st Interest | 9 | 49 | 38 | 40 | .33[a] |
| Political 1st Interest | 67 | 51 | 72 | 65 | .17 |
| Family Stimulated Running | 37 | 64 | 57 | 85 | .30[a] |
| Party & Interest Group Stimulated Running | 58 | 59 | 47 | 50 | .11 |
| Issues Stimulated Running | 33 | 26 | 49 | 20 | .23[b] |
| Own Competence Stimulated Running | 30 | 39 | 45 | 45 | .13 |
| *Socioeconomic Resources* | | | | | |
| College Education | 84 | 82 | 66 | 70 | .19[b] |
| Elite University | 26 | 8 | 4 | 5 | .29[a] |
| Professional Occupation | 75 | 59 | 68 | 75 | .14 |
| Family Income $15,000 | 93 | 95 | 71 | 79 | .29[a] |
| *Self-Confidence* | | | | | |
| Qualifications Above Ave | 72 | 67 | 59 | 85 | .07 |
| Time on Job Above Ave | 86 | 96 | 94 | 100 | .19[b] |
| Personality Above Ave | 83 | 88 | 89 | 89 | .16 |
| *Role Conflicts* | | | | | |
| Married | 95 | 85 | 83 | 80 | .17 |
| Over 3 Children | 76 | 65 | 60 | 90 | .22[b] |
| Child Under 6 | 42 | 23 | 38 | 10 | .24[a] |
| Over 10 Hrs Outside Work | 37 | 28 | 74 | 50 | .38[a] |
| Gets Hshld Help | 86 | 82 | 62 | 90 | .27[a] |
| Hires Hshld Help | 28 | 46 | 26 | 60 | .26[a] |
| Family Obligations Hurt Office | 0 | 39 | 29 | 35 | .42[a] |
| Over 25 1st Interest | 58 | 45 | 41 | 55 | .14 |
| Over 35 1st Ran | 56 | 44 | 47 | 60 | .12 |

[a]Statistically significant at .05 level.
[b]Statistically significant at .15 level.

Table 7.4  Regression Explanations of Spouse Politicization

|  | Spouse Active in Politics | Spouse Interested in Politics When Career Began | Spouse Encouraged Political Career at Beginning |
|---|---|---|---|
| Multiple R | .40[a] | .46[a] | .38[a] |
| *Regression Coefficients* | | | |
| Female | .24[a] | .35[a] | .13[b] |
| Other Relatives Held Office | .14[b] | .14[b] | .21[a] |
| Mainlander | — | -.17[b] | -.24[a] |
| Parents Politically Active | -.23[a] | — | — |
| Father College Education | — | -.23[a] | — |
| Over 45 | — | -.20[a] | — |
| Urban Life | — | — | .19[a] |

[a]Statistically significant at .05 level.
[b]Statistically significant at .15 level.

The finding that women politicians in Taiwan were much more likely to come from politically involved families than were their male counterparts implies that family-related factors should be more important in activating women's political careers. This hypothesis is tested by data from two questions that asked why a respondent first became interested in politics and what groups or people helped persuade her or him to first run for office. Answers to the first were grouped under two categories—family-related reasons (e.g., political activities by various family members or conversations with family and friends) or politically related ones (e.g., interest in issues, candidates, or parties, interest in a public service career, or experiences abroad). Responses to the second question were grouped into four categories—family and friends, party and interest group leaders, issue concerns, and belief in one's own competence and qualifications. Both these questions allowed for multiple answers, permitting a respondent to be included in several, if not all, of the categories for each of these items (e.g., have had both family and political reasons for becoming interested in politics).

As expected, family-related matters were much more important in launching the political careers of women than of men in Taiwan (Table 7.3). Women were over four times more likely than men to cite family-related reasons for becoming interested in politics (42% versus 9%) and were considerably more likely to credit family and friends with stimulating their desire to run (85% for the 1969 assemblywomen and 60% for the contemporary assemblywomen and losing candidates, as opposed to 37% of the assemblymen). In contrast, there was almost no significant difference between men and women in the impact of more politically oriented factors upon their political activation. Women politicians in the ROC, therefore, evidently need the countersocialization of a supportive family environment to pursue a political career. Those women who do enter the electoral arena, though, appear to be no less politically concerned or connected than similar men, in contrast to the predictions of the disadvantaged-status thesis.

Representative regression analyses for the political activation items are reported in Table 7.5. All four of these variables—family-related first political interest, politically related first political interest, party or interest group stimulation to run for office, and stimulation to run because of issue concerns—turn out to be moderately conditioned by the socialization environment, as indicated by Multiple R's ranging between .3 and .5. They confirm that women were more likely than men to embark on political careers for family-related reasons, but that the sexes did not differ in the degree of political influences. Thus, even after the other relevant independent variables were controlled, women were 22% more likely than men to attribute their initial political interest to family or friends, but gender was completely unrelated to the other three dependent variables. In terms of socioeconomic effects, those with higher incomes, professional occupations, and affiliation with Christian churches were in general more likely to have become involved in politics for political reasons. However, politicians from families with incomes under $15,000 were more likely to stress issue concerns than were their wealthier colleagues, suggesting the possibility of a nascent "class consciousness" that most observers of Taiwan's political scene have yet to discern.

Table 7.5  Regression Explanations of Political Activation

|  | First Interest | | Stimulation to Run | |
|---|---|---|---|---|
|  | Family-Related | Politically-Related | Party/Interest Group | Issues |
| Multiple R | .47[a] | .31[a] | .44[a] | .43[a] |
| *Regression Coefficients* | | | | |
| Female | .22[a] | .01 | -.05 | -.04 |
| Over 45 | -.17[a] | — | — | -.29[a] |
| Mother Political Interest | .19[b] | — | — | .14[b] |
| Other Relatives Active | .15[b] | — | .30[a] | — |
| Spouse Active | .21[a] | — | — | — |
| Spouse Initially Encouraged | — | -.23[a] | -.30[a] | — |
| Professional Occupation | — | .22[a] | .19[a] | — |
| Family Income $15,000 | — | — | .17[a] | -.25[a] |
| Christian | — | — | — | .20[a] |

[a]Statistically significant at .05 level.
[b]Statistically significant at .15 level.

The results in Table 7.5 on the impact of family-related independent variables are quite interesting. For the most part, having a politically active family stimulated family-related influences and inhibited politically related ones, as might well have been expected. There were two major exceptions to this pattern, though. While having other relatives active in politics and the role model of a politically interested mother increased the probability of becoming interested in politics for family reasons, these factors were also associated with being stimulated to run for office by, respectively, party and interest group leaders and by the respondent's own issue concerns. While mother's role model had surprisingly little childhood socialization effects, therefore, it seems to be more important in adult socialization. In addition, coming from an extended political family evidently helped integrate a new candidate into existing party and interest group networks. Thus, family ties and political ties in Taiwan are not necessarily antithetical, but can interact to provide a firm foundation for engaging in local politics.

The data on socioeconomic resources and self-confidence in Table 7.3 provide support for both the countersocialization and disadvantaged-status perspectives. As the former predicts, women politicians in Taiwan (as well as their male counterparts) rank quite high in terms of socioeconomic status. For example, among current assemblymen and assemblywomen, over 80% had college educations and over 90% had family incomes of over $15,000, with the other two groups being only slightly lower (67% had a college education and 74% had family incomes of at least $15,000). In addition, 75% of the assemblymen and 59% of the assemblywomen were in professional occupations, with the other two groups approximating the higher figure. Thus, as confirmed by multiple regression results not presented here, these women politicians had high socioeconomic status that was only slightly (and insignificant statistically) behind their male colleagues. Presumably as a result, they also exhibited strong self-confidence that differed little from that of assemblymen. For example, in the entire sample, 68% believed their personal qualifications to be above-average, 87% felt their personalities were above average, and 94% said that they devoted an above-average amount of time to their job. Given the stereotype of women's submissiveness in Chinese society,[6] these results are little short of astonishing.

These data have another positive implication as well. Obviously, substantial upward socioeconomic mobility had occurred among these politicians—three-quarters of them had college degrees, compared with a fifth of their fathers. Moreover, regression analysis not presented in these tables showed that father's education and social origin, the two indicators of class advantage, had no impact whatsoever on college education or occupation and income, again indicating substantial intergenerational mobility. While results from a group of elite politicians certainly cannot be generalized to the whole society, other studies have found that substantial opportunities exist for upward mobility in Taiwan even for the poorest segments of society.[7] Given this flux, considerable opportunities should exist for women in both the political and professional spheres, at least in theory.

However, the data on socioeconomic resources also indicate two important practical limitations on these theoretical opportunities for women's mobility. First, the extremely elite nature of politicians in the ROC means that women's disadvantage in the eligibility pool (those with administrative and professional occupations, as discussed in Chapter 4) constitutes a daunting constraint on breaking into politics. Second, while there was little difference in college attendance between men and women, the same could not be said for access to the elite universities (National Taiwan or National Chengchi) where lasting political and professional ties are made among the fastest-rising stars in Taiwan's politics—men were almost five times as likely (26% to 6%) to have attended one of them. Thus, evidence of women's disadvantaged status in Taiwan's politics can certainly be adduced.

The final set of adult socialization variables (Table 7.3) concerns role conflicts. Here the theoretical expectations are contradictory. Countersocialization theory would predict that female politicians would have fewer role conflicts than males because their absence would help provide the countersocialization needed to stimulate a woman's political career. In contrast, the disadvantaged-status perspective would anticipate women legislators to have more role conflicts than men, thus sapping the time and effort that they can devote to their political careers. At first blush, the data on objective indicators of role conflict seem to support the countersocialization hypothesis: Women were less likely than men to be married, to have over three children, to have paid household help, and (for current holders of assembly seats) to have children under six and to work more than ten hours a week at outside jobs.

However, further consideration raises questions about most of these differences. First, almost all the respondents were married; given the importance of family support for women's political careers that emerged in the preceding analysis, it is hard to argue that the absence of a family is a political advantage for women. Second, multiple regression analysis not presented here showed that the two variables involving children were almost entirely a function of age. That is, older parents had more children because of the demographic shift to smaller families in Taiwan. Of course, younger parents would be expected to have younger children (although the much lower proportion of assemblywomen than losing candidates having young children, 23% to 38%, suggests that role conflicts may cause problems in the campaigns of female candidates). Third, there was little difference between the sexes (except for the 1983 losing candidates) in their nearly universal reporting of getting extra help with household work from relatives or hired help.

Furthermore, unlike in many other countries (e.g., the United States) where role conflicts delay women's entry into political careers, there was almost no difference between male and female politicians in the ROC in terms of their age when they had their initial political interest or first experience on the hustings. The multiple regression results confirm that men and women entered politics at almost the same age (Table 7.6). In fact, there was even a slight tendency for women to become interested in politics earlier than men—women were 11% less likely than men to have become first interested in politics after they became 25. Another interesting result is that mother's political interest had the greatest impact on the factor of age at time of first political interest, with the role model of a politically interested mother promoting involvement at a younger age.

The regressions reported in Table 7.6 for two central objective indicators of role conflict—working more than ten hours a week outside the home and hiring household help—also found no difference between men and women, but a closer examination suggests at least a little support for the countersocialization approach. The regression for working (other than in politics) includes only active legislators, since others would obviously not face a conflict between their occupational and political careers. Substantial outside work is most common for those with professional jobs ($b = .39$), and younger people also work longer hours ($b = -.19$). One of the measures of spouse support (spouse initially encouraged political career), though, has a significant negative impact (b = -.21), indicating that a supportive family is less demanding about sacrificing political commitments for earning power. Since women were about 20% more likely to have such supportive spouses, this suggests an indirect countersocialization effect. Likewise, the most important determinant of hiring household help was having an office-holding spouse ($b = .30$). Since almost no men fell into this category, this again implies special support for assemblywomen, this time regarding the conflict between family and political duties.

In sharp contrast, though, a subjective measure of role conflict—the

Table 7.6 Regression Explanations of Role Conflicts

|  | Over 25 First Political Interest | Work Outside Over 10 Hours Per Week[a] | Hired Household Help | Family Obligations Hurt Political Career |
|---|---|---|---|---|
| Multiple R | .43[b] | .48[b] | .40[b] | .50[b] |
| *Regression Coefficients* | | | | |
| Female | -.11[c] | .01 | .05 | .34[b] |
| Over 45 | .21[b] | -.19[b] | .15[b] | — |
| Christian | .17[c] | — | .25[b] | — |
| Income of $15,000 | .13[c] | — | .19[b] | — |
| Mother Political Interest | -.25[b] | — | — | — |
| Buddhist | .15[c] | — | — | — |
| Professional Occupation | — | .39[b] | — | — |
| Spouse Intially Encouraged Political Career | — | -.21[b] | — | — |
| Spouse Politically Active | — | — | .30[b] | — |
| In-laws Politically Active | — | — | — | .47[b] |

[a]Only current legislators included in analysis.
[b]Statistically significant at .05 level.
[c]Statistically significant at .15 level.

belief that family obligations detract from the performance of one's official duties—presents a completely different picture. A third of the women held this view, in contrast to none of the men. The multiple regression for this item in Table 7.6, furthermore, shows that gender has a major independent impact on this belief (women were 34% more likely than men to hold it) and that such role strains are exacerbated by having the extended family involved in politics ($b = .47$). Thus, despite the relatively limited differences in objective indicators of role conflicts, conflicts between family and political career appear to be considerable for women in Taiwan politics. Two reasons may be adduced for this difference between the objective and subjective indicators. First, role conflicts were limited by the fact that women politicians came from elite backgrounds that enabled them, for example, to hire household help. Second, the sharing of household and child-care duties was presumably far from equal—women politicians no doubt had to devote far more time than their male colleagues to family duties.

Adult socialization, therefore, appears quite significant for women's political careers in Taiwan, although specific factors follow the different logics of the countersocialization and disadvantaged-status hypotheses. Countersocialization could clearly be seen in the effects that a politically active and supportive family had on women's careers and in the large amount of socioeconomic resources upon which most of these women could draw. This is similar to the situation in the United States, incidentally, since family support has been found to help women's political careers even in an advanced industrial society.[8] The existence of significant countersocialization is also implied by the absence of the expected differences in objective indicators of role conflict between the sexes and by the fact that women's entries into politics were as politically motivated as men's. In contrast, women's disadvantaged status was also apparent in their general exclusion from elite universities and in their much greater perceptions of role conflicts between family and political obligations.

## Socialization Differences Between Analytic Groups

A major test of the importance of these childhood and adult socialization factors is their ability to discriminate between the three sets of analytic groups on which our study is oriented: assemblywomen compared with assemblymen, assemblywomen compared with losing 1983 candidates, and old-generation compared with new-generation women. Socialization theory would predict that women legislators should experience more countersocialization and status disadvantage than their male colleagues. Similarly, one might apply these premises to differentiating successful and unsuccessful candidates by hypothesizing that winners should have greater countersocialization to make them more aggressive and more socioeconomic resources and fewer role conflicts to spur their campaigns. Finally, assuming that modernization in Taiwan has lowered the barriers to women's entrance into public life over time, it would be expected that older women would have had to experience more countersocialization to overcome greater cultural obstacles and that younger women would possess more socioeconomic resources.

The three discriminant analyses testing these hypotheses are presented in Tables 7.7 to 7.9. Only the socialization variables that had a statistically significant discriminating effect are included in the final equations. There are three basic results contained in these tables: (1) the canonical correlation, which shows how well the variables in combination discriminate between the two groups; (2) the group centroid, which shows which group scores positively and which negatively on the discriminant function; and (3) the standardized discriminant coefficient, which measures each variable's independent contribution to the discriminant function (see Chapter 6 for a more detailed discussion of this technique).

The results in the discriminant analysis for female versus male current legislators in Table 7.7 are quite striking. The canonical correlation is a very high .76, indicating that assemblymen and assemblywomen had quite divergent socialization experiences. Both countersocialization and disadvantaged-status factors proved to be quite important. In terms of the latter, women were much more likely to feel role conflicts between their family and political lives ($dc = .72$) and less likely to have attended an elite university ($dc = -.39$). They also were much more likely to have experienced the countersocialization of a supportive family environment. Thus, women were much more likely to have become interested in politics for family-related reasons ($dc = .58$) and somewhat more likely to have a spouse who had held an official post ($dc = .35$). Also, as modernization theory would suggest, women politicians tended to live in an urban environment ($dc = .44$). In addition, assemblywomen were significantly less likely to have young children ($dc = -.39$). Thus, while Taiwan differs from the U.S. pattern of women legislators being older than their male colleagues because they postpone political careers to avoid family role conflicts,[9] this certainly suggests that having young children is a significant role conflict that inhibits women's public activism.

The hypotheses about differences between assemblywomen and losing candidates were generally supported as well (see Table 7.8). The canonical correlation is a moderate .48, indicating that the differences between the socialization experiences were significant but not as great as those between assemblymen and assemblywomen. As predicted, assemblywomen had greater resources, as indicated by college education ($dc = .65$), and fewer role conflicts, as indicated by hiring household help ($dc = .36$). assemblywomen also had a much greater propensity to have other relatives active in politics ($dc = .49$), presumably reflecting both countersocialization from politicized families and access to broader political networks. Likewise, successful women candidates were much less likely to be Christians ($dc =$

-.33), who cannot benefit from the politically important religious networks in Taiwan's local politics.[10] Finally, women whose campaigns were stimulated by issue concerns were much less successful than those that lacked such motivation ($dc = -.57$), again indicating the traditional nature of politics in Taiwan. Thus, as might well have been expected, resource factors were much more important than countersocialization ones in differentiating successful and unsuccessful legislative aspirants among women.

Table 7.7 Discriminant Analysis for Women Versus Men Legislators

| | |
|---|---|
| *Canonical Correlation* | .76 |
| *Group Centroids* | |
| Assemblywomen | 1.19 |
| Assemblymen | -1.13 |
| *Discriminant Function Coefficients* | |
| Family Obligations Hurt Legisslative Duties | .72 |
| Family-Related 1st Political Interest | .58 |
| Urban Life | .44 |
| Elite University | -.39 |
| Child Under 6 | -.39 |
| Spouse Politically Active | .35 |

*Note:* Canonical correlation is significant at the .0001 level. Statistical significance of individual discriminant function coefficients cannot be computed, but all entered the discriminant equation at the .05 level.

Table 7.8 Discriminant Analysis for Women Winners Versus Losers

| | |
|---|---|
| *Canonical Correlation* | .48 |
| *Group Centroids* | |
| Assemblywomen | .57 |
| Losing Candidates | -.52 |
| *Discriminant Function Coefficients* | |
| College Education | .65 |
| Issues Stimulated Running | -.57 |
| Other Relatives Active | .49 |
| Hired Household Help | .36 |
| Christian | -.33 |

*Note:* Canonical correlation is significant at the .002 level. Statistical significance of individual discriminant function coefficients cannot be computed, but all entered the discriminant equation at the .05 level.

Table 7.9 examines the generational differences in socialization among female politicians. While there is scant support for the original hypothesis that older women would experience more countersocialization and have less socioeconomic resources (in fact, they were more likely to hire household help), a substantial and politically important difference emerges between older and younger women (canonical correlation = .65): Younger women appear to be more self-motivated in entering politics, as opposed to the more co-opted pattern of older ones. Thus, women politicians under age 45 were much more likely to have become interested in politics for political reasons ($dc = -.68$), to have run for office because of interest in issues ($dc = -.57$), to have first run at a younger age ($dc = .45$), and to have been encouraged to enter politics by their husbands ($dc = -.40$) These findings, therefore, do support the supposition that over time the modernization processes in Taiwan have reduced cultural barriers to women's participation in politics and made women more activist. Thus, just as in the United States, the traditional gender gap in the recruitment patterns of male and female political leaders seems to be narrowing.[11] However, as the results of the previous discriminant analysis of women winners and losers showed, the continuing traditional nature of electoral politics in Taiwan places the younger, more politically oriented female candidates at something of a disadvantage.

Table 7.9 Discriminant Analysis for Old- Versus New-Generation Women

| Canonical Correlation | .65 |
|---|---|
| *Group Centroids* | |
| Over 45 | .71 |
| Under 45 | -1.02 |
| *Discriminant Function Coefficients* | |
| Politically-Related 1st Political Interest | -.68 |
| Issues Stimulated Running | -.57 |
| Over 35 1st Ran | .45 |
| Hired Household Help | .40 |
| Spouse Initially Encouraged Political Career | -.40 |
| College Education | -.43 |

*Note:* Canonical correlation is significant at the .002 level. Statistical significance of individual discriminant function coefficients cannot be computed, but all entered the discriminant equation at the .05 level.

## Implications

This chapter has analyzed the socialization processes that have helped shape the perspectives of politicians in Taiwan. The theory of countersocialization posits that if women are to become involved in politics, most of them must have unusual socialization experiences in order to surmount cultural norms against their participation in the public sphere. Our findings certainly indicate that this theoretical perspective can be applied to Taiwan. However, the countersocialization processes that operate there must be considered "selective" for several reasons. First, particularly in regard to childhood socialization, some factors (e.g., elite or nontraditional family status and belonging to an extended family that is highly involved in politics) were important, but other factors that are normally considered to provide counter-socialization (e.g., a politicized nuclear family and especially a positive maternal role model) turned out to be insignificant. Second, in regard to adult socialization, countersocialization could be observed in the effects of family politicization and the possession of socioeconomic resources, but the disadvantaged-status perspective applied as well to role conflicts and entrance to elite universities. Moreover, mother's political role model appeared important for adult but not childhood socialization when, if anything, the reverse should have been expected. Third, adult socialization in general appeared to be more effective than childhood experiences. Finally, the expected status and resource disadvantage of women politicians did not emerge in certain areas (i.e., objective indications of role conflicts and entering politics for political reasons), but this can be explained by the culture's barriers to women's participation in public life that limit women candidates to a narrow social elite.

More theoretically, different explanatory patterns existed in each of the three basic comparisons between different types of politicians. Assemblymen and assemblywomen differed greatly in terms of exposure to countersocialization and to role conflicts; access to socioeconomic resources (including existing political networks) formed the prime distinction between successful and unsuccessful women candidates; and the processes of modernization and secularization created significant divisions between younger and older women, particularly in the more self-activating nature of the former's political careers. Thus, socialization factors are important for women politicians in Taiwan, but they operate in a fairly varied and selective manner.

## Notes

1. Diane L. Fowlkes, "Developing a Theory of Countersocialization: Gender, Race, and Politics in the Lives of Women Activists," *Micropolitics* 3:2 (No. 2, 1983) pp. 181–225.
2. Hill Gates, "Ethnicity and Social Class," in Emily Martin Ahern and Hill Gates, eds., *The Anthropology of Taiwanese Society* (Stanford, Calif.: Stanford University Press, 1981) pp. 241–281.
3. R. Darcy and Sunhee Song, "Women and Korean Politics: Political Access and Role Conflict," paper presented at the Annual Meeting of the International Society of Political Psychology, University College, Toronto, June 24–27, 1984.
4. Ahern and Gates, *The Anthropology of Taiwanese Society*; J. Bruce Jacobs, "A Preliminary Model of Particularistic Ties in Chinese Political Alliances: *Kan-ch'ing* and *Kuan-hsi* in a Rural Taiwanese Township," *China Quarterly* 78 (June 1979) pp. 237–273; and Arthur J. Lerman, *Taiwan's Politics: The Provincial Assemblyman's World* (Washington, D.C.: University Press of America, 1978).
5. Virginia Sapiro, *The Political Integration of Women: Roles, Socialization, and Politics* (Urbana: University of Illinois Press, 1983).
6. Margery Wolf and Roxane Witke, "Introduction," in Margery Wolf and Roxanne Witke, eds., *Women in Chinese Society* (Stanford, Calif.: Stanford University Press, 1975) pp. 1–11.
7. David C. Shack, "Socioeconomic Mobility and the Urban Poor in Taiwan,"

*Modern China* 15:3 (July 1989) pp. 346–373; and Charlotte Shiang-yun Wang, "Social Mobility in Taiwan," in James C. Hsiung, ed., *Contemporary Republic of China: The Taiwan Experience, 1950–1980* (New York: Praeger, 1981) pp. 246–257.

8. Susan J. Carroll, "The Personal Is Political: The Intersection of Private Lives and Public Roles Among Women and Men in Elective and Appointive Office," *Women & Politics* 9:2 (Summer 1989) p. 57.

9. Robert A. Bernstein, "Why Are So Few Women in the House," *Western Political Quarterly* 39:1 (March 1986) p. 159; and Jeane Kirkpatrick, *Political Women* (New York: Basic Books, 1974) p. 55.

10. Lerman, *Taiwan's Politics*, Chp. 5.

11. Denise L. Baer and John Jackson, "Are Women Really More 'Amateur' in Politics Than Men?" *Women & Politics* 5:2 (Summer 1985) pp. 79–92; and Joan Hulse Thompson, "Career Consequences: Election of Women and Men to the House of Representatives, 1916–1975," *Women & Politics* 5:1 (Spring 1985) pp. 69–90.

CHAPTER EIGHT

# Political Characteristics: Similar Resources but Significant Gender Discrimination

Legislative behavior, of course, should be strongly influenced by the political characteristics and attitudes of assemblywomen and assemblymen. This chapter, therefore, examines two primary types of political characteristics. The first concerns the political resources legislators or candidates possess: their affiliation or nonaffiliation with the dominant Nationalist (Kuomintang) Party, their previous political experience, and their relationship to organized groups in Taiwan's society. The second focuses upon several key political orientations of the respondents: their political liberalism, their perceptions of discrimination against women in electoral politics, and their views concerning the role of women in Taiwan's politics.

A priori, the theoretical discussion in Chapter 2 would predict that women would have far less political resources than their male colleagues and would be much more sensitive to gender discrimination and to their own contributions to political life in the Republic of China. However, the empirical results from the preceding chapter suggest that these hypotheses might have to be modified. The examination of the social environment from which Taiwan legislators come found that the careers of women politicians were stimulated by selective countersocialization experiences. The hypothesized status and resource disadvantage of women, however, turned out to be much less pronounced than anticipated, in large part because a key component of countersocialization was that almost all women legislators and candidates were part of a narrow social elite in the ROC.

The social environment should obviously have a considerable impact upon the political characteristics of leaders, though this should not affect the hypothesis about political orientations. If anything, the expected attitudinal differences should be reinforced because selective countersocialization should make women politicians especially assertive and self-confident. The impact upon women's presumed access to political resources is more ambiguous, though. On the one hand, differences in political resources might be less than anticipated given the elite nature of women politicians. On the other hand, many assemblywomen may have been co-opted into the political arena to compete for legislative seats that had to be filled by members of their sex. This implies that such female legislators might be viewed as second-class citizens among the political elites and, thus, might be given proportionately far less political resources in comparison to their fairly equal social background ones. An examination of these items, then, should produce a good comparative test of the countersocialization and disadvantaged-status models.

## Political Resources

The possession of political resources is a key to a politician's success. Thus, we would expect those who rank higher on these items to have a better chance of winning elections and to be more active and successful in Taiwan's assemblies. Three types of political resources are examined here: membership in the dominant KMT party, previous political experience, and ties with organized groups. Table 8.1 presents the percentages of assemblymen, assemblywomen, losing female candidates, and 1969 assemblywomen possessing each of these resources.

Table 8.1  Political Resource Differences Among Respondent Groups

|  | Male Legislator (%) | Female Legislator (%) | Female Loser (%) | Female 1969 Legislator (%) | V |
|---|---|---|---|---|---|
| *Party* | | | | | |
| KMT | 79 | 77 | 51 | 85 | .29[a] |
| *Substantial Political Experience* | | | | | |
| Electoral | 77 | 77 | 4 | 65 | .66[a] |
| Appointive | 16 | 10 | 0 | 0 | .27[a] |
| Party | 42 | 33 | 11 | 45 | .30[a] |
| *Member in Group* | | | | | |
| Political | 42 | 77 | 47 | 80 | .33[a] |
| Religious | 49 | 44 | 37 | 45 | .10 |
| Civic | 56 | 54 | 38 | 35 | .18 |
| Professional | 35 | 28 | 15 | 30 | .18 |
| Leisure | 30 | 23 | 21 | 30 | .09 |
| Two or More Types | 63 | 72 | 51 | 60 | .16 |
| *Group Helped Campaign* | | | | | |
| Political | 16 | 41 | 13 | 30 | .28[a] |
| Religious | 37 | 21 | 13 | 5 | .28[a] |
| Civic | 21 | 8 | 11 | 5 | .18 |
| Professional | 19 | 18 | 9 | 20 | .13 |
| Leisure | 5 | 15 | 6 | 5 | .16 |

[a]Statistically significant at .05 level.

Membership in the KMT, which won 70% of the vote during the early and mid-1980s and had overwhelming majorities in all the assemblies, is obviously a political plus. The expected relationship between KMT membership and gender is somewhat ambiguous: On the one hand, less in the mainstream, groups such as aspiring women politicians, should be attracted to the more liberal opposition groups; on the other, the Nationalists might be expected to be more aggressive in recruiting women to run for the reserved seats because of their "machine's" ability to support full slates of candidates. These contrasting logics result in there being little association between gender and party affiliation. Slightly over three-quarters of assemblymen and assemblywomen, both current and past, belonged to the KMT, in contrast to just half the losing women candidates. Thus, party appears related to electoral success, as would certainly be expected, but not to gender per se.

This conclusion is supported by the regression results in Table 8.2 that explain party affiliation by the respondents' socioeconomic and socialization characteristics. There is a slight tendency for women not to belong to the Kuomintang (11%). However, this is a misleading result of the fact that the only losing candidates in the sample were women; when losing-candidate status is included as a separate control variable in a regression for KMT membership, the negative relationship between gender and party membership vanishes.[1]

Table 8.2   Regression Explanation of KMT Membership

| | |
|---|---|
| Multiple R | .56[a] |
| *Regression Coefficients* | |
| Female | -.11[b] |
| Over 35 1st Ran | .28[a] |
| Mainlander | .23[a] |
| Issues Stimulated Running | -.22[a] |
| Family Income $15,000 | .21[a] |
| Politically Related 1st Political Interest | -.17[a] |
| Buddhist | .14[a] |

[a]Statistically significant at .05 level.
[b]Statistically significant at .15 level.

With respect to influences on party affiliation, several of the socialization factors are fairly strongly associated with joining the KMT or running as an independent, as indicated by the Multiple R of .56 in Table 8.2. As would be expected, Kuomintang members appear to be part of the political establishment, while the opposition attracts more politically oriented outsiders. Thus, non-KMT respondents were 17% more likely to have become interested in public affairs for political reasons and 22% more likely to have run for office because of personal concern about political issues. In contrast, Nationalist candidates were wealthier ($b = .21$), more likely to be Mainlanders ($b = .23$) and Buddhists ($b = .14$), and to have first run for office at an older age ($b = .28$). They seem, therefore, to have possessed more socioeconomic resources, to have had stronger ties with traditional political networks, and perhaps to have been co-opted into politics later in their lives.

In addition to membership in the dominant KMT, previous political experience should also provide a considerable political resource, since it should generally create both stronger ties with existing political networks and name recognition with the general public. Political experience is measured here by three indices of previous office-holding in electoral, appointive, and party posts. These indices were calculated by adding together the number of previous offices weighted on a scale of 1 to 4 by the geographic level of the office (local, county or city, provincial, and national). For this analysis, these three scales were divided into respondents who had substantial previous experience and those who did not, with more than four points (i.e., the equivalent of one national and one other office) denoting substantial experience.

The data in Table 8.1 comparing the proportion of each respondent group who had substantial experience in each of the three types of positions appear conclusive in several respects. First, experience certainly is important for electoral success. Losing female candidates had little experience, while assemblymen and assemblywomen were many more times likely to have substantial experience on all three dimensions. Thus, incumbency exerts the same strong impact on electoral success that it does in many other nations, such as the United States.[2] Second, as for KMT membership, the differences in experience between assemblymen and both current and past assemblywomen were marginal at most, suggesting that women incumbents were fairly equal to their male colleagues in terms of possessing political resources.

It is also clear that legislators' experience in Taiwan varies greatly among these three types of posts. They have extensive electoral experience —approximately three-quarters of the assemblymen and women (compared with a meager 4% of the female losers) ranked as having substantial electoral experience. Since this entails having held at least two offices, it also suggests that electoral careers in Taiwan are based on moving from one office to another, as experience and exposure at one level make competition at higher levels easier. In stark contrast, very few legislators had much history of holding appointive office, implying that electoral and bureaucratic careers are quite distinct in the ROC. Party experience falls in between these two extremes; about 40% of the legislators (compared with 11% of the losing women) ranked high on this dimension. Thus, party experience may give electoral careers some boost, but bureaucratic appointments do not— probably because those with government positions are primarily interested in an administrative career.[3]

These conclusions receive further support from the multiple regression results in Table 8.3. All three experience indices have fairly strong Multiple R's of about .50 with social and family characteristics, political activation, and party affiliation, indicating that political careers are structured by these background factors. The impact of these independent variables upon electoral and party experience is fairly similar, but an almost totally different causal pattern exists for service in appointive posts, confirming the distinctiveness of this political career pattern.

Table 8.3 Regression Explanations of Political Interest

|  | Electoral Experience | Appointive Experience | Party Experience |
|---|---|---|---|
| Multiple R | .55[a] | .46[a] | .51[a] |
| *Regression Coefficients* | | | |
| Female | -.23[a] | -.04 | -.09 |
| KMT | — | .09[b] | .25[a] |
| Over 45 | .27[a] | — | .23[a] |
| Father College Education | -.24[a] | — | -.18[a] |
| Mainlander | -.21[a] | — | — |
| Elite University | .19[b] | — | — |
| College Education | .16[b] | — | — |
| Issues Stimulated Running | -.15[b] | — | — |
| Hired Household Help | .15[b] | — | .19[a] |
| Family Stimulated Running | — | -.15[a] | — |
| Christian | — | -.13[a] | — |
| Urban | — | -.08[b] | — |
| Buddhist | — | -.08[b] | — |
| Spouse Now Politically Interested | — | -.07[b] | — |
| Spouse Held Political Office | — | — | -.21[a] |

[a]Statistically significant at .05 level.
[b]Statistically significant at .15 level.

These regression results also show that women were surprisingly equal to men in the possession of this particular type of political resource. Women scored only slightly lower (insignificant statistically) than male legislators in terms of previous experience in appointive and party posts. Women were 23% less likely than men to have had substantial electoral experience. However, this was again an artifact of only female losing candidates being included in the survey—gender had no relationship at all to electoral experience after losing-candidate status was entered into the regression as a control variable. Assemblywomen's previous political careers, therefore, differed little from those of their male counterparts.

In terms of the other explanatory variables, both age and membership in the dominant Nationalist Party would certainly be expected to have a positive impact on length of political service. Respondents over age 45 were 27% more likely to have substantial electoral experience and 23% more likely to have a substantial record in party offices, but age was unrelated to appointive experience. Belonging to the KMT did have the greatest effect on party experience ($b = .25$), which reflects the prohibition of opposition groups from forming formal parties. However, KMT membership surprisingly had no independent impact on electoral experience and was only marginally related to appointive office-holding. Thus, despite their minority status, independents were able to establish careers and longevity comparable to those of KMT legislators. Moreover, the few respondents who had had administrative careers before entering the electoral arena must have done so at a fairly young age, and some may have switched party allegiance because most administrative appointments would presumably have gone to KMT members.

There are some other interesting relationships revealed in Table 8.3. First, assemblymen and assemblywomen with more electoral and party experience tended not to have fathers who had a college degree and to have hired help for their housekeeping. This suggests that political careers in Taiwan, as in many other countries, may be used as a route for upward mobility and that the absence of role conflicts helps sustain a political career. Second, the possession of socioeconomic resources (as indicated by having attended an elite university and having a college degree) and favorable political characteristics (as indicated by being an Islander—a disadvantage in bureaucratic infighting but an advantage in electoral politics) exerted a considerable positive influence on political longevity. Third, legislators who had substantial administrative experience were less likely to have entered electoral politics for family-related reasons, suggesting a politically motivated career switch. Finally, respondents who had substantial party experience were 21% less likely to have a politically active spouse than those who did not. This implies that co-optation into electoral politics by an active spouse occurs directly, rather than indirectly through an intermediary stage of party work.

The third type of political resource considered here is involvement in nonpolitical groups. Participation in organized interest groups is generally viewed as helping politicians' careers in two distinct but interrelated ways. First, participation in nonpolitical groups engenders skills in human relations, leadership, and organizational dynamics that are invaluable in the political arena. Second, interest groups can provide direct campaign aid in terms of contributions and voter mobilization that may mean the difference between victory and defeat at the polls. Given the importance of traditional political networks in Taiwan's electoral politics,[4] group membership should be especially important for politicians in the ROC. Furthermore, the male-dominated norms in Chinese society imply that women should be fairly disadvantaged in terms of their ability to participate in such voluntary organizations.

The survey included questions concerning whether a respondent belonged to one or more of five types of groups—political (including women's groups), religious, civic (including such issue-oriented groups as consumers and environmental ones), professional (including business, labor, and alumni ones), and leisure—and whether such groups had helped in their campaigns. The data in Table 8.1 demonstrate that politicians in Taiwan, like their counterparts in many other countries, are certainly joiners. Approximately 60% were members of political groups, 45% members of religious or civic groups, and 25% members of professional and leisure groups. Moreover, 60% of the sample belonged to at least two different types of groups (and this does not count multiple group memberships within a single type). In contrast, group involvement in legislative campaigns was less extensive, although still quite significant. Slightly over a fifth of these politicians reported that they had been helped by either a political or a religious group, while between 8% and 15% had received aid from one of the other three types. Thus, at least up through the mid-1980s, direct involvement of interest groups in campaigning was far less in the ROC than in most advanced industrial societies.

The gender differences in group membership were much more muted than expected. About 60% of both women and men were active in two or more types of groups, and women were even much more likely than men to belong to a political group (64% to 42%), reflecting the fact that women's groups were classified as political ones. More men than women belonged to the other four types of groups, but these differences were fairly small and not statistically significant. In terms of actual campaign support, however, women did appear to be at a significant disadvantage. Both religious and civic groups were twice as likely to support male than female candidates, despite the fact that gender differences in membership were much smaller. Political groups were much more prone to support women than men, but this generally reflects the fact that women were more likely to belong to such groups. The importance of group support for electoral success is also clear, since losing women candidates were much less likely to be members of or receive support from organized groups (especially political and business ones) than were assemblywomen and assemblymen.

These initial interpretations are confirmed by the more complex regression results presented in Tables 8.4 and 8.5. Table 8.4 examines the influences on joining political and religious groups (the two types with the greatest involvement in legislative politics in Taiwan) and on being a "group activist" (as denoted by belonging to two or more types of groups). Table 8.5 seeks to explain what factors make political and religious groups likely to support an assembly candidate.

The data in these tables are suggestive in several respects. First, introducing other control variables in the multiple regressions does not change the relationship between gender and group linkages. Women were 22% more likely than men to be members of political groups and a slight 9% more likely to have joined at least two different types of groups, while men were 14% more likely to be members of civic groups. Political groups were 25% more likely to help women than men, while this was counterbalanced by the greater involvement of religious and civic groups in the campaigns of male candidates. Thus, while women might have been expected to be less well politically connected than men (because many of them were evidently co-opted into electoral politics to take advantage of the reserved-seats system), they showed similar involvement in organized groups, although they were somewhat disadvantaged by organized groups' involvement in campaign activities.

Table 8.4  Regression Explanations of Group Memberships

|  | More Than Two Types | Political | Religious |
|---|---|---|---|
| Multiple R | .45[a] | .61[a] | .32[a] |
| *Regression Coefficients* | | | |
| Female | .09 | .22[a] | .00 |
| KMT | .26[a] | .41[a] | — |
| Spouse Held Political Office | -.35[a] | — | -.29[a] |
| Party/Interest Group Stimulated Running | .23[a] | — | — |
| Substantial Appointive Experience | — | -.28[a] | — |
| Substantial Party Experience | — | .18[a] | — |
| Child Under 12 | — | -.17[a] | — |
| Mainlander | — | .17[b] | — |
| Issues Stimulated Running | — | — | -.20[a] |
| College Education | — | — | .17[a] |

[a]Statistically significant at .05 level.
[b]Statistically significant at .15 level.

Table 8.5  Regression Explanations of Groups Helping Campaign

|  | Political | Religious |
|---|---|---|
| Multiple R | .49[a] | .31[a] |
| *Regression Coefficients* | | |
| Female | .25[a] | -.17[a] |
| KMT | .15[a] | — |
| Substantial Electoral Experience | .22[a] | — |
| Over 35 1st Ran | .20[a] | — |
| Family-Related 1st Political Interest | -.13[b] | — |
| Over 25 1st Political Interest | — | .15[a] |

[a]Statistically significant at .05 level.
[b]Statistically significant at .15 level.

Second, those who were active in two or more groups or just in political and, to a lesser degree, religious groups seemed to belong to the traditional political networks. KMT members were 26% more likely to belong to two or more types of groups and 41% more likely than nonmembers to belong to a political group, reflecting the party control over most organized groups that existed until the mid-1980s.[5] Quite understandably, respondents whose candidacies had been stimulated by party or interest group leaders had extensive group ties, as indicated by membership in several different types of groups ($b = .25$), and Mainlanders and those with substantial party experience were more likely to join political groups. Somewhat surprisingly, there was a strong negative relationship between appointive experience and membership in political groups ($b = -.28$), providing more support for the conclusion that administrative and electoral political careers are quite divergent in Taiwan. Political groups, in turn, tended to support establishment candidates—KMT members ($b = .15$) and those who had substantial electoral experience ($b = .22$)—again indicating the importance of incumbency in the ROC. They also were more likely to support candidates who began their electoral careers later in life, which, as discussed earlier, appears to be associated with traditional politics in the ROC.

Membership in religious groups is usually seen as part of the traditional political network in Taiwan, but the evidence from the regressions is not as strong in support of this supposition for several reasons. Social and political background factors in general had a lesser impact on joining and being supported by religious groups (the two Multiple R's are a weak .32) than on political and multiple group membership (which had moderate to fairly strong R's of between .45 and .61). Several key independent variables, such as party and political experience, were unrelated to association with religious groups. Still, some evidence of traditional ties can be found: People who ran because of issue concerns were less likely than others to join religious groups, and religious groups tended to support men and politicians who did not become interested in politics until they were 25.

Third, having a spouse who had held a political office had a pronounced negative impact on belonging to two or more groups ($b = -.35$) or joining a religious group ($b = -.29$), similar to the tendency for these people to have less experience in party offices. Thus, the more traditionally oriented career patterns discussed in the last chapter can seemingly be divided into two types. In one, a legislator is integrated into existing family, party, and interest group networks. In the other, the primary stimulus to running for office evidently comes from a spouse already holding a political post and does not involve the broader participation in traditional political networks and organizations entailed by the first. Since this second pattern was almost entirely limited to women, it suggests an important effect of the reserved-seats system. In the United States, widows taking the seats of their deceased husbands have provided an important family-connected route to legislative service.[6] In Taiwan, in contrast, many political activists encourage their wives to run for assembly positions that must be filled by a woman.

These results, therefore, indicate that women's disadvantage in terms of political resources compared with men is fairly limited and that the possession of political resources confers a strong advantage in electoral politics. These suppositions are supported by the discriminant analyses presented in Table 8.6. The possession of political resources differentiates winning and losing women candidates extremely well (canonical correlation = .75). By far the most important such resource is having substantial experience in elective office ($dc$ = .98) being a member of the Kuomintang confers a moderate advantage as well ($dc$ = .36). These relationships are certainly not unexpected. However, given the KMT's domination of Taiwan's electoral politics up through the mid-1980s, the relative strength of their discriminating effects is at least a little surprising and underlines the strong effect of incumbency in electoral politics, even for members of minority parties.

In sharp contrast, political resource factors had only a moderate ability

Table 8.6 Discriminant Analyses for Political Resource Items

| WOMEN VERSUS MEN LEGISLATORS | |
|---|---|
| *Canonical Correlation* | .46 |
| *Group Centroids* | |
| Assemblywomen | .49 |
| Assemblymen | -.49 |
| *Discriminant Function Coefficients* | |
| Member Political Group | .83 |
| Substantial Party Experience | -.44 |
| Religious Group Helped Campaign | -.43 |
| Leisure Group Helped Campaign | .42 |
| **WOMEN WINNERS VERSUS LOSERS** | |
| *Canonical Correlation* | .75 |
| *Group Centroids* | |
| Assemblywomen | 1.22 |
| Losing Candidates | -1.12 |
| *Discriminant Function Coefficients* | |
| Substantial Electoral Experience | .98 |
| KMT Member | .36 |
| **OLD- VERSUS NEW-GENERATION WOMEN** | |
| *Canonical Correlation* | .49 |
| *Group Centroids* | |
| Over 45 | .50 |
| Under 45 | -.63 |
| *Discriminant Function Coefficients* | |
| Member Political Group | .75 |
| Substantial Electoral Experience | .35 |
| Substantial Party Experience | .25 |

*Note:* Canonical correlation is significant at the .001 level. Statistical significance of the individual discriminant function coefficients cannot be computed but all entered the discriminant equation at the .05 level.

to distinguish between assemblymen and assemblywomen and between old-generation and new-generation women (canonical correlations = about .45). Furthermore, women were actually advantaged vis-à-vis men on two of the four resource variables that entered the discriminant equation—belonging to a political group ($dc = .83$) and having their campaign helped by a leisure group ($dc = .42$). For their part, assemblymen were more likely to have had substantial experience in party offices ($dc = -.44$) and to have their campaigns helped by a religious group ($dc = -.43$). These results suggest that men do have some advantage in political resources, since religious groups were two and a half times more likely than leisure groups (21% to 8%) to become involved in campaigns and since party experience appears to have given a boost to electoral chances.[7] Still, these differences were much less than would have been anticipated given the status of women in Chinese society.

Finally, older women have significantly more electoral experience ($dc = .35$) and party experience ($dc = .25$) than younger ones. By far the most important discriminating factor, though, was the much greater propensity of older women to belong to political groups ($dc = .75$). These results confirm earlier ones that a change has occurred in the nature of women politicians in the ROC: They have moved from being co-opted into existing political networks, as indicated by the traditional political groups, toward being more self-motivated (that is, concerned about political issues) and becoming involved in politics at an earlier age. The latter characteristic, then, accounts for the relatively modest discriminating impact of political experience for the two generations of women politicians.

## Political Orientations

The general political orientations of legislators can be important for structuring their legislative activities. For example, especially among women, those who are more liberal and more positive about women's political roles should be more active and assertive in the assemblies. In addition, the perceptions of legislators and legislative candidates can be used to test the presumption that significant gender discrimination exists in the ROC. This section, then, examines liberal values, perceptions of gender discrimination, and beliefs about the contributions of women to Taiwan's political life.

The respondents to the survey were asked to place themselves on a five-point scale of political ideology, from strongly liberal to strongly conservative, Table 8.7 reports the percentage of respondents in each of the four subsamples who called themselves liberals or strong liberals. Our principal working hypothesis was that women would be more liberal than men. For example, studies of women office-holders in the United States and Western Europe have shown that they are relatively liberal on social issues, regardless of their political party affiliation.[8] Given the nature of Chinese society and politics on Taiwan, even larger differences in ideology would be expected there. In addition, we presumed that 1969 assemblywomen would be less liberal than younger women because of the changing socialization environment and that losing women would be more liberal than assemblywomen because of their issue concerns and weaker affiliation with the KMT.

Table 8.7  Political Attitude Differences Among Respondent Groups

|  | Male Legisator (%) | Female Legisator (%) | Female Loser (%) | Female 1969 Legisator (%) | V |
|---|---|---|---|---|---|
| *Ideology* | | | | | |
| Liberal | 47 | 56 | 72 | 75 | .24[a] |
| *Gender Discrimination* | | | | | |
| Male Party Leaders Discriminate | 41 | 71 | 70 | 75 | .29[a] |
| Voters Discriminate | 56 | 46 | 49 | 30 | .16 |
| Women Equal Chance to Be Leaders | 37 | 26 | 33 | 25 | .11 |
| Women's Image Helps Campaign | 23 | 13 | 15 | 5 | .16 |
| Bias v Women Affects Campaign | 26 | 31 | 30 | 30 | .05 |
| Male Freedom Affects Campaign | 19 | 28 | 15 | 10 | .16 |
| Family Obligations Affect Campaign | 0 | 8 | 11 | 15 | .20[b] |
| Ambition Helps Campaign | 23 | 5 | 9 | 5 | .24[a] |
| *Reserved-Seats System* | | | | | |
| Guarantee for Women | 14 | 67 | 49 | 55 | .41[a] |
| Increases Male Competition | 61 | 3 | 2 | 0 | .68[a] |
| Ceiling for Women | 2 | 15 | 15 | 30 | .25[a] |
| Increases Party Control | 5 | 13 | 11 | 15 | .12 |
| *Women's Contribution* | | | | | |
| Women as Qualified Officials | 74 | 95 | 94 | 90 | .27[a] |
| Women Make Important Political Contribution | 63 | 97 | 96 | 95 | .43[a] |
| Women More Honest | 44 | 80 | 70 | 75 | .30[a] |
| Women Less Influenced by Interest Groups | 30 | 72 | 66 | 75 | .37[a] |
| Women Better at Human Relations | 35 | 41 | 57 | 30 | .21[b] |
| Women Spend More Time on Politics | 28 | 56 | 32 | 50 | .25[a] |
| Women Less Tricky | 42 | 67 | 75 | 55 | .27[a] |
| Women Less Political | 63 | 46 | 53 | 45 | .14 |

[a]Statistically significant at .05 level.
[b]Statistically significant at .15 level.

The first and third hypotheses were strongly confirmed. Current assemblywomen were significantly more liberal than their male colleagues (56% to 47%), and losing female candidates were much more liberal (72%) than victorious females. However, in direct contradiction to the second hypothesis, the 1969 assemblywomen were the most liberal group—three-quarters of them professed a liberal ideology. Thus, the more conservative socialization environment that they faced, rather than making them more conservative, meant that only women with special attitudes and characteristics could overcome traditional norms against entering public life, again supporting the countersocialization perspective.

The regression analysis of liberalism on background political and social factors in Table 8.8 confirms that women were substantially more liberal (21%) than men. However, these results are somewhat surprising—other social and political factors have only a limited influence on political ideology. Social class, socialization experiences, and particularly political experience and affiliation normally condition a person's ideology and policy opinions.[9] This is true to some extent in Taiwan. Younger politicians were more liberal ($b = -.22$), as were those less deeply involved in organized groups ($b = -.15$). In addition, wealthier respondents were much more likely to be liberal ($b = .24$). While the direction of this relationship is the opposite from the one that normally exists in most countries (i.e., richer people are more conservative), this is explicable by the character of Taiwan's politics at that time. The major issue was probably democratization of the authoritarian political system rather than bread-and-butter economic and social issues (see Chapter 3), and the middle class had assumed a leading role in supporting democratization.[10]

Table 8.8  Regression Explanation of Political Liberalism

| | |
|---|---|
| Multiple R | .36[a] |
| *Regression Coefficients* | |
| Female | .21[a] |
| Family Income $15,000 | .24[a] |
| Over 45 | -.22[a] |
| Member 2 Groups | -.15[b] |

[a]Statistically significant at .05 level.
[b]Statistically significant at .15 level.

Despite these usual influences on liberalism, social and political factors had only a limited impact on ideology, as indicated by the weak to moderate Multiple R of .36. Furthermore, party affiliation and political experience had no impact whatsoever on this indicator of political orientations. This is certainly striking, since members of the Nationalist Party and those with extensive party and administrative experience would certainly be expected to be among the more conservative segments of the political spectrum in Taiwan. Evidently, involvement in electoral politics brings a commitment to democratization that transcends normal political cleavages and also helps to account for the surprisingly high level of liberal beliefs in the whole sample (discussed earlier in Chapter 6). In particular, KMT assemblymen and women probably saw further democratization as promoting their position vis-à-vis more conservative elements in the party and the regime.[11]

The survey contained several questions related to gender discrimination in Taiwan's politics. First, individual questions specifically asked whether male party leaders or voters discriminated against women and whether women had an equal chance to become political leaders. Second, other questions touched upon whether women in election campaigns had advantages (e.g., a positive image) or suffered from several disadvantages (i.e., biases against women, role conflicts with family duties, and greater male social freedom). Third, another question, which focused on the effects of the reserved-seats system, could also be used to discern gender discrimination.

The data in Table 8.7 provide strong support for our two basic hypotheses that women still face considerable discrimination in electoral politics in the Republic of China and that women are much more sensitive than men to this discrimination. Thus, three-quarters of the women and a substantial minority (41%) of the men agreed that male party leaders engaged in gender discrimination; about half the sample believed that voters were biased against women candidates (although, surprisingly, men were slightly more likely to have said so than women). Consequently, only about a third of the sample felt that women had an equal chance to become political leaders in Taiwan, with men only a bit more likely than women to believe this. Certainly, a goodly amount of gender discrimination is implied by these perceptions of both men and women who were directly involved in electoral politics.

The data on gender biases in campaigning and the election system are far less overwhelming, but do suggest that women have yet to attain complete equality. About 30% of the respondents felt that women suffered from some biases during campaigning; another 20% said that the greater social freedom of men gave them a significant campaign asset. Interestingly, there was almost no difference by sex in these attitudes. In addition, 10% of the women, but no men, reported that family obligations detracted from their campaign activities. Men were about twice as likely to believe (23% to 12%) that women's image helped them in campaigning, while men were more than three times more likely than women (23% to 7%) to say that their personal ambition was a campaign asset. In terms of the reserved-seats system per se, a majority of the women said that it constituted a guarantee for women's election, while a majority of the men argued that it increased competition for men. That is, the system could be seen as a bias for women's candidacies. However, about 15% of the women, as opposed to only about 3% of the men, felt that the reserved-seats system contained other biases that hurt women's electoral chances as well—first, by setting a ceiling on the number of women who could be elected and providing an excuse for not voting for women; second, by increasing the control over nominations by party leaders, who were widely perceived to discriminate against female candidates. Overall, therefore, the evidence is fairly strong that women continue to be subjected to significant discrimination in Taiwan's politics, in line with the disadvantaged-status hypothesis.

This general line of argument is supported by the multivariate analysis in Table 8.9 of two central perceptions about discrimination: that male party leaders discriminated against women and that women had an equal chance to become political leaders. (The Multiple R's are in the moderate .40–.50 range.) Women clearly were much more sensitive to gender discrimination than were men—they were 24% more likely to say that male party leaders discriminated and 16% less likely to believe that the sexes had an equal chance to assume leadership roles.

Table 8.9 Regression Explanations of Perceptions of Gender Discrimination

|  | Male Leaders Discriminate | Women Equal Chance to be Leaders |
|---|---|---|
| Multiple R | .51[a] | .40[a] |
| *Regression Coefficients* | | |
| Female | .24[a] | -.16[b] |
| KMT | -.29[a] | — |
| Father College Education | .22[a] | — |
| Child Under 12 | -.20[a] | — |
| College Education | .18[a] | — |
| Politically Related 1st Political Interest | .15[b] | — |
| Hired Hshld Help | — | .25[a] |
| Family Obligations Hurt Legislative Duties | — | -.16[b] |
| Substantial Electoral Experience | — | -.16[b] |
| Urban | — | .15[b] |
| Above-Ave. Personal Qualifications | — | -.11[b] |

[a]Statistically significant at .05 level.
[b]Statistically significant at .15 level.

While none of the other independent variables had a significant effect on both discrimination items, a common theme that emerges is that discrimination was more likely to be felt by respondents who had more resources and a lesser degree of role conflicts. For example, perceptions of discrimination among party leaders were higher among people who had college degrees, whose fathers were college graduates, and who did not have young children. The belief that women had an equal chance to become leaders tended to be held by those who had hired household help, who did not feel that family obligations detracted from their official duties, who had less experience in electoral office, and who had higher self-confidence (as reflected in the belief that their personal qualifications were above average). Thus, discrimination was most likely to be felt by those who would be expected to be most aggressive and successful, suggesting that it is a real barrier to activists.

In addition, Kuomintang members were much less likely (29%) to report gender discrimination than were independents. This was not the result of "sour grapes" from losing candidates—adding that status to the regression results reported in Table 8.9 did not change them at all. There are two somewhat contradictory interpretations for this. On the one hand, leaders among independents might have been less solicitous of women candidates because they are less concerned with running a full slate than is the KMT. On the other hand, independent candidates might have been referring to perceived discrimination by KMT leaders, since they represented the major legal party at the time of the survey. Unfortunately, the data do not permit us to weigh these rival interpretations.[12]

The final set of variables presented in Table 8.7 includes attitudes about women's contribution to politics in the ROC. Two questions elicited an overall evaluation of women's political role in Taiwan's politics that turned out to be quite high. Approximately two-thirds to three-quarters of the men and well over 90% of the women believed that women were as qualified as men to be political officials and that women had made an important contribution to political life in the Republic of China. The other items in this set queried whether women possessed desirable political qualities more so than men did on a number of dimensions. As would be expected, agreement here was substantially lower than for the first two questions. Still, majorities of between 50% and 75% of the women and significant minorities of between 30% and 45% of the men believed that women in comparison with men were more honest, less influenced by interest groups, better at human relations, willing to spend more time on politics, and less tricky. Thus, despite the evident discrimination against women in Taiwan's politics, they appear to be accepted as legitimate and equal actors in electoral politics.

Table 8.10 Regression Explanations for Perceptions of Women's Political Abilities

|  | Women Make Important Contribution to Politics | Women As Qualified Officials As Men |
| --- | --- | --- |
| Multiple R | .44[a] | .36[a] |
| *Regression Coefficients* | | |
| Female | .33[a] | .18[a] |
| Liberal | — | .19[a] |
| Member 2 Groups | — | .12a |

[a]Statistically significant at .05 level.
[b]Statistically significant at .15 level.

The regressions in Table 8.10 indicate that women were much more likely than men to hold these attitudes. In fact, gender was the only independent variable to have a significant impact on the belief that women had made a significant contribution to politics in the ROC. This is at least partially consistent with the countersocialization approach because it implies that women politicians have been socialized to see certain issues as reflecting their own special interests.

In addition, people who were active in interest groups (as indicated by belonging to two or more types of groups and to a political group) were more likely to feel that women were as qualified as men to be political leaders. Thus, women evidently play a strong part within these organizations, again implying gender-neutral behavior because of successful countersocialization. Liberals were also more likely to see no difference between men's and women's leadership capacities, indicating that the liberal concern with democratization extends to the gender front as well.

In direct contrast to the political resource variables, therefore, these political orientations should differentiate assemblymen and assemblywomen much better than the other two sets of analytic groups. The results from the discriminant analyses in Table 8.11 confirm this supposition. The canonical correlation for distinguishing assemblymen from assemblywomen is a fairly strong .63, while the other two are about .40.

The primary difference between assemblywomen and assemblymen is that the former were quite understandably much more positive about women's political role in Taiwan. For example, female legislators were more likely than their male colleagues to say that women made an important contribution to Taiwan's politics ($dc = .50$), that women were as qualified as men to be officials ($dc = .42$), and that women were less subject than men to interest group manipulations ($dc = .48$). Another important distinguishing factor was the women's greater belief that male party leaders engaged in gender discrimination ($dc = .45$). Men, for their part, were more likely to say that their ambition helped their campaigns. Assemblymen and assemblywomen, therefore, differed sharply in terms of their valuation of women's contribution to politics and perceptions of discrimination against women.[13]

The differences between older and younger women are consistent with earlier findings about generational differences among women politicians in Taiwan. Women over age 45 were more likely than younger ones to believe that women spent more time than men on politics ($dc = 1.04$) and that family obligations hurt campaigning ($dc = .57$), while younger women were more sensitive to gender discrimination by party leaders ($dc = -.40$). These findings imply that in earlier times women had to work harder than men to establish their political legitimacy, again suggesting the special "pioneer" status of this generation of women leaders. The more self-motivated nature of the careers of younger women also seems consistent with their lesser sensitivity

Table 8.11  Discriminant Analyses for Political Orientation Items

### WOMEN VERSUS MEN LEGISLATORS

| | |
|---|---|
| *Canonical Correlation* | .63 |
| *Group Centroids* | |
| Assemblywomen | .76 |
| Assemblymen | -.83 |
| *Discriminant Function Coefficients* | |
| Ambition Helps Campaign | -.52 |
| Women Make Important Political Contribution | .50 |
| Women Less Influenced by Interest Groups | .48 |
| Male Party Leaders Discriminate Against Women | .45 |
| Women As Qualified Officials | .42 |

### WOMEN WINNERS VERSUS LOSERS

| | |
|---|---|
| *Canonical Correlation* | .40 |
| *Group Centroids* | |
| Assemblywomen | .46 |
| Losing Candidates | -.42 |
| *Discriminant Function Coefficients* | |
| Women Spend More Time on Politics | .68 |
| Women Better at Human Relations | -.57 |
| Male Social Freedom Affects Campaign | .48 |
| Liberal | -.43 |

### OLD- VERSUS NEW-GENERATION WOMEN

| | |
|---|---|
| *Canonical Correlation* | .42 |
| *Group Centroids* | |
| Over 45 | .40 |
| Under 45 | -.51 |
| *Discriminant Function Coefficients* | |
| Women Spend More Time on Politics | 1.04 |
| Family Obligations Affect Campaign | .57 |
| Male Party Leaders Discriminate Against Women | -.40 |

*Note:* Canonical correlation is significant at the .004 level. Statistical significance of the individual discriminant function coefficients cannot be computed, but all entered the discriminant equation at the .05 level.

to role conflicts and their greater assertiveness in denouncing discriminatory political practices.

The discriminant results for winning and losing female candidates are more ambiguous, though, in the sense that they appear to be only partially related to electoral success per se. Winning candidates were less liberal ($dc = -.43$), which was probably an advantage given the presumably fairly conservative opinions of the electorate. Winners were also more likely to say that women spent more time than men on politics ($dc = .68$), but this was probably related more to their greater realization of what legislative life involved than to greater campaign efforts per se. In contrast, the tendency for winning women to believe that men's social freedom was a campaign advantage ($dc = .48$) and that women were not better than men at human relations ($dc = -.57$) implies, if anything, disadvantages on the hustings. Thus, these attitudinal differences do not appear very significant for explaining how women overcome political barriers in Taiwan.

## Implications

This study of the political orientations of legislators and legislative candidates, therefore, has both optimistic and pessimistic implications about women's political role in the Republic of China. On the one hand, there is strong evidence that women suffer from significant status disadvantage in Taiwan's politics. Thus, they continue to face substantial discrimination at the hands of male party leaders, which in itself constitutes a formidable barrier to improving women's representation in Taiwan's legislative bodies, not to mention the more powerful executive institutions. On the other hand, the picture is far from entirely bleak. Women are surprisingly well accepted in Taiwan's politics, even by assemblymen, and the absence of the expected inequalities in the possession of important political resources also implies that women's status in the political elites might improve significantly in the future.

In general, the countersocialization hypothesis about gender differences in political orientations was well supported by these data. Clearly, women were significantly more liberal, sensitive to gender discrimination, and appreciative of their sex's contribution to political life in the ROC. Additional evidence was also adduced for countersocialization theory in that the older-generation women appear to have been in the vanguard, with special attitudes that helped them to overcome the cultural barriers against women's movement into public life.

## Notes

1. Note that it makes no sense theoretically to include "losing status" as a predictor of party membership, since the causal impact should be in the other direction (i.e., Kuomintang members should have a better chance of winning). However, because only women losing candidates were included in our sample, some spurious relationships may emerge unless this fact is controlled for statistically.

2. William J. Keefe and Morris S. Ogul, *The American Legislative Process: Congress and the States*, 7th Ed. (Englewood Cliffs, N.J.: Prentice-Hall, 1989)

Chp. 4.

3. This interpretation is also supported by the correlations among these three indices. Thus, party experience has a moderate association with electoral officeholding ($r = .42$), but experience in appointive posts is only weakly correlated with electoral ($r = .21$) and party ($r = .14$) positions.

4. Arthur J. Lerman, *Taiwan's Politics: The Provincial Assemblyman's World* (Washington, D.C.: University Press of America, 1978) Part II.

5. Hung-mao Tien, *The Great Transition: Political and Social Change in the Republic of China* (Stanford, Calif.: Hoover Institution Press, 1989) Chp. 3.

6. Jeane Kirkpatrick, *Political Women* (New York: Basic Books, 1974) pp. 106–135.

7. As mentioned in Footnote 3, there is a moderate bivariate correlation of .42 between electoral and party experience. Much more importantly, when party experience is added to the multiple regression explaining electoral experience presented in Table 8.3, it turns out to have the greatest explanatory impact.

8. Marilyn Johnson and Susan Carroll, *Profile of Women Holding Office II* (New Brunswick, N.J.: Center for the American Woman and Politics, Rutgers University, 1978) pp. 35A–38A; and Joni Lovenduski, *Women and European Politics: Contemporary Feminism and Public Policy* (Amherst: University of Massachusetts Press, 1986) Chp. 6.

9. Gerald M. Pomper, *Voters, Elections, and Parties: The Practice of Democratic Theory* (New Brunswick, N.J.: Transaction Books, 1988) Part I.

10. Tun-jen Cheng, "Democratizing the Quasi-Leninist Regime in Taiwan," *World Politics* 41:4 (July 1989) pp. 471–499; and Hsin-huang Michael Hsaio, "Development, Class Transformation, Social Movements, and the Changing State-Society Relations in Taiwan," paper presented at the 18th Sino-American Conference on Mainland China, Stanford University, June 8–11, 1989. However, Tun-jen Cheng, "Is the Dog Barking? The Middle Class and Democratic Movements in the East Asian NICs," *International Studies Notes* 15:1 (Spring 1990) pp. 10–16, argues that middle-class support for democratic movements in East Asia dwindles when democratization challenges elite economic interests.

11. Jurgen Domes, "Political Differentiation in Taiwan: Group Formation Within the Ruling Party and Opposition Circles, 1979–1980," *Asian Survey* 21:10 (October 1981) pp. 1011–1029 argues that the Nationalist government had three major segments or factions: conservatives primarily interested in national security, technocrats primarily concerned with state-led economic development, and electoral politicians pushing for greater democratization and responsiveness to the public.

12. It might also be thought that independent candidates would be more sensitive to gender discrimination because of their presumed greater liberalism. However, this interpretation does not appear tenable: As described earlier, there was surprisingly little ideological difference between KMT and independent respondents, and liberalism per se was unrelated to perceptions of discrimination against women by party leaders.

13. In addition, assemblywomen and assemblymen differed considerably on the two images that the reserved-seats system either provided a guarantee for women or resulted in increased competition for men. These variables were not included in the discriminant analysis, however, because the tremendous split between this assessment of the reserved-seats system by assemblymen and assemblywomen overshadowed other important differences between them.

# CHAPTER NINE
# Legislative Activities: Selective Emphases

Surely, calls for women (or any other minority group) to receive more equal representation are based on the premise that people holding public office will affect public policy. Thus, if the achievement of "descriptive representation" for women is to be more than marginal window-dressing, women legislators must participate actively and have some influence over actual decisions. Only then can the special policy interests and styles of political activity that have been attributed to them (see Chapter 2) be effectively represented in the social and political life of a nation.

Research in the United States, for example, suggests that women's effectiveness in legislative settings was significantly limited in the past both by their small numbers and by their lower levels of ambition and activity compared with men's. During the 1970s and 1980s, however, the gender gap in this regard closed noticeably. Women scored important gains in their office-holding; male-female differences in ambition and activity narrowed greatly and perhaps even vanished; and secular trends, such as increasing legislative professionalism, enhanced women's effectiveness as well, although significant problems remained.[1] Women's position in Taiwan's assemblies would be expected to be somewhat worse than in the United States for several reasons. Women's active participation should be inhibited by the more patriarchal Chinese society; women's wide-scale involvement in the industrial economy and in electoral politics is of much shorter duration in the ROC; and the reserved-seats system itself suggests that assemblywomen may be treated as tokens.

This chapter, therefore, examines women's activities in the assemblies of the Republic of China in some detail. The first section focuses upon what may be termed legislative orientations, such as special training for legislative office, the role definitions of assemblymen and assemblywomen, the areas of their committee assignments, and the areas of the legislation that they sponsored. The second is concerned with levels of activity and effectiveness, such as amount of participation in several legislative duties, perceptions of legislative success, problems associated with office-holding, and ambition for future office.

If the presumed gender gap in legislative behavior exists in Taiwan, then, women should receive less party training, have role definitions that are less assertive, confine their legislative endeavors to areas of traditional women's interests, be less active and successful in the legislative arena, be more prone to experience difficulties in office-holding, and have less ambition concerning their future political careers. As will be seen, some of these hypotheses hold true. However, many of the expected differences between the sexes fail to materialize. Thus, women in Taiwan politics seemingly have built upon their socioeconomic and political resources, which the last two chapters showed to be surprisingly equal to those of their male colleagues, to attain near equality in selected areas of legislative activities.

## Orientations Toward Legislative Activities

This section describes several types of political orientations that are important for legislative behavior. In terms of background preparation and attitudes, receiving training for holding party office could well make an assemblywoman or assemblyman more capable and successful within the legislative arena, and self-definitions of what are important legislative roles should channel assembly members into different types of activities. In addition, the legislators' interests are generally reflected in the committee assignments they receive and especially in the subjects in which they show interest by sponsoring resolutions or amendments.

Both the Kuomintang Party and the more informal and only semilegal organizations associated with the opposition (*tangwei*) provided various types of training for legislators. As can be seen from the figures in Table 9.1, the male advantage in receiving such training and support expected by the disadvantaged-status model clearly existed. Among current assembly members, men were twice as likely as women to have received such training (28% versus 15%), while only 5% of the losing female candidates and 1969 assemblywomen had received training from party or quasi-party organizations. Thus, the reluctance of party organizations to provide legislative training opportunities to women provides empirical verification for the widespread perceptions that male party leaders discriminate against women. Fortunately, however, the effects of this evident discrimination appear rather limited because, quite surprisingly, receiving party training had no independent impact whatsoever on any other dimension of legislative behavior analyzed here.

The disadvantaged status of women in terms of this type of support from their party or quasi-party organizations is confirmed by the multiple regression results presented in Table 9.2 that seek to explain party training by a respondent's social and political background. The Multiple R is a moderate .44, even though only three independent variables had a statistically significant impact at the .05 level.[2] Even after other explanatory factors were controlled, women were 30% less likely than men to have received party training, underlining a significant type of party discrimination. The other two independent variables that affected party training were having other relatives besides spouse or parents who had held political office ($b = .25$) and becoming interested in politics for politically related reasons ($b = -.25$). This pattern of impact, then, implies that party training was most readily available to those with contacts in traditional political networks. In addition, the fact that party affiliation was unrelated to training shows that the *tangwei*'s unofficial organizations had become quite extensive by the mid-1980s.

Table 9.1 Legislative Orientation Differences Among Respondent Groups

|  | Male Legislator (%) | Female Legislator (%) | Female Loser (%) | Female 1969 Legislator (%) | V |
|---|---|---|---|---|---|
| *Preparation* | | | | | |
| Party Training | 28 | 15 | 6 | 5 | .26[a] |
| *Role Definitions* | | | | | |
| Adminstrative Oversight | | | | | |
| Important | 65 | 69 | 55 | 50 | .14 |
| Decisionmaking | 49 | 64 | 68 | 60 | .16 |
| Constituent Service | 70 | 92 | 81 | 90 | .23[a] |
| Subordinate to Others | 16 | 28 | 21 | 40 | .18 |
| *Committee Assignments*[b] | | | | | |
| Economic Affairs | 61 | 62 | 36 | 45 | .19 |
| Interior & Civil Affairs | 26 | 44 | 43 | 40 | .17 |
| Finance, Budget, & Local | | | | | |
| Government | 35 | 33 | 36 | 40 | .05 |
| Education & Culture | 26 | 49 | 36 | 45 | .21[c] |
| Legal & Judicial | 16 | 13 | 36 | 15 | .19 |
| Foreign Affairs & Defense | 9 | 15 | 7 | 10 | .10 |
| Ethnic & Overseas Chinese | 5 | 5 | 0 | 0 | .12 |
| *Resolutions*[b] | | | | | |
| Economic Affairs | 37 | 15 | 7 | 25 | .26[a] |
| Public Works | 19 | 5 | 50 | 20 | .34[a] |
| Local Development | 33 | 54 | 50 | 40 | .19 |
| Education & Culture | 14 | 18 | 43 | 25 | .22[c] |
| Elections, Civil & Human | | | | | |
| Rights | 15 | 13 | 15 | 25 | .12 |
| Foreign Affairs & Defense | 0 | 3 | 0 | 0 | .13 |
| All Areas | 37 | 23 | 0 | 10 | .31[a] |

[a]Statistically significant at .05 level.
[b]Percentages computed for only those 14 losing candidates who had previously held some legislative office.
[c]Statistically significant at .15 level.

The role definitions of these legislators and legislative candidates were inferred from their answers to a question about what they believed to be the most important functions of assemblywomen and assemblymen. The answers to these questions were grouped into four major categories: (1) administrative oversight (e.g., oversight of the executive branch and making government more efficient); (2) decisionmaking (e.g., sponsoring legislation, developing policy, making independent decisions, and getting issues on the public agenda); (3) constituent relations (e.g., constituent case work, discovering the public will, and educating the public); and (4) subordination to leaders (e.g., representing the party, seeking out colleagues' opinions, and maintaining regular attendance). Since up to six responses were coded for this question, an individual could consider several or even all of these role definitions as important.

Table 9.2  Regression Explanation of Receiving Party Training for Legislative Office

| | |
|---|---|
| Multiple R | .44[a] |
| *Regression Coefficients* | |
| Female | -.30[a] |
| Other Relatives Held Office | .25[a] |
| Politically Related 1st Political Interest | -.25[a] |

[a]Statistically significant at .05 level.

The data on these role definitions in Table 9.1 are striking in two important regards. First, despite the subordinate status of legislative bodies vis-à-vis the executive in the ROC, these legislators and legislative candidates had very active role definitions. Approximately 60% of them believed that administrative oversight and decisionmaking were important, and over 80% were concerned with constituent service. In contrast, only about a quarter of the sample expressed any interest in being more subordinate to others. Clearly, these politicians believed that representative bodies should assume a more activist and participant place within Taiwan's polity.

Second, the hypothesis that women would be less activist than men in their role orientations finds only a slight amount of empirical support. Women were considerably more likely than men to cite subordinate roles (27% versus 16%), but they were also more likely to stress both decisionmaking (65% versus 49%) and constituent service (86% versus 70%). The multiple regressions for these role definitions in Table 9.3, moreover, show that gender had no independent impact at all on either administrative oversight or decisionmaking, that women's greater acceptance of subordinate roles (10%) was not statistically significant, and that even after controlling other relevant causes, women were somewhat more likely than men (16%) to be concerned about relations with their constituencies. Women, therefore, differed little from their male colleagues in how they approached their legislative duties. Thus, the role orientations of assembly members in the ROC fall much closer to the predictions of the gender neutral than the disadvantaged-status model.

Table 9.3  Regression Explanations of Role Definitions

|  | Administrative Oversight | Decisionmaking | Constituent Service | Subordinate to Others |
|---|---|---|---|---|
| Multiple R | .41[a] | .41[a] | .45[a] | .41[a] |
| *Regression Coefficients* | | | | |
| Female | .04 | .03 | .16[a] | .10 |
| KMT | -.25[a] | -.21[a] | — | — |
| Substantial Electoral Experience | -.20[a] | .16[a] | — | — |
| Substantial Appointive Experience | — | — | -.30[a] | — |
| Substantial Party Experience | — | — | — | .18[a] |
| Elite University | .29[a] | — | — | — |
| Over 45 | -.20[a] | — | — | .15[a] |
| Mainlander | — | — | — | .29[a] |
| Member Religious Group | — | — | .18[a] | — |
| Professional Occupation | — | — | -.18[a] | — |
| Father College Education | — | — | -.17[a] | — |

[a]Statistically significant at .05 level.

The social and political correlates of activist roles for Taiwan's assembly members are consistent with general interpretations of political liberalization in the Republic of China in several ways. First, independents were much more concerned with administrative oversight ($b = -.31$) and decisionmaking ($b = -.21$) than were KMT members. Their emphasis on increasing the power of representative bodies is most understandable, of course, in light of the Kuomintang's domination of the other branches of government. Second, assemblywomen and men with greater legislative experience were more supportive of assemblies being involved in administrative oversight and decisionmaking, indicating that legislative experience inculcates institutional loyalty rather than acquiescence to executive or party domination. Third, administrative oversight was stressed by those who had attended elite universities ($b = .29$) and were younger than 45 ($b = -.20$). Since public interpellation sessions of executive officials were one of the leading methods for trying to increase democratic pressure on the regime in the mid-1980s,[3] this confirms the image of young upper-middle-class professionals as the leaders of the political liberalization movement in Taiwan.[4]

The influences on constituent service and subordinate roles are significant as well. Respondents who had had substantial experience in appointive posts were 30% less likely than those who lacked such experience to believe that constituent service was important, indicating a wariness of administrators about mixing with the masses. Likewise, people with more elite characteristics, as indicated by having a professional occupation or father who went to college, put less emphasis on maintaining contacts with their constituents. In contrast, legislators and candidates who were members of religious groups were more likely to have a constituent-service orientation. Religious groups, along with political ones, were the types of groups most likely to support campaign activities (see Chapter 8). Since many political groups in Taiwan at that time tended to be organized by the regime,[5] religious groups represented an important traditional source of grass-roots pressure, thus accounting for this relationship. Finally, subordinate roles were stressed by respondents who might well have been expected to have been socialized into accepting authority—Mainlanders, those with substantial experience in party office, and older people.

The third type of legislative orientation (Table 9.1) focuses on the areas of committee assignments held by assemblymen and assemblywomen (only the 14 losing female candidates who had previously held legislative posts could be included in this analysis). Seven specific types of committee assignments were delineated: (1) economic affairs, (2) interior and civil affairs, (3) finance, budget, and local government, (4) education and culture, (5) legal and judicial affairs, (6) foreign affairs and defense, and (7) ethnic and overseas Chinese affairs. Economic affairs was by far the most popular, as over half the respondents had served on this type of committee, followed by interior, finance, and education, each of which had just over 33% participation. In contrast, only a fifth of the legislators had served on legal committees and less than a tenth had been connected with the last two types of committees that were concerned with foreign affairs.

The working hypothesis that there would be major gender differences in the legislators' committee assignments receives only partial support. It was anticipated that men would be more represented on high-visibility and more prestigious committees (e.g., economic affairs and foreign or defense policy) and women on less prestigious ones or on committees concerned with traditional women's issues (e.g., education and culture). Women were more likely (about 43% to 26%) to have served on both education and interior committees (see Table 9.1). The former is clearly within the purview of women's traditional issue concerns, and some of the responsibilities of the latter are as well. Interior committees deal with the police, elections, and urban planning; hence, they discuss some of the social and civil rights policies of presumed interest to women. More men then women had been members of economic affairs committees, but there was no difference between current assemblymen and assemblywomen. Otherwise, the committee assignments were almost the same for the two sexes. The regression results in Table 9.4, furthermore, show that when other explanatory factors are taken into account, women were 32% more likely than men to have served on education committees and 18% more likely to have been on interior committees, while gender had no statistically significant difference in other areas. Thus, women clearly had a special interest in educational and cultural issues and, perhaps, in the social affairs and civil rights that come under interior committees (although government involvement here is low by international standards). However, other expected male and female emphases in committee work failed to emerge.

The multiple regression results in Table 9.4 are presented in somewhat abbreviated form because a plethora of independent variables affected the tendency to serve on the various committees. However, the major determinants for most types of committee service included gender, political experience, legislative role definitions, and ties to political groups. Thus, these independent variables are included in the table; a few other important explanatory factors for specific items are noted in the text. The Multiple R's are all moderate, ranging from .38 to .51.

Table 9.4  Regression Explanations of Committee Assignments

|  | Multiple R | Regression Coefficients | | | |
|---|---|---|---|---|---|
|  |  | Female | Experience[a] | Role Definitions[b] | Group Ties[c] |
| Economic | .50[d] | -.06 | — | Sub -.18[d] | Pol Mem .28[d] |
| Interior | .38[d] | .18[d] | — | — | Pol Hlp .26[d]<br>Mem 2+ .16[d] |
| Finance | .48[d] | -.09 | El -.18[a] | Ad Ov .28[d] | Pol Hlp -.24[d] |
| Education | .42[d] | .32[d] | — | — | — |
| Legal | .44[d] | -.05 | El -.26[d]<br>Ap .41[d] | — | — |
| Foreign Affairs | .51[d] | .10 | El .19[d] | Sub .19[d] | Rel Mem -.12[e] |
| Overseas Chinese | .46[d] | .02 | — | Cs Sv -.12[e] | Mem 2+ -.09[e] |

[a]Ap is appointive; El is electoral.
[b]Ad Ov is administrative oversight; Cs Sv is constituent service; Sub is subordinate roles.
[c]Mem 2+ is member of two or more types of groups; Pol Hlp is political group helped campaign; Pol Mem is member of political group; Rel Mem is member of religious group.
[d]Statistically significant at .05 level.
[e]Statistically significant at .15 level.

In most legislatures, parliamentarians with the most experience seek and gain choice committee assignments, either because of formal seniority rules or more informal political power.[6] Thus, the relationship between experience in electoral office and committee memberships can be viewed as a potential measure of committee prestige and/or desirability. Assemblywomen and men with more experience were more likely to have been on foreign affairs and defense committees and less likely to have been on ones concerned with legal and judicial affairs or with finance, budget, and local government. The image of the former as a high-prestige area and the latter two as low-prestige assignments needs a little modification, though. Those serving on foreign affairs and defense committees tended to subscribe to subordinate role definitions, probably because of the extreme executive domination of foreign policy by the national executive; rather surprisingly, Mainlanders were no more prone than Islanders to serve in this area. In addition, the finance and judicial affairs committees were attractive to certain types of assembly members. Those who saw their role as promoting administrative oversight tended to serve on finance, budget, and local government committees; the few legislators who had substantial appointive experience were much more likely than those who did not to have been on judicial affairs committees, suggesting that many of those who switched from administrative to legislative careers may have had legal training.

Legislators who had ties to political and/or religious groups tended to serve on economic and interior committees, where policies involve material benefits for business interests and other constituencies (infrastructure construction projects come under the control of interior committees). Strikingly, Islanders, who dominate Taiwan's economy, were 47% more likely than Mainlanders to have been associated with economics committees. Conversely, they were less likely than the average assembly member to be associated with finance, foreign affairs, and overseas Chinese committees. In addition, members of economics committees were more assertive in the sense that they rejected subordinate roles, and legislators with constituent-service orientations quite understandably avoided service on overseas Chinese and ethnic affairs committees. Thus, group activities in Taiwan's legislative politics seem more than tangentially involved with "patronage politics."[7] In another area, people with a presumed interest in education also appear to have sought out service in this area. In addition to women, this included those with college educations and high incomes, while those having ties with traditional political networks (as indicated by having other relatives who had held political office) avoided education committees.

Perhaps one of the most striking findings is that political orientations, as measured by party affiliation and ideology, were almost completely unrelated to committee service. Kuomintang and independent legislators displayed exactly the same pattern of committee membership, and the only impact of ideology on the seven dependent variables was a modest tendency for liberals not to have belonged to committees dealing with overseas Chinese and ethnic affairs. Thus, committee assignments in Taiwan appear remarkably free of partisan or ideological considerations.

While a few exceptions can be noted, therefore, committee service in Taiwan's legislatures appears to be shaped by the political characteristics of assembly members in ways that reflect their political interests and ties. In terms of women per se, they were overrepresented on two types of committees that were concerned with what are conventionally considered women's issues (for interior committees, this association is only partial, though), while they were not underrepresented on any types of committee. Thus, women do not suffer from any bias in the assignment of committee slots. For committee assignments, hence, there is some evidence of counter-socialization in the tendency of female assembly members to serve on committees dealing with women's issues, but overall these results are most consistent with the gender-neutral model.

A much different picture emerges, however, when we look at another indicator of areas of interest that should, a priori, be even more directly tied to the concerns of individual assembly members. This is participation in assembly proceedings by introducing specific pieces of legislation. Executive dominance over legislation is much greater in Taiwan than in most advanced industrial societies.[8] Still, assemblymen and women can and do sponsor resolutions or amendments to pending bills. The respondents were asked to list the subjects on which they had introduced resolutions or amendments— (1) economic and business affairs, (2) public works, (3) local development, (4) education and culture, (5) elections and civil and human rights, (6) foreign affairs and defense, and (7) all or most of these areas. (See Table 9.1.)

Local development resolutions were by far the most popular as 43% of the respondents said they had sponsored such initiatives, indicating that promoting projects of benefit to a legislator's home community is an important constituent service even in the fairly authoritarian politics that existed in the ROC at the time. At the other end of the scale, only one of the 149 respondents had ever sponsored a legislative initiative in foreign and defense affairs, which strongly confirms the executive domination in this field. About a fifth to a quarter of the sample indicated that they had sponsored resolutions and amendments in the other four specific fields. Overall, these legislators seemed fairly active given the normal image of quite constrained legislative politics in Taiwan, since a quarter of them reported introducing legislation in most of these areas.

Women clearly were disadvantaged relative to men in sponsoring legislation, unlike their position of equality in terms of committee membership. According to the data in Table 9.1, men were over twice as likely as women to have introduced resolutions and amendments (37% to 16%) both in the activist category of all areas and in the important field of economic affairs. Women did introduce more legislation in two fields, but the gender gap was not as greatly in their favor—local development (49% to 33%) and education (25% to 14%). The regression results in Tables 9.5 and 9.6, moreover, show that after other explanatory factors are controlled, men were much more likely to introduce legislation in all areas (27%) and economic affairs (45%), while women's advantage in local development and education was a fairly modest 11%. If actual behavior is more important than formal committee assignment for affecting policy, as might well be assumed, these findings substantiate the hypothesis that women would be less active and effective than men in the ROC's assemblies. As argued later, however, this supposition seems at least a little problematic.

Normally, a strong correlation would be expected between committee membership and the areas in which legislation was sponsored. Both presumably measure interest in specific subjects, and committee members should develop more expertise in their fields of competence. For these Taiwan legislators, though, this linkage is somewhat tenuous. Members of education committees compared with the average assembly member were more likely to sponsor resolutions and amendments concerning education ($r = .43$), and members of interior committees disproportionately initiated legislation in the field of elections and human rights ($r = .32$). Otherwise, however, there was no correlation of even .20 between committee membership and area of legislative activity. Two reasons for this may be adduced. First, the pressure to help constituents, especially business interests, might be so diffused that most legislators, not just those on the relevant committees, would try to promote favorable initiatives in the potential patronage areas of economics, public works, and local development. Second, political influence by committee members may be exercised informally and indirectly upon the drafters and implementors of laws in the executive branch, rather than in the direct sponsorship of legislation. If either of these speculations is true, then, introducing amendments and resolutions may be less important than committee membership for influencing policy formation and especially how policies are applied in individual cases.

The regression results in Table 9.5 explaining sponsorship of legislation in specific areas (foreign affairs and defense are not included because there was only one initiative in this area) provide some indirect evidence that resolution introduction is less tied than committee membership to actual policy influence. This is suggested by the fact that sponsoring legislation is not as structured as committee service in the sense that the normal influences on policy predispositions have much less of an impact. Thus, overall the Multiple R's in Table 9.5 are somewhat lower than in Table 9.4; much more importantly, the experience, role definition, and group affiliation factors that were so important for explaining committee assignments had much less influence here. First, elections and human rights committees, which have little linkage with patronage politics, were the only area where belonging to an organized group or receiving group campaign support had an impact,[9] in contrast to the strong linkage between group ties and service on committees with patronage potential. Second, economic resolutions were totally unaffected by a legislator's constituency characteristics and linkages, with the exception that they were more likely to be introduced by urban representatives. Third, group membership and campaign support were totally unrelated to introducing resolutions and amendments concerning the prime patronage area of public works, although people who sponsored this type of legislation were more likely than others to have had their careers stimulated by party or interest group support. Finally, party membership and ideology were almost completley unrelated to this dimension of assembly activity.

Sponsorship of resolutions was more structured in the areas of education and local development. In addition to women, liberals, college graduates, and those who had become interested in politics for nonfamily-related reasons were the most likely to sponsor education legislation. In conjunction with the findings about service on educational committees, this implies that education is a special subject area of greater interest to women and highly educated professionals than it is to legislators in the traditional political networks, who are more concerned with material benefits and patronage opportunities.

Table 9.5 Regression Explanations of Offering Resolutions in Specific Areas

| | Multiple R | Regression Coefficients | | |
|---|---|---|---|---|
| | | Female | Experience[a] | Role Definitions[b]/ Group Ties[c] |
| Economic | .45[d] | -.45[d] | — | — |
| Public Works | .40[d] | -.06 | El -.16[d] | — |
| Local Development | .46[d] | .11[e] | Pty .22[d] | Cs Sv .18[d] |
| Education | .47[d] | .11[e] | — | — |
| Elections, Human Rights | .33[d] | .04 | — | Pol Hlp .21[d] |

[a]El is electoral; Pty is party.
[b]Cs Sv is constituent service.
[c]Par/Grp Stim is first candidacy stimulated by party or interest group leaders; Pol Hlp is political group helped campaign.
[d]Statistically significant at .05 level.
[e]Statistically significant at .15 level.

Assemblywomen and men with greater party experience and constituent-service role orientations were the most likely to introduce local development resolutions. This suggests that local development is of special concern to those legislators trying to cultivate support from the electoral constituencies (e.g., experience in party office might bring greater realization about the favors needed to curry popular support). If this is true, it is quite significant that women were more likely than men to adhere to constituent-service role definitions and to be involved in local development issues. Since democratization is increasing the importance of electoral politics, the new style of politics is demanding precisely these orientations and activities.

The full regression results reported in Table 9.6 define the characteristics of the activists who introduced resolutions and amendments in most of the individual subject areas. Such activists were much more likely to be males ($b = -.27$) and to come from wealthier families ($b = .29$), a result consistent with normal models of participatory differences among elites. The other three independent variables, however, indicate that the idiosyncratic nature of legislative politics in the Republic of China exerts several effects too. First, independents were 29% more likely than Kuomintang members to sponsor legislation in a wide variety of areas. Thus, this type of legislative activity appears to be a means that the opposition employs for publicizing and pushing its issues to a significant extent, rather than a way for the dominant party to implement its will.[10] Second, introducing resolutions in multiple areas was more common among legislators who subscribed to subordinate roles and whose careers were not stimulated by party or interest group leaders—characteristics not usually attributed to the most assertive and aggressive politicians. While introducing legislation is certainly important in Taiwan, therefore, there are several indications that it may not be as dominant a strategy for exercising legislative influence as it is in many other nations.

Table 9.6  Regression Explanation of Offering Resolutions in All Areas

| | |
|---|---|
| Multiple R | .48[a] |
| *Regression Coefficients* | |
| Female | -.27[a] |
| KMT | -.29[a] |
| Family Income $15,000 | .29[a] |
| Subordinate Roles Important | .23[a] |
| Party/Interest Group Stimulated Running | -.16[a] |

[a]Statistically significant at .05 level.

The discriminant results for the differences between assemblymen and assemblywomen on these political orientations are presented in Table 9.7. (Discriminant analyses were not computed for the other two analytic groups because data on actual legislative activities were only available for 14 losing women candidates.)[11] These results indicate that role definitions were the most important factors distinguishing assemblymen from assemblywomen (the canonical correlation was a moderate .52). Female legislators were much more likely than their male colleagues to believe that constituent-service was important ($dc = .56$) and to accept subordinate roles ($dc = .47$). Women tended also to serve on education and interior committees, while men were more likely to sponsor public works and economics legislation. Thus, women appear more willing to appeal directly to voters and to be interested in women's issues, such as education, while male legislators focus on economic issues, where favors can potentially be distributed to the business community.

This discussion of the legislative orientations of assembly members and candidates in the ROC, therefore, did find some evidence in line with the disadvantaged-status hypothesis that women would be less assertive and active. They were disadvantaged in terms of party training, more willing to consider subordinate roles within the assembly important, and clearly less active in sponsoring legislation. Yet women stressed active roles for the assemblies (i.e., administrative oversight and decisionmaking) just as much as men did, were even more likely to consider constituent service important, did not appear to suffer any disadvantage in committee assignments, and pursued their own interests in such areas as education and local development projects. Furthermore, their dearth of party training did not seem to affect any other aspect of legislative behavior, and sponsoring resolutions seemed less important in some regards in Taiwan than in most parliaments. Thus, given the expectation that women legislators would be particularly passive in the ROC, these findings suggest that they have made considerable progress in overcoming inequality in the legislative arena and that the gender-neutral perspective receives a surprising amount of support.

Table 9.7 Discriminant Analysis for Women Versus Men Legislators on Legislative Orientations

| | |
|---|---|
| *Canonical Correlation* | .52 |
| *Group Centroids* | |
| Assemblywomen | .60 |
| Assemblymen | -.60 |
| *Discriminant Function Coefficients* | |
| Constituent Service Important | .56 |
| Subordinate Roles Important | .47 |
| Sponsored Public Works Resolutions | -.46 |
| Education Committee Member | .44 |
| Interior Committee Member | .44 |
| Sponsored Economic Resolutions | -.36 |

*Note:* Canonical correlation is significant at .001 level. Statistical significance of individual discriminant function coefficients cannot be computed, but all entered the discriminant equation at the .05 level.

## Legislative Activity and Success

The level of activity and success within Taiwan's assemblies is perhaps the touchstone for assessing the degree of gender equality. If women's representation is to be meaningful, there should be few differences in legislative effectiveness between them and their male colleagues. However, our working hypothesis that was adumbrated at the beginning of the chapter predicted the opposite—that women would be less active and successful (i.e., subjected to a disadvantaged status) in the assemblies of the Republic of China because of the cultural norms and development level of its Chinese society.

This section begins, therefore, by examining several dimensions of activism within the assemblies and several measures of legislative success. It then considers two types of more indirect measures of success: perceived problems with holding office and ambition to run for future elected office. Each of the latter three blocks of variables is considered to be potentially dependent upon the previous ones, as well as upon the legislative orientations considered in the previous section and the social and political characteristics described in Chapters 7 and 8 (with the exception of attitudes about women's roles and discrimination against women).

Three measures of legislative activism were included in the survey. The first, time on the job was measured by whether a respondent spent more than 50 hours a week on official duties; the second concerned active participation in legislating as measured by whether a respondent sponsored over 15 resolutions and amendments per legislative session; and the third was related to decisionmaking within the assemblies as measured by whether a respondent had held two or more committee chairmanships during her or his political career. Three indicators of legislative success were also used: (1) whether legislators felt they had above-average influence in the assembly; (2) whether they reported a 60% or better adoption record for the legislation they sponsored; and (3) whether they said they enjoyed holding public office.

The intercorrelations among these measures were surprisingly low, indicating that several dimensions of activity and success exist. There was a moderate correlation of .42 between time spent on assembly duties and introducing legislation. Thus, while there is some evidence (as discussed in the previous section) that sponsoring legislation may not be as important in Taiwan as in many other parliamentary situations, it clearly is tied to broader dimensions of legislative activism. On the other hand, holding committee chairmanships is only weakly related to introducing amendments and resolutions ($r = .24$) and was almost completely uncorrelated with time devoted to official duties. Assuming leadership positions, then, does not appear to be as time-consuming as other facets of a legislator's work, such as maintaining good relations with voters and interest groups. The associations among the three indicators of legislative success were even more modest. There was only a weak correlation of .21 between perceived legislative influence and resolution success rate, and enjoyment of an assembly position was unrelated to the other two success indicators.

The data in Table 9.8 on these six variables support two central conclusions. First, despite the conventional image of weak assemblies in Taiwan, legislators in the ROC claim to be quite active and successful. Over half stated that they devoted more than 50 hours a week to their official duties; almost half had chaired at least two assembly committees at some level; and half the assemblymen and a third of the assemblywomen sponsored over 15 legislative initiatives during an average session. In terms of legislative success, 74% of the sample enjoyed holding office, 59% felt that they had above-average influence (which obviously suggests some misperceptions about what "average influence" was), and 44% said that well over half of their resolutions and amendments ultimately passed. Clearly, these assemblywomen and men felt that they constituted far more than a rubber stamp for an authoritarian executive.

Second, the expectation that women would be less active and successful than men generally does not hold except for the much greater propensity of men to sponsor resolutions. There was almost no difference between men and women in time devoted to legislative service or in the number of committee chairs held; women even claimed to be more successful than men within the assemblies on all three indicators used here. Moreover, these simple percentage comparisons between the sexes in Table 9.8 are confirmed by the more complex multivariate results presented in Tables 9.9 and 9.10. Thus, while women were clearly less likely to sponsor legislation, these data suggest a surprising degree of gender equality on other important dimensions of legislative endeavors.

Table 9.8  Legislative Activity and Success Differences Among Respondent Groups

|  | Male Legislator (%) | Female Legislator (%) | Female Loser (%) | Female 1969 Legislator (%) | V |
|---|---|---|---|---|---|
| *Activity Level*[a] | | | | | |
| Work Over 50 Hrs/Wk | 49 | 59 | 60 | 47 | .11 |
| Two Committee Chairs | 44 | 41 | 50 | 50 | .07 |
| Over 15 Resolutions/Session | 52 | 34 | 17 | 41 | .24[b] |
| *Legislative Success*[a] | | | | | |
| Above-Average Influence | 51 | 54 | 86 | 68 | .24[b] |
| Over 60 Resolutions Passed | 35 | 46 | 64 | 47 | .19 |
| Enjoy Public Office | 56 | 85 | 64 | 100 | .38[c] |
| *Problems with Office*[a] | | | | | |
| No Sense/Accomplishment | 40 | 56 | 64 | 50 | .18 |
| Powerlessness | 30 | 26 | 14 | 10 | .18 |
| Duties Too Great | 9 | 15 | 14 | 5 | .12 |
| Political Conflicts | 33 | 18 | 29 | 10 | .21[b] |
| Relations with Voters | 44 | 26 | 29 | 10 | .27[c] |
| Role Conflicts | 12 | 26 | 14 | 15 | .16 |
| *Ambition* | | | | | |
| Run for Same Office | 56 | 49 | 51 | 25 | .19[b] |
| Run for Another Office | 47 | 31 | 40 | 15 | .21[b] |
| Run for Either | 72 | 56 | 62 | 25 | .29[c] |

[a]Percentages computed for only those 14 losing candidates who had previously held some legislative office.
[b]Statistically significant at .15 level.
[c]Statistically significant at .05 level.

The multiple regression results for the indicators of legislative activity in Table 9.9 and of political success in Table 9.10 are suggestive about the nature of assemblies in Taiwan in several regards. First, politics in these bodies appears quite fluid. For example, experience in party and even in electoral office had no influence on either activity or success; the most active legislators were neither more nor less likely than their colleagues to be successful. More importantly perhaps, while the legislators who had chaired two or more committees had some characteristics of the politically powerful in Taiwan (i.e., being Mainlanders and Kuomintang members), the strength of this relationship was much more modest than anticipated, as indicated by a fairly weak Multiple R of .31 (in contrast to the R's of approximately .50 for the other five dependent variables). Moreover, party affiliation and Mainlander origin had no impact upon any of the other indicators of activism and success; liberals were even somewhat more likely than conservatives to believe that they were influential, belying the conservative images of Taiwan's politics.

Area of committee service did have some influence on activity and success, though, suggesting some regularity to activity within the parliamentary arena. The previous indications that assemblywomen and men who were interested in education were somewhat out of the legislative mainstream receives further confirmation from the fact that members of education committees had less influence and spent less time than their colleagues on legislative duties. In addition, members of interior and finance committees were much less likely (32% and 26% respectively) to have a high success rate for their legislative initiatives, suggesting that these may be low-status committees. More surprisingly, economics committee members were somewhat less likely (22%) to believe that they had above-average legislative influence than were other assembly members, despite the presumed attractiveness of such assignments for influence over patronage projects. Perhaps, they were frustrated by the widespread practice of other legislators trying to influence policies in this area that was implied by the previously noted lack of correlation between committee membership and sponsoring resolutions in the area of economic affairs.

Second, association with traditional political networks and other ties external to the assemblies themselves appear to have exerted an important influence on several of the success and activity indicators. The surprising finding that people from elite universities were actually 31% less likely than other assembly members to have held multiple committee chairs, thus, might be explained by the power of traditional political groupings in which power derives much more from longterm kinship and social bonds than from the attainment of "modern" and "elite" characteristics.[12] Ties to traditional groups also appeared an asset in gaining support for legislative initiatives since legislators who had other relatives having held political office and who stressed subordinate roles were more successful in getting their resolutions passed than those who did not. The latter relationship again shows that activism does not necessarily breed success and calls to mind the adage from the U.S. Congress: "To get along, go along."[13]

In contrast to these indications that association with traditional networks was an advantage in legislative politics, respondents with two characteristics assumed to be associated with these traditional factional groupings (i.e., receiving campaign help from religious groups and coming from rural areas) enjoyed office much less than did their colleagues. This implies that the transition Taiwan was commencing at that time toward more democratic and media-centered politics had begun to create stress for those whose political ties and skills were successful in the traditional system.

Table 9.9  Regression Explanations of Legislative Activity

| | Over 50 Hrs Legislative Work/Wk | Held 2 or More Committee Chairs | Over 15 Resolutions per Legislative Session |
|---|---|---|---|
| Multiple R | .51[a] | .31[a] | .49[a] |
| *Regression Coefficients* | | | |
| Female | .05 | -.07 | -.21[a] |
| Christian | -.49[a] | — | — |
| Constituent Service Important | .40[a] | — | — |
| Father College Education | .40[a] | — | — |
| Education Committee Member | -.26[a] | — | — |
| Elite University | — | -.31[a] | — |
| Mainlander | — | .24[a] | — |
| KMT | — | .16[a] | — |
| Sponsored Economic Resolutions | — | — | .24[a] |
| Other Relatives Held Office | — | — | .23[a] |
| College Education | — | — | .20[a] |
| Constituent Service Important | — | — | .18[a] |
| Administrative Oversight Important | — | — | .17[a] |
| Politically Related 1st Political Interest | — | — | .17[a] |

[a]Statistically significant at .05 level.


Table 9.10  Regression Explanations of Legislative Success

| | Above-Average Legislative Influence | Over 60% Resolution Success Rate | Enjoys Public Office |
|---|---|---|---|
| Multiple R | .52[a] | .51[a] | .47[a] |
| *Regression Coefficients* | | | |
| Female | .17[b] | .13[b] | .20[a] |
| Education Committee Member | -.34[a] | — | — |
| Liberal | .24[a] | — | — |
| Economics Committee Member | -.22[a] | — | — |
| Above-Ave Personal Qualifications | .20[a] | — | — |
| Subordinate Roles Important | — | .35[a] | — |
| Interior Committee Member | — | -.32[a] | — |
| Finance Committee Member | — | -.26[a] | — |
| Other Relatives Held Office | — | .20[a] | — |
| Religious Group Helped Campaign | — | — | -.29[a] |
| Urban | — | — | .24[a] |

[a]Statistically significant at .05 level.
[b]Statistically significant at .15 level.

Third, several divergent factors evidently stimulate legislators to sponsor resolutions and amendments. First, assembly members who had become interested in politics for political reasons and who had college educations were more likely to introduce legislation, suggesting that the more politicized legislators were more active. Second, more resolutions emanated from respondents who had politically active relatives, who had introduced economic resolutions, and who were concerned with constituent service. This indicates that ties with traditional political networks and the patronage politics of economic projects associated with it, as well as more general concern about appealing to voters, stimulate legislative activity. Third, legislators who were concerned with administrative oversight were also more active, demonstrating that modifying executive initiatives is an important method for exercising such checks against the regime's authority. Finally, even after these diverse motives for sponsoring initiatives are controlled, women remained 21% less likely than men to score highly on this dimension of legislative activity.

It is also worth noting that except for the tendency for members of education committees to devote less time than their colleagues to legislative duties, the influences on spending more than 50 hours a week on official work are not related to activities inside the assemblies. The external orientations and associations of legislators are clearly the most important factor in determining how much time they put in on the job. Thus, those who emphasize constituent service worked longer, while Christians (who would be expected to be less well connected with traditional groups) were much less likely than non-Christians to spend more than 50 hours a week in their political pursuits. In addition, upper-class assembly members (as denoted by having a father with a college education), who might be expected to be under less pressure to earn money from private business activities, were able to devote more time to legislative duties. By the mid-1980s, hence, the assemblies in the Republic of China appeared to be significantly on their way toward making a transformation toward representative bodies for which ties to and service for external constituencies were major functions, if not the primary one.

Frustration with legislative office and ambition to continue a career in electoral politics form two, more indirect measures of legislative success. Several questions touched upon problems with holding assembly office. The answers to them were combined in six categories: (1) receiving no sense of accomplishment in public service; (2) suffering from feelings of powerlessness; (3) being overwhelmed by political duties that became too great; (4) feeling frustrated by political conflicts with other leaders; (5) suffering from conflicts in relations with voters; and (6) perceiving role conflicts with family or business responsibilities. Political ambition was measured by whether a respondent was considering running for the same office again or running for another office in the future.

The data in Table 9.8 show that although these assemblywomen and assemblymen reported significant stress in their political careers, none of the six factors appears to have been overwhelming. Half said they felt no sense of accomplishment, but the other problems were much less likely to be cited. A third had experienced conflicts with voters; about a fifth were bothered by political conflicts, role conflicts, or feelings of powerlessness; and only a tenth complained that their political duties were too great. Furthermore, these perceived problems did not seem to dampen the respondents' ambition for pursuing electoral careers. Except for the 1969 assemblywomen, who quite understandably were much less interested in running for office in the future, half the respondents said they would run for the same office; 40% indicated interest in seeking another elected post. In the combined answers to these two questions, over 60% of the sample (excluding the 1969 assemblywomen) said they would probably run for some office in the future.

Our working hypothesis—that women would experience more problems in office-holding and be less ambitious than their male colleagues—receives partial but far from full support from the percentages in Table 9.8 and the multivariate results in Table 9.11, which contains the Multiple R and regression coefficient for gender in the final regression equations for these variables. (Full regression results for selected dependent variables are presented in Tables 9.12 and 9.13.)

In terms of the raw percentages, women were more likely to cite three types of problems with holding legislative office—no sense of accomplishment, duties too great, and role conflicts. Men were more likely to cite the other three—powerlessness, political conflicts, and relations with voters. However, this image of a balance between the sexes, with men and women facing an equal number of different problems, is challenged by the multivariate results. Once other explanatory factors are taken into account, women were significantly more likely than men to suffer from two of these problems (21% for no sense of accomplishment and 14% for duties too great), while men were more sensitive only to one problem (19% for political conflicts). Thus, women do seem to experience somewhat greater strains in carrying out their assembly duties.

Men clearly were more ambitious than women. The difference between the sexes was fairly minor in terms of the desire to run for reelection to the same assembly post. However, men were significantly more likely than women to want to run for another office, thus displaying more ambition to climb the political ladder than simply to continue in the same seat. When the two questions were combined, 72% of the men, compared with 60% of the women, indicated that they wanted to run for some office (either the same one or another); after other independent variables are controlled, men were 21% more likely than women to express the desire to enter the electoral lists again. Thus, just as in the United States,[14] women politicians tend to be less ambitious than their male counterparts, a finding in line with the disadvantaged-status hypothesis.

Table 9.11  Effects of Gender in Regressions for Legislative Problems and Ambition for Office

|  | Multiple R | Gender Regression Coefficient |
|---|---|---|
| *Legislative Problems* |  |  |
| No Sense of Accomplishment | .38[a] | .21[a] |
| Powerlessness | .34[a] | -.07 |
| Duties Too Great | .40[a] | .14[a] |
| Political Conflicts | .41[a] | -.19[a] |
| Relations with Voters | .41[a] | -.04 |
| Role Conflicts | .41[a] | .01 |
| *Ambition* |  |  |
| Run for Same Office | .56[a] | -.08 |
| Run for Another Office | .38[a] | -.16[b] |
| Run for Either | .47[a] | -.21[a] |

[a]Statistically significant at .05 level.
[b]Statistically significant at .15 level.

The full regression results in Table 9.12 for three of the legislative problems imply that members of the political establishment in the Republic of China have fewer problems, while those who are more politically concerned have higher degrees of alienation. Urban legislators and those with substantial party experience, both probable marks of establishment status, were, respectively, 25% and 27% less likely than their colleagues to feel no sense of accomplishment in politics; members of finance committees, which previous analysis showed to be comparatively low-status ones, were more likely than others to experience feelings of powerlessness. On the other hand, members of the establishment Nationalist Party were more frustrated than independents in the sense of not taking any pride in their political accomplishments,[15] suggesting a negative reaction to the new political reforms that were challenging the KMT's dominant role in Taiwan's politics (see Chapter 3).

The issue-oriented and more experienced assembly members were the most prone to feelings of powerlessness, implying that the legislators who were most involved in assembly politics were the most frustrated by executive dominance in a fairly authoritarian polity. Likewise, respondents who thought that decisionmaking was an important assembly function were involved in (or at least aggravated by) the most political conflicts, although legislators who held the most committee chairs tended to see political conflicts as less of a problem. This suggests that these committee chairs either had developed the political skills to manage clashing interests within the legislative arena or had the requisite political contacts to deal with executive officials.

Table 9.12  Regression Explanations of Legislative Problems

| | No Sense of Accomplishment | Powerlessness | Political Conflicts |
|---|---|---|---|
| Multiple R | .38[a] | .34[a] | .41[a] |
| *Regression Coefficients* | | | |
| Female | .21[a] | -.07 | -.19[a] |
| Substantial Party Experience | -.27[a] | — | — |
| Urban | -.25[a] | — | — |
| KMT | .25[a] | — | — |
| Issues Stimulated Running | — | .22[a] | — |
| Substantial Electoral Experience | — | .16[a] | — |
| Finance Committee Member | — | .15[a] | — |
| Decisionmaking Important | — | — | .24[a] |
| Held 2 Committee Chairs | — | — | -.22[a] |

[a]Statistically significant at .05 level.

The multiple regression in Table 9.13 for desire to run for either the same or another elected office draws an interesting picture of what may be termed the "assembly careerist" in Taiwan's politics—that is, people most interested in a full-time career in elective office. First, candidates with the economic and social advantages denoted by a professional occupation ($b = -.22$) and having a father with a college education ($b = -.19$) were less desirous of future office, implying that their greater socioeconomic resources made them less eager for a political career. Similarly, those who may have been co-opted into politics by a politically active spouse were less ambitious as well ($b = -.19$). Second, such careerists did not enter politics because of issue concerns or because they had become politicized. Rather, their first interest in politics stemmed from family-related reasons ($b = .22$). Third, the more ambitious politicians tended to devote more time to their legislative duties ($b = .16$). Since activities external to the assemblies, such as constituent service, were the major determinants of whether legislators worked more than 50 hours a week (see Table 9.9), this implies that ambition drives assembly members to appeal to voters and interest groups, in line with the logic of democratic theory. Finally, as would be expected, younger politicians were more likely to want to run for office in the future ($b = -.19$).

As in the United States, where the distinction between "professional" and "amateur" politicians was first made,[16] therefore, many politicians in our sample seemed interested in legislative offices basically for career-related reasons, rather than because of ingrained interest in issues and politics per se. This interpretation is supported by some of the factors that did not have any effect on political ambition. Normally, it would be expected that legislators who were more successful in their assembly posts would be the most likely to run for office again. However, none of the measures of legislative success or role difficulties had any impact on ambition, nor did almost any facet of life within the assemblies. In addition, such variables as party affiliation and ideological preference were unrelated to ambition, indicating that careerism spanned the political spectrum in Taiwan.

Table 9.13  Regression Explanation of Political Ambition

|  | Plan to Run for Same or Another Office |
|---|---|
| Multiple R | .47[a] |
| *Regression Coefficients* |  |
| Female | -.22[a] |
| Family-Related 1st Political Interest | .22[a] |
| Professional Occupation | -.22[a] |
| Over 45 | -.19[a] |
| Spouse Held Political Office | -.19[a] |
| Father College Education | -.19[a] |
| Over 50 Hrs Legislative Work/Wk | .16[a] |

[a]Statistically significant at .05 level.

The working hypothesis in this section was that women, compared with their male colleagues, would be less active and successful within Taiwan's assemblies and less ambitious in pursuing their political careers. These expectations found partial support in the data analysis. Women were clearly less active in sponsoring legislation, somewhat more prone to complain about the difficulties associated with legislative service, and, in particular, less ambitious in pursuing further careers in electoral politics. On the other hand, there was no difference between the sexes on other dimensions of activism within the assemblies; furthermore, women scored higher than men on all the other indicators of legislative success, providing a surprising degree of support for the gender-neutral model.

This picture is confirmed by the discriminant analysis results in Table 9.14 for these activity and success indicators. The ability of these items to distinguish between assemblywomen and assemblymen was fairly strong, with a canonical correlation of .61. However, the two strongest items showed that women enjoyed public office more than did men ($dc = .71$) and spent more time than their male colleagues on their legislative work ($dc = .59$), in direct contrast to a priori expectations. The other four discriminating variables had the anticipated effects, though. Women were more likely to have serious role conflicts between their political and nonpolitical lives ($dc = .55$) and to get no sense of accomplishment out of politics ($dc = .53$), while men were more prone to sponsor resolutions ($dc = -.50$) and to want to run for some office again in the future (dc = -.34). It is noteworthy that when other aspects of the differences between current male and female legislators are controlled, the gender gap on role conflicts is revealed as much wider than suggested by the initial comparison between the sexes, reaffirming previous findings in Chapter 7 that women politicians were much more subject to role conflicts than were men.

Table 9.14 Discriminant Analysis for Women Versus Men Legislators on Legislative Activity and Success

| | |
|---|---|
| *Canonical Correlation* | .61 |
| *Group Centroids* | |
| Assemblywomen | .84 |
| Assemblymen | -.70 |
| *Discriminant Function Coefficients* | |
| Enjoy Public Office | .71 |
| Over 50 Hrs Legislative Work/Wk | .59 |
| Role Conflicts Legislative Problem | .55 |
| No Sense of Accomplishment | .53 |
| Sponsored Over 15 Resolutions per Session | -.50 |
| Run for Some Office in Future | -.34 |

*Note:* Canonical correlation is significant at .0001 level. Statistical significance of individual discriminant function coefficients cannot be computed, but all entered the discriminant equation at the .05 level.

We are, hence, again left with the question of whether the glass is half empty or half full. In many ways, assemblywomen differed little from their male colleagues in their legislative activities, a finding that bodes well for achieving the equitable representation of women. They certainly appear to have been far more effective than would have been predicted from the nature of the Chinese society and polity on Taiwan. Still, significant problems in their positions can be found as well. Their lower ambition means that over time women may avail themselves of the tremendous advantages of incumbency less than men; women's reluctance to sponsor legislation must hurt their name recognition and appeal to interest groups; and their greater role conflicts and lesser abilities to find meaning in their political careers put additional strain on their motivation to build upon the political resources they have accumulated.

## Implications

The description and analysis in this chapter about legislative behavior in the Republic of China produced some interesting and even surprising results both about the role of assemblies in Taiwan's politics and about the role of women in legislative life. Taiwan's legislatures clearly have a significant, albeit circumscribed, role in the overall political system. Assembly members appear much more active, at least in certain regards, than might have been expected given the regime's authoritarian image at that time. Many legislators evidently were deeply involved in such normal representative functions as helping traditional political groups and using economic and local development legislation to help constituents; the opposition (*tangwei*) used the assemblies for publicizing and promoting their cause; and there was strong support for involving the assemblies in important decisionmaking and administrative oversight activities. On the other hand, many assembly members were clearly frustrated by the extent of executive dominance, indicating growing legislative activism and challenge to the established way of doing things.

There were several indications that assembly life was becoming more democratic and issue-oriented as the domination of political life in Taiwan by the Kuomintang Party and traditional political networks eroded. As a result, assembly politics appeared to be fairly unstructured by comparison with the much more institutionalized legislatures in advanced industrial democracies. For example, activity and success within the assemblies were not related to each other, and neither had much impact on political ambition. Also, while political orientations and characteristics influenced committee service in a predictable manner, they had little association with several other important dimensions of legislative activity (e.g., sponsoring resolutions or holding committee chairmanships).

Women's roles in Taiwan's legislatures were surprisingly equal to men's in sevaral important ways, perhaps reflecting the lack of institutionalization of power relationships suggested previously. Assemblywomen and assemblymen differed little in terms of role orientations, most types of legislative activities, and self-reported success within the assemblies. On the other hand, women were less likely than their male colleagues to receive special party training, to sponsor resolutions and amendments, and to be ambitious about running for future elective office.

However, despite these instances of disadvantaged status, the gender-neutral model appears more applicable overall. In fact, women's greater concern with constituent service and local development projects compared with men's suggests that women may even be better at adapting to the new democratic and competitive political environment. Certainly, the gender gap in legislative effectiveness has closed much faster in Taiwan than in the United States (see the U.S. findings cited at the beginning of this chapter). The basic reason for this striking amount of gender equality, of course, lies in the countersocialization factors discussed in Chapters 7 and 8. This raises a possible paradox, though. If women's representation is to increase greatly, a much wider spectrum of women must run for office, but if they do, they may not have the countersocialization resources to act so equally within the legislative arena.

## Notes

1. Irene Diamond, *Sex Roles in the State House* (New Haven: Yale University Press, 1977) Chps. 4 & 5; Marilyn Johnson and Susan Carroll, *Profile of Women Holding Office II* (New Brunswick, N.J.: Center for the American Woman and Politics, Rutgers University, 1978) Parts II and III; Carol Mueller, "Women's

Organizational Strategies in State Legislatures," in Janet A. Flammang, ed., *Political Women: Current Roles in State and Local Government* (Beverly Hills, Calif.: Sage, 1984) pp. 156–176; and Jeanie R. Stanley and Diane D. Blair, "Gender Differences in Legislative Effectiveness," paper presented at the Annual Meeting of the American Political Science Association, Atlanta, Georgia, August 31–September 3, 1989.

2. Because of the very large number of potential explanatory factors for the legislative behavior items examined in this chapter, the final regression equations are limited to only those independent variables (in addition to gender) that were statistically significant at the .05 level.

3. Richard L. Engstrom and Chu Chi-hung, "The Impact of the 1980 Supplementary Elections on Nationalist China's Legislative Yuan," *Asian Survey* 24:4 (April 1984) pp. 446–458; and Hung-mao Tien, *The Great Transition: Political and Social Change in the Republic of China* (Stanford, Calif.: Hoover Institution Press, 1989) Chp. 6.

4. Tun-jen Cheng, "Democratizing the Quasi-Leninist Regime in Taiwan," *World Politics* 41:4 (July 1989) pp. 471–499.

5. Tien, *The Great Transition*, Chp. 3.

6. Charles O. Jones, *The United States Congress: People, Place, and Policy* (Homewood, Ill.: Dorsey, 1982) Chps. 8 & 10.

7. Arthur J. Lerman, *Taiwan's Politics: The Provincial Assemblyman's World* (Washington, D.C.: University Press of America, 1978) Chps. 8 & 9; and Tien, *The Great Transition*, Chps. 3 & 6. The correlation between group support and responsibility for patronage areas is not perfect, though, since group ties are unrelated to membership on finance committees whose power over banking and financial institutions is viewed as a prime patronage plum (Tien, *The Great Transition*, p. 158).

8. Tien, *The Great Transition*, Chp. 6.

9. It will be recalled that political groups generally have close ties to the regime in Taiwan. The legislators who both received help from political groups and introduced resolutions concerning elections or civil rights tended to be KMT members and conservatives. Thus, even in the mid-1980s, insurgent independents and liberals had not yet begun challenging authoritarian political structures by formally introducing legislation.

10. Yangsun Chou and Andrew J. Nathan, "Democratizing Transition in Taiwan," *Asian Survey* 27:3 (March 1987) pp. 280–282; and Alexander Ya-li Lu, "Future Democratic Developments in the Republic of China on Taiwan," *Asian Survey* 25:11 (November 1985) pp. 1085–1092.

11. Obviously, excluding 23 of the 47 losing candidates makes the remaining 14 unrepresentative for purposes of statistical comparison. In addition, because almost all of the losing candidates were under age 45, excluding them from the discriminant analysis also skews the results in the generational comparison.

12. See Lerman, *Taiwan's Politics*, Part II; J. Bruce Jacobs, "A Preliminary Model of Particularistic Ties in Chinese Political Alliances: *Kan-ch'ing* and *Kuan-hsi* in a Rural Taiwanese Township," *China Quarterly* 78 (June 1979) pp. 237–273; Tien, *The Great Transition*, pp. 164–171; and Edwin A. Winckler, "Roles Linking State and Society," in Emily Martin Ahern and Hill Gates, eds., *The Anthropology of Taiwanese Society* (Stanford, Calif.: Stanford University Press, 1981) pp. 50–86.

13. See the discussion of the "informal rules" of Congress by Malcolm E. Jewell and Samuel C. Patterson, *The Legislative Process in the United States*, 3rd Ed. (New York: Random House, 1977) pp. 331–338. This particular quote from former Speaker of the House of Representatives Sam Rayburn is on p. 332.

14. Janet Clark, Charles D. Hadley, and R. Darcy, "Political Ambition Among Men and Women State Party Leaders: Testing the Countersocialization Perspective," *American Politics Quarterly* 17:2 (April 1989) pp. 194–207.

15. Since KMT members were much more likely to have substantial experience in party posts than nonmembers, there is the possibility that this unexpected positive relationship is an artifact of "multicollinearity" (i.e., very high intercorrelation between two independent variables in a multiple regression that distorts the statistical results). However, tests for multicollinearity showed that this is not a problem here.

16. C. Richard Hofstetter, "Organizational Activists: The Bases of Participation in Amateur and Professional Groups," *American Politics Quarterly* 1:2 (April 1973) pp. 244–276; and James Q. Wilson, *The Amateur Democrat: Club Politics in Three Cities* (Chicago: University of Chicago Press, 1962).

# PART FOUR
# CONCLUSION

CHAPTER TEN

# The Taiwan Experience and Overcoming Barriers to Women's Political Participation and Representation

Women have been forced to assume a subordinate role in almost every society known to man (and especially to woman). They are subordinated within patriarchal families, suffer from sex segregation into less desirable occupations within both agricultural and industrial economies, and remain largely excluded from positions of political leadership. Thus, many people have concluded that only radical cultural, social, economic, and political change can free women from their bondage. Whether such change should start with sociocultural values, the structure of the economy, or political institutions is more controversial and ambiguous, however.

Whether political change is possible in the absence of cultural or economic transformations is a judgment not made here, but women's gross underrepresentation in almost every government in the world certainly appears a key factor in the perpetuation of their second-class status. Given the ability of public policy to shape economic and social institutions, women's equality will probably be kept off the serious public agenda until women move much closer to equitable political representation than they are today. As discussed in Chapter 2, therefore, women are in particular need of receiving "descriptive representation," both because they have their own interests that are inadequately represented by men and because their approach to politics differs significantly from the current male-dominated style of decisionmaking. Thus, the question of how women can overcome the existing barriers against their participation in the political processes appears central to redefining their place in society.

The twentieth century has witnessed a revolution in women's political participation, although women clearly remain second-class citizens in terms of political representation in every government in the world. During this century, women gained the suffrage in almost all nations, and by the mid-1980s women constituted about a tenth of the members elected to national legislatures. Their representation was best in the socialist countries, both developed and developing, where they held over a fifth of the seats, and clearly better in the developed world, where they scored major gains during the 1970s and 1980s, than in the nonsocialist Third World nations (see Table 1.1).

There are two conflicting theoretical traditions for interpreting these data. Modernization theory argues that industrialization and the accompanying social change inevitably create gender equality through a three-step process: Women move out of the home into independent employment, become interested in the public sphere, and ultimately run for and are elected to political leadership positions. In sharp contrast, feminist theory contends that industrialization continues, if not intensifies, the subordination of women. Women's economic positions are marginalized, and capitalism reinforces patriarchal norms. Thus, there is a fundamental disagreement as to whether women's representation is a glass one-tenth full or nine-tenths empty.

Writing within the feminist tradition, Margaret Leahy provides an interesting perspective upon these data with her argument that both industrialization and a revolution in gender roles are necessary for women to move toward equality. Thus, women have much lower representation in parliaments of capitalist societies than in socialist ones because the demands of capitalism's "economic efficiency" premise preclude the transformation of gender roles.[1] Leahy's theoretical perspective can also explain the rapid rise of women's representation in many industrial democracies during the last two decades. Clearly, industrialization itself does not provide the answer— many of these nations had been industrialized for long periods. Rather, the key factor in the 1970s and 1980s was the rise of the women's movement that helped change social norms about gender roles to a considerable extent and promoted women's entrance into the professional occupations that form the basic eligibility pool for political leadership positions.[2] In 1988, for example, 65% of Americans believed that "women should have an equal role with men in running business, industry, and government," while only 13% said that "women's place is in the home"— certainly betokening a rejection of traditional role stereotypes.[3] Ironically, then, the feminist movement itself might be responsible for gainsaying at least a little of the extreme pessimism of feminist theory.

The conclusion that improvements in women's representation are possible but far from certain or inevitable turns our attention to the barriers that prevent women from participating in politics on an equal basis and explain their severe underrepresentation throughout the world. Chapter 2 outlined three such general sets of barriers: (1) socialization norms that inhibit women from entering the alien sphere of public life, (2) discrimination against women by political leaders and the mass citizenry, and (3) structural features of electoral politics (e.g., the advantages of incumbency and different types of electoral systems that either hurt or help the chances of women candidates). Feminists stress the first two (and thus deem the third irrelevant); modernizationists tend to assume that the first two are transitory remnants of traditional society.

## The Taiwan Experience

This book has used the Republic of China on Taiwan as a case study for assessing the problem of women's political underrepresentation. Taiwan has a strongly patriarchal society, a rapidly industrializing economy, and an electoral system that provides a guarantee for a minimum level of women's representation. In combination, these factors have differing implications about the strength of the barriers to women's political participation. Thus, an examination of women's political status on Taiwan should provide an interesting comparison for the differing predictions of the feminist and modernization theories. Furthermore, evaluating the efficacy of Taiwan's reserved-seats system for increasing women's political participation and representation is important in itself because it could serve as a model for other societies concerned with promoting equality for women.

The impact of the ROC's rapid industrialization upon the status of women as described in Chapter 4 was mixed in the sense that it did not fully conform to either the optimism of the modernization approach or the pessimism of feminism. Some women clearly benefited from industrialization—they were able to move into professional and, to a lesser extent, administrative positions, and horizontal sex segregration appears to be surprisingly limited. Just as clearly, however, pronounced problems of vertical sex segregation exist, and women have been marginalized in agriculture and perhaps in labor-intensive manufacturing. Thus, women's position in industrializing Taiwan is dependent upon their class positions and educational attainments.

In terms of political representation, this meant that women now form a significant minority of people in the eligibility pools from which politicians normally emerge. There are several reasons, though, to discount these gains. First, women probably form a much smaller proportion of these eligibility pools than, for example, in the United States, where women's ability to enter the political elites still remains far from overwhelming. Second, Taiwan's patriarchal culture and the recency of its industrial transformation suggest that considerable skepticism may exist over the legitimacy of women's candidates. Finally, the women's movement in Taiwan did not become a salient force in intellectual and political life until the late 1980s; thus, its impact upon public views of gender roles must still be quite limited. In short, socialization and discrimination barriers would be expected to be very high.

In contrast, one structural aspect of the electoral system was extremely favorable: The reserved-seats system provided a quota of about one-tenth of the seats in legislative bodies at all levels of government. The fundamental question that this raises is whether the women who assumed these seats were co-opted tokens or were more individualistic activists. An important part of the answer to this question, of course, is whether women politicians could get elected in their own right. The election data in Chapter 5 indicate that this was somewhat doubtful for the 1950s and 1960s because women could win scarcely any seats beyond their quota. By the end of the 1980s, however, women were winning well more than their reserved minimums in assemblies at all levels of government and beginning to make some inroads into unreserved elected executive posts. Thus, having women serve in assemblies during the 1950s and 1960s might have served a function analogous to the one performed by the women's movement in the West of legitimizing and stimulating women's assumption of new social and political roles.

This turns analytic attention to the actual attitudes and behaviors of women politicians in Taiwan. We tapped these through an in-depth survey of assemblywomen and several comparator groups in 1985 that examined seven broad characteristics: childhood socialization, adult socialization, political resources, ideology, attitudes about women's political roles, orientations toward legislative behavior, and legislative effectiveness. We then analyzed differences among the comparator groups to test three broad models that might explain the situation of female legislators in Taiwan: (1) the implication of extreme modernization theory that politics should be gender-neutral; (2) the argument of extreme feminist theory that women would universally be subjected to *disadvantaged-status* conditions; and (3) the expectation of a more moderate feminist approach that most women politicians would have to experience significant *countersocialization* in order to overcome cultural barriers against political participation in a patriarchal society.

Tables 10.1 and 10.2 summarize these empirical results. The first table examines each of the seven principal types of legislator characteristics analyzed here in terms of which of the three models of women's political situation proved applicable and of which explanatory variables were most important, comparing these results with the hypotheses developed in Chapter 6. Table 10.2 then summarizes the primary distinctions between the two groups in each of the three sets of analytic groups on which the study was based: (1) assemblywomen versus assemblymen, (2) winning versus losing female candidates, and (3) old-generation versus new-generation women.

Political recruitment obviously lies at the heart of women's representation. The summary of results in Tables 10.1 and 10.2 provide strong support for countersocialization theory. Assemblywomen, compared with their male colleagues, had far more countersocialization experiences (e.g., coming from a supportive or politicized family), and winning women candidates were significantly more likely than losing ones to be exposed to countersocialization. In addition, strong countersocialization is also implied by the failure of several predicted behavioral and attitudinal differences to emerge between old-generation and new-generation women politicians. This implies that the women who pioneered in Taiwan's politics were very special because of factors that helped them to overcome the barriers against them in traditional Chinese society.

Furthermore, because of some aspects of countersocialization, in particular having an elite family background, women and men were surprisingly equal in the possession of political resources. The importance of this for political success is certainly indicated by the fact that among just women socioeconomic and political resources had a strong impact on whether an individual candidate won or lost. Women did have a dis-

Table 10.1  Summary of Results About Seven Basic Factors in Assemblywomen Study

|  | Explanatory Models | Determinants of Behavior |
|---|---|---|
| Childhood Socialization | *Countersocialization* | — |
| Adult Socialization | *Countersocialization*<br>family support<br>self-confidence<br><br>*Gender-Neutral*<br>socioeconomic resources<br>objective role conflicts<br>(from countersocialization)<br><br>*Disadvantaged-Status*<br>elite university<br>subjective role conflicts | Childhood socialization as predicted |
| Political Resources | *Gender-Neutral*<br>group, party, experience<br>(from countersocialization)<br><br>*Disadvantaged-Status*<br>group campaign support | Socioeconomic resources and adult roles as predicted |
| Ideology | *Countersocialization* | Political resources and adult roles but weaker than predicted |
| Women's Roles | *Disadvantaged-Status*<br>discrimination<br><br>*Countersocialization*<br>women's contributions | Political resources not predicted; Ideology but weaker than predicted<br>Adult roles as predicted |
| Legislative Orientations | *Gender-Neutral*<br>role definitions<br>committee service<br><br>*Disadvantaged-Status*<br>party training<br>resolutions | Political resources as predicted; Ideology but much weaker than predicted<br>Adult roles but slightly weaker than predicted |
| Legislative Effectiveness | *Gender-Neutral*<br>success, activities<br>except resolutions<br><br>*Disadvantaged-Status*<br>ambition, resolutions | Political resources but different than predicted (group ties, not party) |

advantaged status on several important aspects of the recruitment process, though. There was widespread agreement that women continued to suffer from political discrimination; interest groups were somewhat less willing to support female than male candidates; and women were somewhat less ambitious than men to run for future office, vitiating their incumbency status a little. However, such disadvantages have not proven crippling to women's political ambitions, as their growing success at the polls indicates. On balance, therefore, countersocialization in the self-selection of women politicians produced a surprising gender-neutrality access to socioeconomic and political resources that, in turn, helps explain women's increasing representation over the last decade or so. In contrast, the efficacy of this countersocialization does raise a potential problem—substantially expanding the number of women political leaders will almost inevitably entail recruiting women who have not had such extensive countersocialization.

Table 10.2 Summary of Factors Differentiating Analytic Groups

|  | Assemblywomen/ Assemblymen | Winning/Losing Women Candidates | Old/New Generation Women |
|---|---|---|---|
| Childhood Socialization | Little independent difference | | |
| Adult Socialization | More role conflicts & counter-socialization | More resources & countersocialization | Less self-stimulation |
| Political Resources | Counterbalanced | More resources | More resources |
| Ideology | Little independent difference | | |
| Women's Roles | More positive | Ambiguous | More effort & role conflicts |
| Legislative Orientations | More constituent service, women's issues, and subordinate roles; fewer resolutions | Insufficient data | |
| Legislative Effectiveness | Split on activity and success indicators | Insufficient data | |

*Note:* Characteristics listed above were associated with the first of the two comparison groups (i.e., assemblywomen, winning women candidates, and old-generation women).

The survey data also indicate that a significant change is occurring in the nature of Taiwan's electoral politics and the patterns of recruitment to legislative office. Until recently, traditional political groups based on kinship ties and patronage politics played the central role, with recruitment based on co-optation into these groups.[4] In contrast, democratization, urbanization, and media-centered politics have increased the importance of politicians with greater independence whose primary skills lie in appealing to the general electorate rather than in acting within closed traditional political networks. For women, this change is evident in that younger female candidates were more self-stimulated and issue-oriented than older ones. Thus, while our data suggest that new-style candidates were still at a disadvantage in electoral politics in the mid-1980s, this could well have changed in more recent elections.

In theory, this changing nature of politics in the ROC would seem ambiguous concerning women's electoral chances. On the one hand, traditional political groupings might well be something of a bastion for patriarchal norms; on the other, women would be expected to be more hesitant than men to mix with the people because of Confucian stereotypes about sex roles. In practice, however, both these negative factors appear limited. Women have succeeded in gaining leadership positions in several important traditional groups.[5] Even more importantly, the greater willingness of women, compared to their male colleagues and competitors, to perform constituent-service functions and sponsor local development projects suggests that they may be very well in tune with the expanding democratic processes in the Republic of China.

Women's representation or gaining office, of course, is important because we assume that women will act in ways that benefit their gender group. For them to do this, they must be fairly active and effective in performing their legislative duties. Taiwan's culture and development level, though, would lead one to expect that women would have a very pronounced disadvantaged status in terms of actual political and legislative behavior. They were in fact considerably less prone to sponsor legislation and more likely to suffer from role conflicts. Yet the primary image that Tables 10.1 and 10.2 convey fits the countersocialization model in political attitudes and the gender-neutral model on most aspects of legislative activity, success, and effectiveness, despite the pressures of greater role conflicts.

The comparability of women's and men's political activities derives from the basic countersocialization processes previously noted. Because of the very special nature of women who enter politics in Taiwan, their socioeconomic and political resources are not markedly inferior to those of male politicians. In turn, men and women in politics evidently utilize their resources in fairly equal manners to produce surprisingly similar outcomes by gender on all the principal indicators of legislative effectiveness except sponsoring resolutions and amendments. Thus, as indicated in Table 10.1, the causal hypotheses that we outlined in Chapter 6 about how the seven basic factors influence one another were generally supported—countersocialization in the social background factors ultimately produce gender-neutral outcomes in legislative orientation and effectiveness.

In Taiwan, therefore, women have made significant strides in their political participation and representation over the last several decades that rival the progress that took nearly a century in the United States and Western Europe. The key to this progress in the West was countersocialization both for women candidates and the people who decided their fate (i.e., male party leaders and voters). The women's movement produced a key element in the countersocialization of women politicians and general societies during the 1970s and 1980s, and through the worldwide mass media, some of these effects undoubtedly rubbed off on Taiwan.

For the Republic of China, in contrast, the key element that started the countersocialization revolution was a structural element in the electoral system—the reserved-seats system, which guaranteed that a minimum number of women would hold legislative seats. This provided incentives both for political parties and traditional factions to find women candidates and for women to get involved in politics. Over the last four decades, then, women have seemingly been transformed from primarily tokens to being increasingly activists in two extremely important senses. First, they now win far more than their reserved quota, indicating that they have become competitive political actors on their own. Second, they now seemingly act as independently and effectively within assemblies as do their male colleagues. Women have become so successful, in fact, that many people now question the need for the reserved-seats system.

In terms of broader theoretical implications, the experience of the Republic of China appears closest to the arguments of the liberal-feminist tradition. The gains that women made were almost certainly largely the result of a conscious policy to promote women's representation through the reserved-seats system that, in turn, provided a significant countersocialization experience for women over several decades. On the one hand, this strongly implies that the "automatic" processes of development stressed in modernization theory cannot be left to their own wiles in the achievement of equitable representation. On the other hand, it belies the despair of socialist feminism about achieving any progress in a capitalist and patriarchal society and shows that women can achieve significant progress without retreating to a separate sphere.

Thus, the history of the reserved-seats system in Taiwan should serve as a clarion call for women to act decisively about improving their political and social status. If progress could occur in developing Taiwan with its highly patriarchal Confucian culture, it should be possible almost anywhere. Taiwan's experience also suggests that there is no single path to successful countersocialization. The reserved-seats system served as an analogue to the women's movement in North America and Western Europe for expanding women's demands upon and participation in the polity. Thus, women in other societies should be sensitized to the need *both* for organizing and for promoting institutional change.

In sum, the structural feature of the reserved-seats system has clearly helped women in Taiwan's politics overcome what must have appeared to have been insurmountable barriers of socialization and discrimination at the beginning of the postwar period. Consequently, mandating women's involvement in politics can be very beneficial, even in a highly patriarchal society. This certainly argues for seriously considering Taiwan's election system as a model for other developing societies where women continue to be largely marginalized and underrepresented. The experience of the ROC certainly shows that more than rhetorical support can be given for the UN Decade for Women and that practical steps are available for beginning the integration of women into the polity. While major payoffs may be several decades away, this seems far better than either blindly trusting the impersonal processes of modernization to create equality for women or, conversely, arguing that continuing patriarchy is inevitable no matter what social and political change occurs.

## Notes

1. Margaret E. Leahy, *Development Strategies and the Status of Women: A Comparative Study of the United States, Mexico, the Soviet Union, and Cuba* (Boulder, Colo.: Lynne Rienner, 1986).

2. Barbara Sinclair Deckard, *The Women's Movement: Political, Socioeconomic, and Psychological Issues*, 3rd Ed. (New York: Harper & Row, 1983); Mary Fainsod Katzenstein and Carol McClarg Mueller, eds., *The Women's Movements of the United States and Western Europe: Consciousness, Political Opportunity, and Public Policy* (Philadelphia: Temple University Press, 1987); and Ethel Klein, *Gender Politics: From Consciousness to Mass Politics* (Cambridge: Harvard University Press, 1984).

3. Charles Prysby and Carmine Scavo, *Voting Behavior: The 1988 Election* (Washington, D.C.: American Political Science Association, 1989) p. 55.

4. See Arthur J. Lerman, *Taiwan's Politics: The Provincial Assemblyman's World* (Washington, D.C.: University Press of America, 1978) Part II; J. Bruce Jacobs, "A Preliminary Model of Particularistic Ties in Chinese Political Alliances: *Kan-ch'ing* and *Kuan-hsi* in a Rural Taiwanese Township," *China Quarterly* 78 (June 1979) pp. 237–273; Hung-mao Tien, *The Great Transition: Political and Social Change in the Republic of China* (Stanford, Calif.: Hoover Institution Press, 1989) pp. 164–171; and Edwin A. Winckler, "Roles Linking State and Society," in Emily Martin Ahern and Hill Gates, eds., *The Anthropology of Taiwanese Society* (Stanford, Calif.: Stanford University Press, 1981) pp. 50–86.

5. Carl Chang, "Detailed Platform," *Free China Review* 39:12 (December 1989) p. 21.

# Selected Bibliography

## Women in Politics and Society

Anker, Richard, and Catherine Hein, eds. 1986. *Sex Inequalities in Urban Employment in the Third World.* New York: St. Martin's.

Baxter, Sandra, and Marjorie Lansing. 1980. *Women and Politics: The Invisible Majority.* Ann Arbor: University of Michigan Press.

Blaxall, Martha, and Barbara Reagan, eds. 1976. *Women and the Workplace: The Implications of Occupational Segregation.* Chicago: University of Chicago Press.

Boles, Janet K. 1979. *The Politics of the Equal Rights Amendment: Conflict and Decision Process.* New York: Longman.

Boneparth, Ellen, and Emily Stoper, eds. 1988. *Women, Power, and Policy: Toward the Year 2000.* 2nd Ed. New York: Pergamon.

Boserup, Ester. 1970. *Women's Role in Economic Development.* London: Allen & Unwin.

Boulding, Elise. 1977. *Women in the Twentieth-Century World.* Beverly Hills, Calif.: Sage, 1977.

Bridges, William A. 1980. "Industry Marginality and Female Employment: A New Appraisal," *American Sociological Review* 45:1 (February) pp. 58–75.

Carroll, Susan J. 1985. *Women As Candidates in American Politics.* Bloomington: Indiana University Press.

Carter, April. 1988. *The Politics of Women's Rights.* New York: Longman.

Chaney, Elsa M. 1983. *Scenarios of Hunger in the Caribbean: Migration, Decline of Smallholder Agriculture, and the Feminization of Farming.* East Lansing: Michigan State University, Women in Development Program, Working Paper #18.

Charlton, Sue Ellen M. 1984. *Women in Third World Development.* Boulder, Colo.: Westview.

Dale, Jennifer, and Peggy Foster. 1986. *Feminists and State Welfare.* London: Routledge and Kegan Paul.

Darcy, R., Susan Welch, and Janet Clark. 1987. *Women, Elections, and Representation.* New York: Longman.

Deckard, Barbara Sinclair. 1983. *The Women's Movement: Political, Socioeconomic, and Psychological Issues.* 3rd Ed. New York: Harper & Row.

Diamond, Irene. 1977. *Sex Roles in the State House.* New Haven: Yale University Press.

———, ed. 1983. *Families, Politics, and Public Policy: A Feminist Dialogue on Women and the State.* New York: Longman.

Duverger, Maurice. 1955. *The Political Role of Women.* Paris: UNESCO.

Eisenstein, Zillah H., ed. 1979. *Capitalist Patriarchy and the Case for Socialist*

*Feminism.* New York: Monthly Review Press.
Elshtain, Jean Bethke. 1981. *Public Man, Private Woman: Women in Social and Political Theory.* Princeton: Princeton University Press.
Ferree, Myra Marx, and Beth B. Hess. 1985. *Controversy and Coalition: The New Feminist Movement.* Boston: Twayne.
Flammang, Janet A., ed. 1984. *Political Women: Current Roles in State and Local Government.* Beverly Hills, Calif.: Sage.
Fowlkes, Diane L. 1983. "Developing a Theory of Countersocialization: Gender, Race, and Politics in the Lives of Women Activists," *Micropolitics* 3:2 (No. 2) pp. 181–225.
Freeman, Jo. 1975. *The Politics of Women's Liberation: A Case Study of an Emerging Social Movement and Its Relation to the Policy Process.* New York: David McKay.
Gelb, Joyce. 1989. *Feminism and Politics: A Comparative Perspective.* Berkeley: University of California Press.
Gelb, Joyce, and Marian Lief Palley, eds. 1986. *Women and Public Policies.* Revised and Expanded Ed. Princeton: Princeton University Press.
Gilligan, Carol. 1982. *In a Different Voice: Psychological Theory and Women's Development.* Cambridge: Harvard University Press.
Githens, Marianne, and Jewel L. Prestage, eds. 1977. *A Portrait of Marginality: The Political Behavior of the American Woman.* New York: David McKay.
Haavio-Mannila, Elina, et al. 1985. *Unfinished Democracy: Women in Nordic Politics.* New York: Pergamon.
Hartmann, Susan M. 1989. *From Margin to Mainstream: American Women and Politics Since 1960.* New York: Alfred A. Knopf.
Hess, Beth B., and Myra Marx Ferree, eds. 1987. *Analyzing Gender: A Handbook of Social Science Research.* Beverly Hills, Calif.: Sage.
Iglitzin, Lynne B., and Ruth Ross, eds. 1986. *Women in the World: 1975–1985, The Women's Decade.* 2nd Revised Ed. Santa Barbara, Calif.: ABC-Clio.
Jacobs, Jerry A. 1989. *Revolving Doors: Sex Segregation and Women's Careers.* Stanford, Calif.: Stanford University Press.
Jaquette, Jane S. 1982. "Women and Modernization Theory: A Decade of Feminist Criticism," *World Politics* 34:2 (January) pp. 267–284.
Johnson, Marilyn, and Susan Carroll. 1978. *Profile of Women Holding Office II.* New Brunswick, N.J.: Center for the American Woman and Politics, Rutgers University.
Katzenstein, Mary Fainsod, and Carol McClarg Mueller, eds. 1987. *The Women's Movements of the United States and Western Europe: Consciousness, Political Opportunity, and Public Policy.* Philadelphia: Temple University Press.
Kelly, Rita Mae, and Mary Boutilier. 1978. *The Making of Political Women: A Study of Socialization and Role Conflict.* Chicago: Nelson-Hall.
Kirkpatrick, Jeane J. 1974. *Political Woman.* New York: Basic Books.
Klein, Ethel. 1984. *Gender Politics: From Consciousness to Mass Politics.* Cambridge: Harvard University Press.
Kohn, Walter. 1980. *Women in National Legislatures.* New York: Praeger.
Krauss, Wilma Rule. 1974. "Political Implications of Gender Roles: A Review of the Literature," *American Political Science Review* 68:4 (December) pp. 1706–1723.
Lamson, Peggy. 1968. *Few Are Chosen: American Women in Political Life Today.* Boston: Houghton Mifflin.
Lapidus, Gail Warshofsky. 1978. *Women in Soviet Society: Equality, Development, and Social Change.* Berkeley: University of California Press.
Leahy, Margaret E. 1986. *Development Strategies and the Status of Women: A*

*Comparative Study of the United States, Mexico, the Soviet Union, and Cuba.* Boulder, Colo.: Lynne Rienner.
Le Veness, Frank P., and Jane P. Sweeney, eds. 1987. *Women Leaders in Contemporary U.S. Politics.* Boulder, Colo.: Lynne Rienner.
Lovenduski, Joni. 1986. *Women and European Politics: Contemporary Feminism and Public Policy.* Amherst: University of Massachusetts Press.
Lovenduski, Joni, and Jill Hill, eds. 1981. *The Politics of the Second Electorate: Women and Political Participation.* London: Routledge and Kegan.
Mandel, Ruth B. 1981. *In the Running: The New Woman Candidate.* New Haven, Conn.: Ticknor & Fields.
Mansbridge, Jane M. 1986. *Why We Lost the ERA.* Chicago: University of Chicago Press.
Mueller, Carol M., ed. 1988. *The Politics of the Gender Gap: The Social Construction of Political Influence.* Beverly Hills, Calif.: Sage.
Nash, June, and Maria Patricia Fernandez-Kelly, eds. 1983. *Women, Men, and the International Division of Labor.* Albany: State University of New York Press.
Newman, Jody, Carrie Costantin, Judie Goetz, and Amy Glosser. 1984. *Perceptions and Reality: A Study of Women Candidates and Fundraising.* Washington, D.C.: Women's Campaign Research Fund.
Norris, Pippa. 1987. *Politics and Sexual Equality: The Comparative Position of Women in Western Democracies.* Boulder, Colo.: Lynne Rienner.
Owen, Diana, and Jack Dennis. 1988. "Gender Differences in the Politicization of American Children," *Women & Politics* 8:2 (Summer) pp. 23–43.
Poole, Keith T., and L. Harmon Zeigler, 1985. *Women, Public Opinion, and Politics: The Changing Political Attitudes of American Women.* New York: Longman.
Randall, Vicky. 1987. *Women and Politics: An International Perspective.* 2nd Ed. Chicago: University of Chicago Press.
Reskin, Barbara F., ed. 1984. *Sex Segregation in the Workplace.* Washington, D.C.: National Academy Press.
Rix, Sara E., ed. 1988. *The American Woman, 1988–1989: A Status Report.* New York: Norton.
Rogers, Barbara. 1979. *The Domestication of Women: Discrimination in Development.* New York: St. Martin's.
Roos, Patricia A. 1985. *Gender and Work: A Comparative Analysis of Industrial Societies.* Albany: State University of New York Press.
Rule, Wilma. 1987. "Electoral Systems, Contextual Factors, and Women's Opportunity for Election to Parliament in Twenty-three Democracies," *Western Political Quarterly* 40:3 (September) pp. 477–498.
Saffioti, Heleieth I.B. 1983. *The Impact of Industrialization on the Structure of Female Employment.* East Lansing: Michigan State University, Women in International Development Program, Working Paper #15.
Sapiro, Virginia. 1983. *The Political Integration of Women: Roles, Socialization and Politics.* Urbana: University of Illinois Press.
———. 1981. "Research Frontier Essay: When Are Interests Interesting? The Problem of Political Representation of Women," *American Political Science Review* 75:3 (September) pp. 701–716.
Scott, Alison MacEwan. 1986. "Women and Industrialization: Examining the 'Female Marginalization' Thesis," *Journal of Development Studies* 22:4 (July) pp. 649–680.
Scott, Hilda. 1974. *Does Socialism Liberate Women? Experiences from Eastern Europe.* Boston: Beacon.
Sivard, Ruth. 1985. *Women: A World Survey.* New York: Ford, Rockefeller, and Carnegie.

Tinker, Irene, ed. 1983. *Women in Washington: Advocates for Public Policy.* Beverly Hills, Calif.: Sage.
Tinker, Irene, and Michele Bo Bramsen, eds. 1976. *Women and World Development.* Washington, D.C.: Overseas Development Council.
Tolchin, Susan, and Martin Tolchin. 1976. *Clout: Womanpower and Politics.* New York: Capricorn.
Treiman, Donald J., and Heidi Hartmann, eds. 1981. *Women, Work, and Wages: Equal Pay for Jobs of Equal Value.* Washington, D.C.: National Academy Press.
Verba, Sidney, Norman H. Nie, Jae-on Kim, and Goldie Shabad. 1978. "Men and Women: Sex-Related Differences in Political Activity." In Sidney Verba, Norman H. Nie, and Jae-on Kim, eds., *Participation and Political Equality: A Seven-Nation Comparison.* Cambridge: Cambridge University Press, pp. 234–268.
Welch, Susan. 1977. "Women As Political Animals? A Test of Some Explanations for Male-Female Participation Differences," *American Journal of Political Science* 21:4 (November) pp. 711–730.
Wellesley Editorial Committee. 1977. *Women and National Development: The Complexities of Change.* Chicago: University of Chicago Press.

## Economic and Political Development of the ROC

Ahern, Emily Martin and Hill Gates, eds. 1981. *The Anthropology of Taiwanese Society.* Stanford, Calif.: Stanford University Press.
Cheng, Chu-yuan, ed. 1989. *Sun Yat-sen's Doctrine in the Modern World.* Boulder, Colo.: Westview.
Cheng, Tun-jen. 1989. "Democratizing the Quasi-Leninist Regime in Taiwan," *World Politics* 41:4 (July) pp. 471–499.
Clark, Cal. 1989. *Taiwan's Development: Implications for Contending Political Economy Paradigms.* New York: Greenwood.
Clough, Ralph N. 1978. *Island China.* Cambridge: Harvard University Press.
Copper, John F. 1988. *A Quiet Revolution: Political Development in the Republic of China.* Washington, D.C.: Ethics and Public Policy Center.
Copper John F., with George P. Chen. 1984. *Taiwan's Elections: Political Development and Democratization in the Republic of China.* Baltimore: School of Law, University of Maryland, Chp. 2.
Fei, John C.H., Gustav Ranis, and Shirley W.Y. Kuo. 1979. *Growth with Equity: The Taiwan Case.* New York: Oxford University Press.
Galenson, Walter, ed. 1979. *Economic Growth and Structural Change in Taiwan: The Postwar Experience of the Republic of China.* Ithaca, N.Y.: Cornell University Press.
Gallin, Bernard. 1966. *Hsin Hsing, Taiwan: A Chinese Village in Change.* Berkeley: University of California Press.
Gates, Hill. 1987. *Chinese Working Class Lives: Getting By in Taiwan.* Ithaca, N.Y.: Cornell University Press.
Gold, Thomas B. 1986. *State and Society in the Taiwan Miracle.* Armonk, N.Y.: M. E. Sharpe.
Gregor, A. James, with Maria Hsia Chang and Andrew B. Zimmerman. 1981. *Ideology and Development: Sun Yat-sen and the Economic History of Taiwan.* Berkeley: Institute of East Asian Studies, University of California.
Ho, Samuel P.S. 1978. *Economic Development of Taiwan, 1860–1970.* New Haven: Yale University Press.

Hsiung, James C., ed. 1981. *Contemporary Republic of China: The Taiwan Experience, 1950–1980.* New York: Praeger.
Jacoby, Neil H. 1966. *U.S. Aid to Taiwan: A Study of Foreign Aid, Self-Help, and Development.* New York: Praeger.
Kuo, Shirley W.Y. 1983. *The Taiwan Economy in Transition.* Boulder, Colo: Westview.
Kuo, Shirley W.Y., Gustav Ranis, and John C.H. Fei. 1981. *The Taiwan Success Story: Rapid Growth with Improved Distribution in the Republic of China.* Boulder, Colo.: Westview.
Lee, Teng-hui. 1971. *Intersectoral Capital Flows in the Economic Development of Taiwan, 1895–1960.* Ithaca, N.Y.: Cornell University Press.
Lerman, Arthur J. 1978. *Taiwan's Politics: The Provincial Assemblyman's World.* Washington, D.C.: University Press of America.
Li, K. T. 1988. *The Evolution of Policy Behind Taiwan's Development Success.* New Haven: Yale University Press.
Lin, Ching-yuan. 1973. *Industrialization in Taiwan, 1946–1972: Trade and Import-Substitution Policies for Developing Countries.* New York: Praeger.
Myers, Ramon H. 1984. "The Economic Transformation of the Republic of China on Taiwan," *China Quarterly* 99 (September) pp. 500–528.
———. 1987. "Political Theory and the Recent Political Developments in the Republic of China," *Asian Survey* 27:9 (September) pp. 1003–1022.
Sih, Paul K.T., ed. 1973. *Taiwan in Modern Times.* New York: St. John's University Press.
Sutter, Robert G. 1988. *Taiwan: Entering the 21st Century.* Lanham, Md.: University Press of America.
Tien, Hung-mao. 1989. *The Great Transition: Political and Social Change in the Republic of China.* Stanford, Calif.: Hoover Institution Press.
Winckler, Edwin A. 1984. "Institutionalization and Participation on Taiwan: From Hard to Soft Authoritarianism?" *China Quarterly* 99 (September) pp. 481–499.
Winckler, Edwin A., and Susan Greenhalgh, eds. 1988. *Contending Approaches to the Political Economy of Taiwan.* Armonk, N.Y.: M.E. Sharpe.
Wu, Yuan-li. 1985. *Becoming an Industrialized Nation: ROC's Development on Taiwan.* New York: Praeger.
Yang, Martin M.C. 1970. *Socioeconomic Results of Land Reform in Taiwan.* Honolulu: East-West Center Press.

## Women in Taiwan

Chiang, Lan-hung Nora, and Yenlin Ku. 1985. *Past and Current Status of Women in Taiwan.* Taipei: National Taiwan University, Population Studies Center, Women's Research Program, Monograph #1.
Farris, Catherine S. 1986. *The Sociocultural Construction of Femininity in Contemporary Urban Taiwan.* East Lansing: Michigan State University, Women in International Development Program, Working Paper #131.
Gallin, Rita S. 1984. "Women, Family, and the Political Economy of Taiwan," *Journal of Peasant Studies* 12:1 (October) pp. 76–92.
Gates, Hill. 1979. "Dependency and the Part-time Proletariat in Taiwan," *Modern China* 5:3 (July) pp. 381–407.
Greenhalgh, Susan. 1985. "Sexual Stratification: The Other Side of 'Growth with Equity' in East Asia," *Population and Development Review* 11:2 (June) pp. 265–314.

Huang, Shu-huei. 1985. "The Political Participation and Intentions of Female College and High School Students in Taiwan." Unpublished Master's Thesis. Taipei: National Taiwan University.

Kung, Lydia. 1983. *Factory Women in Taiwan*. Ann Arbor, Mich.: UMI Research Press.

———. 1981. "Perceptions of Work Among Factory Women." In Emily Martin Ahern and Hill Gates, eds., *The Anthropology of Taiwanese Society*. Stanford, Calif.: Stanford University Press, pp. 184–211.

Liang, Suan-laine, ed. 1989. *Women and Political Participation*. Taipei: Awakening Foundation.

Tsay, Ching-lung. 1987. "Status of Women in Taiwan: Educational Attainment and Labor Force Development, 1951–1983," *Academia Economic Papers* 15:1 (No. 1) pp. 153–182.

Tsui, E. Y. 1987. *Are Married Daughters "Spilled Water"?—A Study of Working Women in Urban Taiwan*. Taipei: National Taiwan University, Population Studies Center, Women's Research Program, Monograph #4.

Wolf, Margery. 1972. *Women and the Family in Rural Taiwan*. Stanford, Calif.: Stanford University Press.

Wolf, Margery, and Roxane Witke, eds. 1975. *Women in Chinese Society*. Stanford, Calif.: Stanford University Press.

Yao, Esther Lee. 1981. "Successful Professional Women in Taiwan," *Cornell Journal of Social Relations* 16:1 (Spring) pp. 39–55.

# Index

Academia Sinica, interviews by, 105
Activism, 142, 172, 174, 180
Administration, women in, 62, 68
Administrative oversight, 162, 166; problems with, 182; women legislators and, 163, 170, 176
Agriculture, 75(n10); decline of, 43; investments in, 38; women in, 59, 60, 63–68, 74
Alienation, 72
Ambition, 177–180, 182, 191. *See also* Competitiveness
Amendments: introducing, 169, 176; types of, 167; women sponsoring, 167, 172, 193. *See also* Legislation; Resolutions
Aquino, Corazon, 3
Association, importance of, 111
Attitudes: differences in, 71–72; forming, 108
Awakening (feminist group), work of, 94

Bachrach, Peter, work of, 12
Bandaranaike, Sirimavo, 3
Barriers: cultural, 157; political, 118
Bhutto, Benazir, 3
Boserup, Ester, work of, 3, 57
Boulding, Elise, work of, 15
Boutilier, Mary, work of, 17
Brundtland, Gro Harlem, 3
Buddhists, political pursuits of, 123, 141

Carroll, Susan, work of, 13
Center for the American Woman and Politics, questionnaire of, 103–104
Central Committee (KMT), election of, 47
Central Standing Committee (KMT): Kuo and, 90; role of, 47
Ch'en Yi, 48
Chaing Ching-kuo, 45, 48, 49; KMT and, 47; reforms of, 50
Chaing Kai-shek, 44, 47; National Security Council and, 45
*Chengs*, definition of, 88
Christians, political pursuits of, 123, 129, 176
City council: makeup of, 98(n32); reserved-seats system and, 88–89, 93–94; women in, 89–90, 93, 95, 105
Clerical jobs, women in, 63, 73
Colonialism, 15, 34
Commerce, 75(n10); women in, 59, 60, 64–67
Committee assignments: influence of, 174; legislative activity and, 168; patronage and, 168–169; political experience and, 165; seeking, 164–167; types of, 164; women legislators and, 164–165, 170–171, 176
Committee chairmanships, women legislators and, 172–174
Competitiveness: benefits of, 94–95; women's, 93. *See also* Ambition
Confucian capitalism, development of, 40
Constituent-service, 162, 166; women legislators and, 169, 170, 181, 193
Control Yuan, 44, 83; election of, 45–46, 51
Countersocialization, 7, 110–112, 118, 121, 123–125, 132, 155, 182, 190, 192–194; education and, 68–69; family politicization and, 127–129, 133–135; factors of, 107–109; liberalism and, 108; mother political role and, 123; older-generation women and, 157; reserved-seats system and, 194; selective, 136–137, 139–140; spousal support and, 126. *See also* Socialization

Decade for Women: impact of, 195; proclamation of, 1
Decisionmaking, 162; problems with, 178, 182; role definition and, 163; women legislators and, 170, 172, 187
Democratic centralism, 48
Democratic Progressive party (DPP): competitiveness of, 94–95; election results for, 52; formation of, 50. *See also* Opposition parties
Democratization, 33, 43, 46, 51, 151–152, 158(n11); electoral politics and, 169, 174–175, 182, 192–193; support for, 71; women and, 52

203

Demonstration effect, 24
Descriptive representation, 11–12, 159
Directorate-General of Budget, Accounting, and Statistics (DGBAS),59
Disadvantaged-status conditions, 107, 108, 112, 121, 126, 134, 190; family politicization and, 133
Discriminant analysis, using, 116–17
Discrimination, 11, 24, 68, 94–95, 139, 149, 188; campaign, 152–153; government bureaucracy, 90–91; incumbency and, 148; interest group, 155; KMT and, 154, 158(n12); party, 155–157, 161; political, 153–154, 191; underrepresentation and, 19–21; voter, 20; wage, 68

Economic development, 6, 33–43, 57
Education, 73, 125, 126, 153; countersocialization and, 68–69; gender gap and, 67–68, 74; impact of, 113, 116, 119(n5), 130–131; political efficacy and, 69–73; salaries and, 76(n21); women legislators and, 122, 167–169, 176
Efficacy, political: education and, 69–73; women's, 6, 14–15, 43–52, 70, 74, 154–155, 159
Election systems, influence of, 11, 22–24
Electoral politics: barriers to, 118; democratization of, 169, 174–175, 182, 192–193; entering, 121, 188; success in, 176–177
Electoral systems: types of, 188; reserved-seat, 83
Eligibility pool, 19, 103; employment status and, 62–63; entering, 188, 189
Elite status, indicators of, 122, 123
Employers, women as, 59, 63–66
Employment patterns, changes in, 58–68
Employment status: political status and, 74; vertical segregation and, 63–64
Equality, promoting, 5
Equal Rights Amendment, women's movement and, 13
Examination Yuan, 44; appointment to, 46
Executive dominance, 167; frustration with, 178, 182
Executive elections, women and, 83
Executive Yuan, 44, 46, 47, 83
Experience: administrative, 144, 151–152; electoral, 143, 144, 149, 158(n7), 163, 173; party, 142, 143, 144, 149, 151–152, 158(n3), 158(n7), 169, 173, 184(n15); political, 139, 141–142, 149, 165. *See also* Incumbency
Exploitation, feminist theory and, 4
Exports, 40; agricultural, 38; decline in, 41–42; labor-intensive, 39

Family obligations, 113, 114, 116, 122, 133

Female sphere, recreating, 4
Feminist theory, 106–107
Flammang, Janet, work of, 15
*Fu Nu Huei* (Women's Association), reserved-seats system and, 85–86

Gandhi, Indira, 3
Gender-neutral model, building, 106–108, 125
Gender gap, 13, 58, 123; closing of, 69–70, 74, 136, 159, 182; education and, 67–68; industrialization and, 58; political efficacy and, 70, 72, 73; salaries and, 76(n21)
General Rules for Provincial, *Hsien*, and *Shih* Self-Government in Taiwan Province, 87–88
Gilligan, Carol, work of, 14

*Hsiangs*, 98(n32); definition of, 88
*Hsiens*, definition of, 87

Ideology, 190; committee service and, 166–167
Import-substitution, 37–40
Incumbency, 94, 142, 188, 191; advantages of, 11, 21; discrimination and, 148; interest groups and, 147; women and, 181. *See also* Experience, political
Independents: accomplishments of, 178; career longevity of, 144; committee membership and, 166; role definitions of, 163
Industrialization, 5, 43; drive for, 34, 36, 40; feminist theory and, 188; impact of, 39; import-substitution, 37–40; political participation and, 106; women and, 3, 4, 7, 24, 33, 57–60, 67, 73,187–189
Industries: labor-intensive, 39–41; light, 38–40
Inflation, 37–38, 41–42
Integration, vertical, 68. *See also* Segregation
Interest groups, 121, 155, 181, 183n9; gender discrimination by, 155; importance of, 144–147; incumbency and, 147; KMT and, 146–147; Mainlanders and, 147; membership in, 144–145, 147, 149; reserved-seats system and, 146; types of, 144; women and, 145–148. *See also* Networks, political; Religious groups
Interviews, contents of, 103–105
Islanders, 105, 125, 126, 144; committee assignments for, 166. *See also* Mainlanders

Jacobs, Jerry, work of, 74
Judicial Yuan: appointment to, 46; role of, 44

Kelly, Rita Mae, work of, 17
Kirkpatrick, Jeane, work of, 19
KMT (Kuomintang): accomplishments of, 178; Chaing Kai-shek and, 45; committee membership and, 166; competitiveness of,

94–95; Congress, 47; discrimination and, 154, 158(n12); dominance of, 34, 47–49; election results for, 52; interest groups and, 146–147; legislative activity of, 169–170; membership in, 71–73, 86, 108, 116, 139, 141–144, 148; opposition to, 48–49, 182; policy on women of, 5; reserved-seats system and, 86, 90; role definitions of, 45, 163; training by, 160
Kuo, Shirley: success of, 90; work of, 42

Land reform, 38, 41, 49
Leadership: personalities for, 17; subordination to, 162; women's, 154–155
Leahy, Margaret, work of, 4, 188
Lee Teng-hui, 45, 47, 50, 52
Legislation: introducing, 114, 183(n9); local development, 181, 193; women sponsoring, 118, 167–168, 172, 173, 181. *See also* Amendments; Resolutions
Legislative activity, 108, 193; committee membership and, 168; indicators of, 173; KMT, 169–170; women legislators and, 181
Legislative behavior, 6, 139; analysis of, 181; attitudes about, 190; gender gap in, 159–160; political orientation for, 160–171
Legislative effectiveness, 103, 108–109, 193; attitudes about, 190; women and, 171
Legislative success, 178–179, 193; ambition and, 179–180; factors of, 174; indicators of, 172–173, 176–177; women and, 177, 180
Legislative Yuan, 46; debates in, 50; election of, 45; Mainlanders in, 123; membership in, 51–52; reserved-seats system and, 82–84, 86–87; role of, 44; women in, 86, 89–90, 94, 95, 104
Legitimacy, establishing, 155–156
Lei Chen, arrest of, 48
Liberalism, 49–50, 114–116, 139; countersocialization and, 108; discrimination and, 158(n12); women and, 113, 151
Liu Ming-ch'uan, 34
Local government: reserved-seats system and, 88–89; women in, 93
Local politics: religion and, 135; women and, 83, 90–93
Lower houses, election to, 21–22

Mainlanders, 105, 116, 125, 126; committee assignments for, 165–166; influence of, 122, 123, 173–174; interest groups and, 147; KMT, 141; role definition and, 164. *See also* Islanders
Management, women in, 59, 61, 62, 68, 74
Manufacturing, 75(n10); women in, 59, 60, 64–66
Marginalization, female, 58, 59, 63, 188, 189
Martial law: abolition of, 50; declaring, 44
Mass media, politics and, 192, 194
Minorities, reserved-seats for, 82, 83, 86
Modernization, 3, 106, 136, 137, 187; countersocialization and, 134; women and, 3–4, 24, 52
Mother: political role of, 121, 123–125, 130, 132, 137
Multinational corporations (MNC), 40, 43
Multiple regression analysis, 109–110, 114–115, 131

National Assembly, 45, 46; KMT and, 50; Mainlanders in, 123; membership in, 44, 51; reserved-seats system and, 82–86, 93–94; women in, 89–90, 104
Nationalist Party. *See* KMT (Kuomintang)
National Security Act, 50
National Security Council, creation of, 45
Nechemias, Carol, work of, 19
Networks: kinship, 3–4; political, 176. *See also* Interest groups

Occupational groups, reserved-seats for, 82, 83, 86
Occupational hierarchy, 61–62
Opposition parties: formation of, 50; prohibition of, 48–49. *See also* Democratic Progressive party (DPP); *Tangwei*
Orientation: legislative, 159, 171–172; political, 106, 139, 149–157; role, 182
Original Statute on the Election and Recall of Members of the Legislative Yuan, 1947, 86
Overseas Chinese, 84; reserved-seats for, 82, 83, 86

Party affiliation: committee service and, 166–167; impact of, 119(n4) Passivity, 71–72
Patriarchy, 5, 11, 24, 58, 159; overcoming, 69, 73; reinforcing, 188
Patronage, 183(n7), 192; committee assignments and, 168–169, 174; influence of, 176
Peng Ming-min, arrest of, 49
Pitkin, Hanna, work of, 11–12
Political groups. *See* Interest groups
Politicization: family, 121, 123–129, 132, 134–136, 142; spouse, 121, 125, 126, 132, 147. *See also* Spouse connection
Politics. *See* Electoral politics
Privatization. *See* Taiwanization
Professional jobs, women in, 23, 59, 61, 69, 73, 74

Provincial Assembly, 52; election of, 46; KMT dominance of, 49; reserved-seats system and, 88; women in, 89–90, 94, 95, 105

Questionnaires, evaluating, 104–106
Quotas, 97(n5), 98(n31); analysis of, 189–190; decline of, 194; determining, 84; exceeding, 93–94; problems with, 95–96. *See also* Reserved-seats system

Recruitment, political, 190–91
Reelection, women legislators and, 177–178
Religious groups, 144, 149; committee assignments and, 166; local politics and, 135; role definition and, 163–164. *See also* Interest groups
Reserved-seats system, 7, 25, 87, 158(n13); analysis of, 81–82, 89–96, 103, 189–190, 194–195; countersocialization and, 194; discrimination in, 152–153, 159; interest groups and, 146; KMT and, 90; laws implementing, 84–86. *See also* Quotas
Resolutions: introducing, 114–116, 169, 170, 176; local development, 167–169; types of, 167; women sponsoring, 167–169, 171, 193. *See also* Amendments; Legislation
Resources: political, 139, 140–144, 147–149, 160, 190–191; socioeconomic, 121, 134, 135, 137, 141, 144, 160; Taiwan's, 34
Role conflicts, 121, 125, 131–133, 137, 193; ambition and, 179–180; politics and, 18–19; women and, 116, 161–163, 179–180, 190
Rule, Wilma, work of, 4, 21, 23

Sales jobs, women in, 63
Sapiro, Virginia, work of, 12, 17, 126
Savings, 39–43
Segregation: horizontal 59, 60, 61, 67, 189; rank, 59; sex, 57–59, 68, 74, 187; vertical, 59, 61–66, 189. *See also* Integration
Self-confidence, 12, 107, 121, 125, 135, 139, 154
Self-employment, women in, 59, 63–67
Services, 75(n10); women in, 59, 60, 64–66
*Shihs*, definition of, 87–88
Sino-Japanese War, Taiwan and, 34
Socialist governments, women in, 2, 4
Socialization, 6, 11, 104, 141, 188. *See also* Countersocialization
Socialization, adult, 125–133, 190; factors of, 121; mother political role and, 130, 137
Socialization, childhood, 17–18, 109, 121–125, 133, 136, 190; mother political role and, 106, 130
Socialization, sex-role, 69; effects of, 17–19; differences in, 133–136; factors relating to, 107; generational differences in, 114, 135–136; overcoming, 18, 24, 52, 57, 68,
73, 77(n24), 103, 121; political efficacy and, 18, 71, 151; selective, 137
Spouse connection, 118; decreasing importance of, 110–111. *See also* Politicization, spouse
Statistical significance, importance of, 111–112
Statute and Implementation Rules of the Election and Recall of the Delegates of the National Assembly, 1947, 84
Statute and Implementation Rules on the Election and Recall of Public Officials for the Duration of Mobilization to Suppress the Communist Rebellion, 1980, 1983, and 1989, 84
Statute and Implementation Rules on the Election and Recall of Supplementary Legislative Representatives of the Central Government in the Free Area for the Duration of Mobilization to Suppress the Communist Rebellion, 1969 and 1972, 84
Subordination, 58, 162, 165–166; feminist theory and, 4, 188; overcoming, 187; role definition and, 163; women legislators and, 170
Suffrage, gaining, 15–16
Sun Yat-sen, 44; policy on women of, 5, 82

Taiwan Independence Movement, 48
Taiwanization, 40, 49
*Tangwei*, 181; negotiations with, 50; training by, 160–161. *See also* Opposition parties
Technical jobs, women in, 61
Temporary Provisions Effective During the Period of Communist Rebellion, 44, 48, 83; reserved-seats system and, 85, 86
Thatcher, Margaret, 3
"Three Principles of the People," 44
Tokenism, 5, 159; decline of, 189, 194; fighting, 95
Training, 171; party, 160–161

Underrepresentation, 1–4, 6, 13, 23–25, 68, 107, 187–189, 195; consequences of, 11; discrimination and, 19–21; theories explaining, 15–23
Unpaid family workers, women as, 59, 63–65, 67, 68

Voting patterns, 13, 71, 72

Welch, Susan, work of, 19
Women's Association. *See Fu Nu Huei* (Women's Association)
Women's movement, 13, 69; influence of, 188, 189, 193–194; reserved-seats system and, 96

Yen Chia-kan, 45
Yu Kuo-hwa, 49

# About the Book and the Authors

Exploring how women overcome societal and cultural barriers to their political participation in a rapidly modernizing society, this book presents a case study of the Republic of China on Taiwan, where strongly male-dominated social norms have come under increasing pressure from the effects of rapid economic growth over the past 35 years and from the regime's ideological commitment to sexual equality.

The authors base much of their work on extensive interviews with all the women serving in the principal assemblies in Taiwan in 1985, a random matched sample of male legislators, and two smaller samples of women candidates who lost elections and women members of the 1970 assemblies. Their findings have mixed implications. On the positive side, for example, modernization clearly has helped to break down the obstacles of traditional gender roles and socialization patterns in the ROC. At the same time, however, most women became active in politics only with the benefit of special social circumstances, and the continuing discrimination against women points to the practical difficulties involved in enacting institutional reforms that would increase their representation, in Taiwan or anywhere else.

*Chou Bih-er* is research fellow at the Institute of American Culture, Academia Sinica, Taiwan. *Cal Clark* and *Janet Clark* are professors of political science at the University of Wyoming.

ACI-5451

**WITHDRAWN**
From Bertrand Library

DATE DUE

MAY 25 '96